HOW TO PROGRAM
THE AMSTRAD NC100 NOTEPAD

Patrick Hall

SIGMA PRESS – Wilmslow, United Kingdom

Copyright ©, P. J. Hall, 1993

All Rights Reserved. No part of this publication may be reproduced, stored in a retrieval system, or transmitted in any form or by any means, electronic, mechanical, photocopying, recording or otherwise, without prior written permission.

First published in 1993 by

Sigma Press, 1 South Oak Lane, Wilmslow, Cheshire SK9 6AR, England.

British Library Cataloguing in Publication Data

A CIP catalogue record for this book is available from the British Library.

ISBN: 1-85058-511-3

Typesetting and design by

Sigma Press, Wilmslow

Distributed by

John Wiley & Sons Ltd., Baffins Lane, Chichester, West Sussex, England.

Printed and Bound by
Manchester Free Press, Unit E3, Longford Trading Estate, Thomas Street, Stretford, Manchester M32 0JT. Telephone 061 864 4540

Acknowledgement of copyright names

Within this book, various proprietary trade names and names protected by copyright are mentioned for descriptive purposes. Full acknowledgment is hereby made of all such protection.

Preface

The Amstrad Notepad NC100 is a remarkable personal computer, squeezing the maximum from its 8-bit architecture and providing more value for cost than many other current machines. Those readers who require a general introduction to all its facilities could not do better than to purchase the excellent book by Kim Wilson, 'Getting the Best From your Amstrad Notepad', also published by Sigma Press.

This book concentrates upon programming the Notepad. The first ten chapters provide an introduction to the BBC BASIC implemented on the machine. Readers new to BASIC will probably need to read all of this in the order presented. Chapter 1 introduces the concept of input and output and illustrates it with a very simple program. The practical skills required in programming are described, with an explanation of running, listing and saving a program and similar 'housekeeping' tasks. Chapter 2 shows how conditional statements, together with loops, extend the possibilities of any program. This chapter also explains how Boolean logic can be included in program code in order to simplify complicated sets of conditions. Boolean expressions are then employed quite liberally in programs developed subsequently in other chapters. The book stresses the use of structured programming with procedures. Both are introduced in Chapter 3 and a detailed explanation given of algorithm design, pseudocode and flowcharts. Chapter 4 extends the concept of variables in a program and shows various techniques for their manipulation. Chapter 5 then develops program structure further with an explanation of arrays and the use of data statements. More sophisticated input via hot-keys is also described in the chapter.

The BBC BASIC relevant to graphic display on the Notepad's screen is explained in Chapter 6, with the introduction of a number of techniques applied in later programs. Graphics is extended to animated display by Chapter 7, which also illustrates simple use of sound in Notepad programs. File handling is demonstrated in Chapter 8 and a simple database using a file is introduced. The final chapters in the first section of the book then introduce the use of a printer in Chapter 9 and debugging in Chapter 10.

Chapters 11 to 20 do not introduce any further BASIC but instead develop lengthy programs, each of which illustrates concepts explained in the first part of the book.

Each program is documented in great detail. The programs are genuinely useful and provide a variety of utilities and games. Chapter 11 develops a computerised shopping list, as well as being a practical demonstration of flags to monitor internal program states. Chapter 12 turns the Notepad into a digital clock with a very large display. This chapter explains data structures and their practical application. Chapter 13 deals with the concept of sorting with, it is hoped, amusing animation. Chapter 14 shows how the Notepad can be directed towards practical number crunching. A simple hierarchical database is written in Chapter 15 and combined with a graphics display. Chapter 16 then develops a more sophisticated database.

The remaining chapters concentrate on games, as the Notepad's portability and graphics screen encourage such applications! Chapter 17 offers a chase through a maze. Chapter 18 shows how the Notepad can produce wordsearch puzzles from any set of words chosen. Chapter 19 is a logic game and Chapter 20 provides a animated version of the Chinese 'tangram' puzzle. The algorithms in this chapter draw heavily upon mathematical techniques which are, nevertheless, explained without assuming more than a background in simple school algebra.

The book has been written for Amstrad Notepad users, but BBC BASIC runs on any other machine which implements this language. As this includes all Acorn computers, the Cambridge Z88 and any machine using BBC BASIC under emulation, it is hoped that the material given here will be of use to anybody learning programming in BASIC. Those studying for examination at GCSE and A level will also find the book of use, as the material has been tested with students.

I am grateful to Dr. Graham Beech for his continued support during the composition of this book. Similarly I offer my thanks to my friend and former colleague John Scriven, now lecturing at the University of Portsmouth. Without his insistence, many years ago, I would never have confronted my first computer terminal!

I am also grateful to Brother Cyril and the de la Salle Order of Christian Brothers for for both employing me and for providing the excellent computing facilities at St.John's College. Useful comments have been volunteered by various members of staff. Michael Bownass suggested the major topic for Chapter 12 and Kathy Davies thought of material for Chapter 7. Geoff Burwood checked the documentation in Chapter 20. One of my students, Gareth Taylor, offered helpful advice on tangrams.

Happy memories of the programming, and social trips, of the 'St Francis' computer club abound and have encouraged me since. I am indebted to Lucy Hopgood, Mark Beard, Pauline and Andrew Davis, Michelle Willcocks, Andrew Denahy, Sarah Watton, Matthew Loten and Heather Habens. Writing for such an important machine as the Notepad has meant that I have claimed the inspiration of muses drawn from these ranks, Heather, Lucy, Michelle, Pauline and Sarah. This book is dedicated to the memory of my mother, Rita Hall, who died after a lengthy and tragic illness shortly before the Amstrad Notepad was launched.

Patrick Hall, St.John's College, Southsea.

CONTENTS

PART ONE: PROGRAMMING IN BASIC ON THE NOTEPAD

1. Beginning to Program 1
Input and output – INPUT, PRINT, RUN, LIST 2
Tidying the display – CLS 4
Adding useful prompts 4
Text coordinates – PRINT TAB 5
Special effects – VDU 6
Explaining a listing – REM. 7
Adding further lines – RENUMBER 7
Examining sections of a program with LIST. 8
Erasing lines of a program – DELETE. 9
Altering a program line – EDIT. 10
Finishing a program – STOP, END 10
Storing or retrieving a program – SAVE, LOAD. .11
Removing or rescuing a program – NEW, OLD 11
Checking saved programs – *CAT. 11
Erasing a stored program – *DELETE 12
Error messages 12
BBC BASIC's abbreviations. 12
Defining keys 13

2. Decisions and Loops 14
String, numeric and integer variables 14
Assigning a value to a variable 15
Including arithmetic in programs 15
Making decisions – IF, THEN. 15
Extending a decision – ELSE 17
Including program blocks – GOSUB, RETURN .17
A statement to avoid – GOTO. 18
Selecting a subroutine – ON GOSUB. 18
Unconditional loops – FOR, TO, NEXT. 19
Modifying a loop with STEP. 20
Creating a delay with a loop 20
Nested FOR-NEXT loops. 21
Conditional loops – REPEAT, UNTIL. 21

Coding letters – ASC and CHR$................................22
Detecting a keypress – GET....................................22
Detecting a keypress – INKEY.................................23
Nested REPEAT-UNTIL loops...................................24
Arithmetic in exit conditions – MOD, DIV......................25
Multiple exit conditions – AND, OR, NOT......................25
Boolean values – TRUE, FALSE.................................25
Simplifying conditions with Boolean expressions................26

3. Structured Programming..29
Planning an algorithm 30
Pseudocode..31
Flowcharts 31
Coding an algorithm...33
Structured programming..34
Control routine and subroutines................................34
Global and local variables – LOCAL............................35
Structured programs with procedures – PROC, DEFPROC, ENDPROC......36
Calling a procedure with a parameter..........................37

4. Variables...39
Finding the length of a string – LEN..........................39
Manipulating strings – LEFT$, RIGHT$, MID$....................39
Interchanging numerics and strings – STR$, VAL................40
Adding spaces – SPC...42
Telling the time – TIME$......................................42
Removing a decimal – INT......................................42
Removing a minus sign – ABS...................................42
Finding a square root – SQR...................................43
Random numbers – RND..43
Error trapping input..43
Using flags...43

5. Arrays and Data...45
Storing names in a program 45
Introducing arrays – DIM......................................47
Two-dimensional arrays..49
Storing data in programs – READ, DATA, RESTORE................51
Avoiding an error message – ON ERROR..........................53
Monitoring user interaction in a program......................54
Choosing between GET and INKEY................................55
Scanning the keyboard...55
Defining hot-keys with an array...............................56

6. Display and Graphics..58
Generating a display by arithmetic............................60
Producing a display with nested loops.........................61
Analysing the arithmetic......................................63
Storing display coordinates in an array.......................64

Producing a bar chart...66
Using graphics coordinates....................................67
Adding lines with MOVE and DRAW...........................67
Drawing a circle – SIN, COS, DEG and RAD...................68
Creating a pie chart..69
Producing a tabular display – TAN............................71
Drawing a graph..74
Drawing a filled triangle – PLOT 85,X,Y......................76
Drawing a filled rectangle – PLOT 101,X,Y...................77
Drawing a filled circle...77
Filled shapes from coordinate data............................77
Drawing with repeated triangles...............................80

7. Animation and Sound.....................................82
The basic principles of animation.............................82
An animated title..83
Using PLOT 5,X,Y and PLOT 7,X,Y............................85
Animating an outlined shape..................................86
Computer simulation and mathematical models................88
Filled shape animation with PLOT 87,X,Y....................92
Including simple sound effects – VDU 7......................94
Altering the pitch and duration with SOUND.................94
Playing a chord..95
Data statements and music....................................96

8. File Handling with the Notepad..........................98
Using a data file..99
Writing data to a file – OPENOUT, PRINT # and CLOSE #...100
Reading data from a file – OPENIN and INPUT #............101
Detecting the end of file – EOF..............................101
A database using file handling...............................102
Control with a menu..104
Creating a new file...105
Displaying all the records....................................105
Altering a record...105
Inspecting a file with the word processor...................106

9. Using a Printer..107
Using the Lapcat...107
Directing program output to a file...........................108
Documenting a BASIC listing – *SPOOL.....................111
Editing a program with the word processor – *EXEC........112
Obtaining a screen dump.....................................113

10. Troubleshooting..114
Tracing errors..115
Using the BASIC trace – TRACE ON, TRACE OFF............116

PART TWO: PROGRAMS TO TYPE IN

11. A Shopping Utility 117
12. Displaying the Time 129
13. Sorting Numbers and Words 139
14. Useful Number Crunching 151
15. Machine Learning 159
16. Writing a Database 178
17. A Notepad Arcade 188
18. A Customised Wordsearch 203
19. A Game of Logic 215
20. The Tangram Puzzle 227

1

Beginning to Program

Although the Notepad might be bought for its role as a portable word processor and personal organiser, it would be sad if owners did not begin to write programs for it as well. The Notepad is a remarkably powerful machine. It comes complete with its own version of the extremely elegant BBC BASIC, tailored to run on the Notepad's Z80 chip but possessing all the features that led to the language becoming the standard for British schools. The Notepad even has a display which can support impressive graphical output. It also has sound. With a little practice, it is very easy indeed to design and code programs which are really useful.

In order to write a program for the Notepad, it is necessary first to enter BASIC by pressing the <Function> and <B> keys simultaneously. The screen will then appear like this:

```
BBC BASIC (NC100) Version 3.10
(C) Copyright R.T.Russell 1992
>
```

Note that the word 'BASIC' is frequently written in capitals. This is not simply to stress what a marvellous programming language it is. The word is an acronym for Beginner's All-purpose Symbolic Instruction Code, the first word emphasising the fact that it was a simplified version of another computer language, FORTRAN. The greater than sign which appears after the copyright message is the 'BASIC prompt'. It is where anything you type will appear and is the Notepad's way of letting you know that it is ready for further commands. Whenever a program finishes running, the BASIC prompt will reappear.

You can, if you want, give the Notepad a direct instruction at the BASIC prompt. For example, to find the average of 7, 45 and 6 you could type the instruction PRINT, which is the fundamental BASIC word used when you want the Notepad to tell you something, followed by the correct arithmetical expression. The Notepad then gives the answer to seven decimal places, followed by the BASIC prompt again:

```
BBC BASIC (NC100) Version 3.10
(C) Copyright R.T.Russell 1992
>PRINT (7+45+6)/3
19.3333333
>
```

Although this is very convenient if you want to do some incidental calculation while working on a program, normally it would be easier to use the Notepad's calculator. The Notepad begins to show its ability when complicated programs are typed in which can perform sophisticated operations and process the data they are given to produce impressive results.

Input and output – INPUT, PRINT, RUN, LIST

When a computer program is running it is necessary for the user to be able to communicate with the machine and for the machine to respond in some way. Computing is essentially interactive and the two important aspects of BASIC to tackle first are 'input' to the computer and 'output' from it.

Suppose, for example, you want the program you are writing to be able to greet you in an apparently friendly fashion. This will match the reassuring 'User friendly' above the display. Thus it would be rather charming if you could type into the Notepad: 'Hello. My name is Charles Babbage.' It would then be quite spectacular if the Amstrad Notepad could respond back excitedly: 'Daddy...!' This is not the right approach, though. Computers are very pedantic and need to be addressed in an extremely formal way. You can tell your Notepad who you are, but this has to be done by 'assigning a value to a string variable'. A full explanation of all of these terms will be given in Chapter 2, but for the moment accept that:

```
INPUT N$
```

is one way of telling a computer your name. The two symbols, N$, will then represent you in the Notepad's memory, although when asked to repeat your name back to you the computer will politely translate into the correct sequence of letters that spell out whatever name you informed it.

In order to make this BASIC 'statement', INPUT N$, into a program, a number must be placed in front of it. BBC BASIC requires that every separate instruction is numbered. The convention is to number statements as multiples of 10 and so this one line program will be:

```
10 INPUT N$
```

Type this line, pressing <Enter> after typing the N$. (The dollar sign is the same key as 4, but shifted.) Then in order to see what this program does you need to type RUN and then press the <Enter> key. A question mark will appear on the screen. The Notepad always responds to the INPUT statement with a question mark like this. You

Beginning to Program 3

are being requested to type your name. Do this, and press <Enter> again. The screen will now look like this:

```
BBC BASIC (NC100) Version 3.10
(C) Copyright R.T.Russell 1992
>10 INPUT N$
>RUN
? CHARLES BABBAGE
>
```

The reappearance of the BASIC prompt shows that the program is over, but it does not seem to have achieved very much. In fact all you have done is to tell the Notepad that the symbols N$ are linked with the sequence of letter characters forming the words 'CHARLES BABBAGE'. What is needed in order to improve the program is some output. The BASIC instruction for this has already been introduced. It is the word PRINT. With this further command the Notepad can start to act positively. First look at your program again by typing LIST, followed of course by <Enter>. The display is now:

```
BBC BASIC (NC100) Version 3.10
(C) Copyright R.T.Russell 1992
>10 INPUT N$
>RUN
? CHARLES BABBAGE
> LIST
   10 INPUT N$
>
```

Use PRINT to add some output. The next line of the program will be 20. Make this the statement:

```
20 PRINT "HELLO WORLD, BUT IN PARTICULAR"
```

Then add a third line, line 30, which is:

```
30 PRINT N$
```

After each line press <Enter> of course. The "Hello World" joke, faithfully retained on page 153 of the Notepad manual, originated with another programming language called C, but is too charming to ignore. The display will be:

```
>10 INPUT N$
>RUN
? CHARLES
> LIST
   10 INPUT N$
>20 PRINT "HELLO WORLD, BUT IN PARTICULAR"
>30 PRINT N$
>
```

Note how the top two lines of the original display have now been lost. This is inevitable with the Notepad. If you are used to using a computer with a full screen display just accept this initial limitation and believe how quickly you will adjust. Running the program now leads to the display:

```
    10 INPUT N$
>20 PRINT "HELLO WORLD, BUT IN PARTICULAR"
>30 PRINT N$
>RUN
? CLIVE SINCLAIR
HELLO WORLD, BUT IN PARTICULAR
CLIVE SINCLAIR
>
```

Line 20 has added extra text to the program. This has been placed between quotes, the shifted <2> key. Any text you wish to include in a program must be isolated in this way. Line 30 has simply reproduced the value that you gave, or 'assigned' to N$ at line 10.

Tidying the display – CLS

The screen on the Notepad does not have to be as cluttered as suggested by the examples above. Instead of each fresh addition to the display scrolling existing items towards the top, a completely blank screen can be generated by using the instruction CLS. This stands for CLear Screen. Type in this extra line:

```
5 CLS
```

Now list the program. This will be:

```
 5 CLS
10 INPUT N$
20 PRINT "HELLO WORLD, BUT IN PARTICULAR"
30 PRINT N$
```

Note how the additional line has been placed at the beginning of the program. BBC BASIC uses the line numbers to put all statements into numerical order. Now when the program is run the display will be like this:

```
? ALAN TURING
HELLO WORLD, BUT IN PARTICULAR
ALAN TURING
>
```

Adding useful prompts

Including the CLS instruction has improved the appearance of the program, but the initial question mark is still rather vague. It is sensible to use PRINT to add a 'prompt' to the display which tells the user what to do. Obviously this prompt must

Beginning to Program 5

be after the screen is cleared, but before the input is requested. Therefore add this as line 6:

```
6 PRINT "PLEASE TYPE YOUR NAME"
```

If you list the program it will now be:

```
 5 CLS
 6 PRINT "PLEASE TYPE YOUR NAME"
10 INPUT N$
20 PRINT "HELLO WORLD, BUT IN PARTICULAR"
30 PRINT N$
```

Running the program gives:

```
PLEASE TYPE YOUR NAME
? ADA LOVELACE
HELLO WORLD, BUT IN PARTICULAR
ADA LOVELACE
>
```

You do not have to use upper case letters (*apologies for the 'Boffin talk'!*) for the prompts. "Please type your name" is quite acceptable. You can toggle between upper and lower case by pressing the <Shift> key as you type. Remember, however, that BBC BASIC words themselves must be in upper case.

Text coordinates – PRINT TAB

This simple example program can be extended still further to show the way in which the Notepad's display can be tailored to your exact requirements. In particular, output can be placed anywhere that you specify on the screen. To do this, the instruction PRINT must be replaced with PRINT TAB. Two numbers, enclosed in brackets, follow the word TAB. The first number determines how far across the display the output should appear and the second decides how many lines down it should be. Type in a new line 30 to replace the existing one. This line is:

```
30 PRINT TAB(30,4) N$
```

Make sure there is no space between the word TAB and the brackets. The listing is now:

```
 5 CLS
 6 PRINT "PLEASE TYPE YOUR NAME"
10 INPUT N$
20 PRINT "HELLO WORLD, BUT IN PARTICULAR"
30 PRINT TAB(30,4) N$
```

When the program is run in this new version the result will be:

```
PLEASE TYPE YOUR NAME
? MARVIN MINSKY
HELLO WORLD, BUT IN PARTICULAR
                              MARVIN MINSKY
>
```

The 'text coordinates' included in the brackets are a powerful method for controlling the display. The coordinates of the top left hand corner of the screen are (0,0). The top right is (79,0), bottom left is (0,7) and bottom right is (79,7). Of course, printing a long word near the right hand side of the display will lead to wrap around. Similarly printing on the bottom line scrolls the display up one line. Care is required!

PRINT TAB can also be used with just one number in the brackets. It will then indent the printed item by that number of spaces on the current line of the display.

Special effects – VDU

BBC BASIC possesses a VDU statement which permits many additional variations to the display. Two of these can be examined here. Bold font is switched on with VDU 17 and off again with VDU 18. Underlining is toggled on and off with VDU 19 and VDU 20. Practice this by adding lines to make the program listing:

```
 5 CLS
 6 PRINT "PLEASE TYPE YOUR NAME"
10 INPUT N$
15 VDU 19
20 PRINT "HELLO WORLD, BUT IN PARTICULAR"
25 VDU 17
30 PRINT TAB(30,4) N$
40 VDU 18
50 VDU 20
```

The effect of this can be seen:

```
PLEASE TYPE YOUR NAME
? HOWARD AIKEN
HELLO WORLD, BUT IN PARTICULAR
                              HOWARD AIKEN
>
```

Lines 40 and 50 are vital in order to switch off bold font and underlining again. This prevents subsequent screen display from being affected by the program. Also try experimenting with VDU 14 and 15, which create inverse text. These effects will probably be used only occasionally in a program, but they are a way of attracting attention!

Explaining a listing – REM

As a program becomes longer it is quite easy to forget what each line does. One solution to this lapse of memory is to include comments in the listing with REM statements. The Notepad executes a program just as if these were not present, or rather it runs slightly slower, but they make the program listing much easier to understand at a later date. The current program could therefore be extended to become:

```
 5 CLS
 6 PRINT "PLEASE TYPE YOUR NAME"
 9 REM Assign user's name to N$
10 INPUT N$
14 REM Toggle on underlining
15 VDU 19
19 REM Display greeting
20 PRINT "HELLO WORLD, BUT IN PARTICULAR"
24 REM Toggle on bold font
25 VDU 17
29 REM Display name at screen centre
30 PRINT TAB(30,4) N$
35 REM Toggle off underlining
40 VDU 18
45 REM Toggle off bold font
50 VDU 20
```

Naturally you would not include quite so many REM statements in a program as short as this. In a long program they become indispensable.

Adding further lines – RENUMBER

Writing a program with lines numbered in multiples of 10 means that you can insert further lines into the gaps between them. This is how the current listing has been extended. The irregular pattern of line numbers that this creates does look rather untidy though. The solution to this is the instruction RENUMBER, which will restore all the line numbers to multiples of 10. Type:

```
RENUMBER <Enter>
```

When the program is listed again it will now be:

```
10 CLS
20 PRINT "PLEASE TYPE YOUR NAME"
30 REM Assign user's name to N$
40 INPUT N$
50 REM Toggle on underlining
60 VDU 19
70 REM Display greeting
80 PRINT "HELLO WORLD, BUT IN PARTICULAR"
```

```
 90 REM Toggle on bold font
100 VDU 17
110 REM Display name at screen centre
120 PRINT TAB(30,4) N$
130 REM Toggle off underlining
140 VDU 18
150 REM Toggle off bold font
160 VDU 20
```

RENUMBER is a way of covering up your steps so that the program listing looks as if you got everything right the first time! It can also be used to alter the intervals between successive lines. Thus RENUMBER 5 <Enter> would create a program with line numbers increasing in multiples of 5. It is very rare to see any program numbered like this.

Examining sections of a program with LIST

The example has now become quite long. This means that when it is listed all that will appear on the display is:

```
100 VDU 17
110 REM Display name at screen centre
120 PRINT TAB(30,4) N$
130 REM Toggle off underlining
140 VDU 18
150 REM Toggle off bold font
160 VDU 20
```

Fortunately there are ways of using LIST to show chosen sections of a listing. LIST, followed by a line number, will show just a particular line:

```
>LIST 110
 110 REM Display name at screen centre
```

LIST, followed by a pair of line numbers separated by a comma, will list all the lines between them inclusively:

```
>LIST 50,90
  50 REM Toggle on underlining
  60 VDU 19
  70 REM Display greeting
  80 PRINT "HELLO WORLD, BUT IN PARTICULAR"
  90 REM Toggle on bold font
```

LIST, followed by a comma and then a single line number, will list all the lines up to the one selected. Naturally only the last six will fit on to the Notepad's display:

```
LIST ,120
```

(This line now scrolls off the top of the display.)

```
 60 VDU 19
 70 REM Display greeting
 80 PRINT "HELLO WORLD, BUT IN PARTICULAR"
 90 REM Toggle on bold font
100 VDU 17
110 REM Display name at screen centre
120 PRINT TAB(30,4) N$
>
```

Similarly, LIST followed by a line number and then a comma will display all the lines from the one selected onwards. These last two variations on LIST are not very convenient with the Notepad's display and are a fossilised relic of BBC BASIC's ancestry on a computer with a full screen monitor. The first two ways of employing LIST are appropriate for the Notepad. Another way of examining the listing of a program is described in Chapter 9.

Erasing lines of a program – DELETE

When you are writing a program it is unlikely that everything will be correct first time. It is important to be able to alter a listing and to remove program lines as required. The simple way to remove a line of code has already been described. It is to enter another line which has the same number. This will overwrite the previous program line and so remove it completely. If just the line number is entered without anything following it, except <Enter>, the line is totally erased.

Alternatively a whole group of consecutive program lines can be removed from a program by using the instruction DELETE. For example lines 50, 60 and 70 of the current program can be removed with:

```
DELETE 50,70
```

This instruction removes everything between the two lines identified, including them as well. Type DELETE 90,110 and, after <Enter>, DELETE 130,160. The listing is now:

```
 10 CLS
 20 PRINT "PLEASE TYPE YOUR NAME"
 30 REM Assign user's name to N$
 40 INPUT N$
 80 PRINT "HELLO WORLD, BUT IN PARTICULAR"
120 PRINT TAB(30,4) N$
```

Remove line 30 by simply typing 30 <Enter>. After erasing lines like this it is sensible to use RENUMBER to create a continuous numbering in multiples of 10 again.

```
 10 CLS
 20 PRINT "PLEASE TYPE YOUR NAME"
 30 REM Assign user's name to N$
```

```
40 INPUT N$
50 PRINT "HELLO WORLD, BUT IN PARTICULAR"
60 PRINT TAB(30,4) N$
```

Like LIST and RUN, DELETE should not be included as part of a program.

Altering a program line – EDIT

Erasing a line is sometimes too drastic. Instead, it can be altered or edited. Type:

```
EDIT 60
```

The Notepad's display will clear and line 60 will appear at the top. The left and right cursor keys can then be used to select any part of the line and allow different code to be entered, or existing code to be removed with the <Del> keys. Alter the first coordinate to become 25. Press <Enter> to confirm this change and then list the program again. You will see that line 60 has been modified. Running the program will place the name not so far across the screen.

Finishing a program – STOP, END

When the last program line is reached a program will finish automatically and the BASIC prompt appears again on the next line of the display. There are circumstances, though, when it becomes necessary to end the program explicitly with an instruction telling it to go no further. Two BASIC commands have this effect: END and STOP. Add line 70 to the program:

```
70 STOP
```

Run the program. This will be the new display:

```
PLEASE TYPE YOUR NAME
? KONRAD ZUSE
HELLO WORLD, BUT IN PARTICULAR
                              KONRAD ZUSE
STOP at line 70
>
```

Now change the last line to:

```
70 END
```

Run the program again. This time there is no extra message appearing. END is therefore a preferable way of stopping a program, unless you need to know the line where the program halted.

Beginning to Program

Storing or retrieving a program – SAVE, LOAD

You can switch off the Notepad without losing the program, provided that the machine has been configured to do this. Page 61 of the user manual explains how to adjust the system settings to 'Preserve context during power off'. What this does not permit, however, is to retain one program while writing or using another. In order to do this you must save each program that you will want to use again. Choose a name, perhaps "FIRST" for the example program. Then enter:

```
SAVE "FIRST"
```

The program is now saved as a file and can be used again later, even if you have worked on a different program in the meantime. A program stored in this way can be made the current program again with:

```
LOAD "FIRST"
```

Removing or rescuing a program – NEW, OLD

When you start a fresh program it is important to remove any previous program lines. If you forget to do this you will find yourself with a composite program, the first part of which is your new one, overwriting the previous program lines, and the second part of which is surviving lines from the earlier program, not yet replaced. To kill off your earlier program completely, enter the instruction:

```
NEW
```

This will remove the previous program. Nevertheless if you suddenly change your mind and want to return to a program after it has apparently been destroyed with NEW, type:

```
OLD
```

Doing this will take you back to the program, which can then be listed and run again. OLD only works if no other program has been started after NEW was entered. Just one numbered line of a different program removes any chance of reviving the previous one. In other words you need to think pretty fast about whether NEW was the right decision after all!

Checking saved programs – *CAT

When you have saved several programs it is easy to forget what you have stored in the Notepad's memory. In order to see a list of all the work saved, type:

```
*CAT
```

A list of all the program file names will then appear. Other files will also be shown, including, for example, any documents you have written with the word processor. (In Chapter 9 it will be shown how this is a rather useful feature of the Notepad.) *CAT is an example of an operating system command, hence the prefixed asterisk.

Erasing a stored program – *DELETE

At some stage it becomes impossible to save any further program because the Notepad's memory is full up. You will then have to decide which of your stored programs is no longer of any great significance and remove it completely from the Notepad's memory. This can be accomplished with the *DELETE command. If you are certain, enter:

```
*DELETE "FIRST"
```

No further prompt of the 'Are you sure' variety will appear. The program is lost completely. *DELETE does not require the use of the quotes around the program's name. They are optional, but included here for uniformity with the other references to the name. If you prefer you can also remove program files in the usual way described on page 65 of the user manual.

Error messages

Inevitably you will make mistakes as you type in and run programs. The Notepad will respond with polite error messages. From time to time you will see appearing comments like:

```
Mistake at line 50
No such variable at line 70
Syntax error at line 20
```

Fortunately, the Notepad mentions the line at which the error has occurred. Removing the error is therefore not too complicated. Most of the time you will discover that you have not typed what you meant to enter. How to react to more involved errors, produced by lapses in your programming ability, is discussed in Chapter 10.

BBC BASIC's abbreviations

BBC BASIC allows words to be abbreviated. For example, PRINT can be replaced with P. and LIST by L. It is a question of personal taste as to whether using abbreviations aids the programmer. Perhaps beginners should avoid adopting an abbreviation until the full word is well established in their minds. Abbreviations can also confuse other people who may want to study a listing you have written.

Defining keys

If there is a sequence of frequently used instructions you find yourself constantly retyping, you may wish to use the *KEY method for defining a certain key to carry out these instructions automatically. Suppose you want the combination <Symbol> and <A> to cause a program to be renumbered and then listed. *KEY can be used to define this sequence. Type:

```
*KEY 41 RENUMBER |M LIST |M
```

followed by <Enter>. The odd-looking character before the M is the key immediately to the right of the Notepad's space bar, shifted. After you have done this, pressing <Symbol> <A> and will renumber any program and then list it. Other keys could be defined to perform further useful sequences. The <B> key is defined with *KEY 42 and similarly for other keys. Thus <Z> is defined with *KEY 66.

Decisions and Loops

In the program developed in the last chapter, the name entered by the user was represented by the pair of characters N$. The name actually associated with N$ depended upon the user's choice. It was, therefore, not fixed but able to vary, according to the input. This use of N$ is an example of a 'variable' in a BASIC program. Variables play an essential role in computer programs and are the method by which different data can be accepted and processed.

String, numeric and integer variables

BASIC allows the use of three different types of variable. The one already introduced is called a 'string' variable. This is because it can represent a sequence, or string, of characters, like the letters of a name. Any text which will be handled by a program must be represented by string variables. They can immediately be recognised in a program because they always end with a dollar sign. This is pronounced 'string' and not 'dollar'. Typical names for string variables are A$, B$... or whole names followed by a dollar sign, like person$ or word$. The 'reserved' words of BASIC must be avoided in the choice of variable names.

A second type of variable is 'numeric'. This is used to represent a number in a program. The number can be negative or fractional if necessary, or of course a whole number. Typical names for a numeric variable are A, B, price and speed. No dollar sign follows the name.

The third type of variable is an integer variable. This is used to represent whole numbers and the variable name is followed by a percent sign, like A%. Integer variables do not have to be used in a program, but they do use less memory and can make a program execute more quickly.

Assigning a value to a variable

Naturally, variables in a program have to be given a value. They must represent something. One way in which a variable can be 'assigned' a value has been encountered already. It is with the BASIC word INPUT. INPUT A$ or INPUT B will assign a string to A$ or a number to B. Another way of assigning a value to a variable is with the 'equals sign', which should be thought of in this context as an 'assignment operator'. For example, the following BASIC statement assigns the value 'Ford Capri' to the string variable car$:

```
car$ = "FORD CAPRI"
```

This statement assigns the value 23 to the numeric variable mpg:

```
mpg = 23
```

Including arithmetic in programs

The usual arithmetical operations of addition, subtraction, multiplication and division can be performed in a BASIC program. The sign used for multiplication is * ('star') and for division / ('slash'). This program shows how arithmetic can be combined with INPUT and PRINT:

```
10 PRINT "Enter a number"
20 INPUT N
30 PRINT "Twice that is ";
40 PRINT; N*2
```

Note how a semicolon has been placed immediately after the PRINT at line 40. This is to prevent the numerical answer to the calculation from being shifted to the right on the display.

Brackets (shifted <9> and <0> keys) can be used in the usual way in chain calculations. The symbol ^ (shifted <6> key) is used to raise to powers. This will calculate the answer 64:

```
PRINT 4^3
```

Making decisions – IF, THEN

If computer programs were only able to proceed in the systematic way illustrated so far, following every line in strict sequence and not leaving out any of the statements written into the program, very little would be achieved. The versatility and complexity of software depends upon the way in which decisions can be made by a program. Depending upon the current values of one or more variables, the program can branch out in different directions. Very soon extremely involved situations can evolve from an initial set of conditions. It is this which makes programs interesting and useful.

One way in which a decision can be incorporated into a program on the Notepad is by using the two BASIC words IF and THEN. The general form of a statement employing them is like this:

IF [Some condition is true] THEN [Perform some action]

A very simple program can make this clear. It requests the user to type in the name of an animal. After this, provided that the animal is one which has been coded into the program, the correct name of the young is displayed on the screen. Here is the listing:

```
 10 REM Making a decision
 20 CLS
 30 PRINT "Type name of animal"
 40 INPUT A$
 50 PRINT "A young one is a ";
 60 IF A$= "CAT" THEN PRINT "KITTEN"
 70 IF A$="DOG" THEN PRINT "PUPPY"
 80 IF A$="BEAR" THEN PRINT "CUB"
 90 IF A$="HORSE" THEN PRINT "FOAL"
100 IF A$="COW" THEN PRINT "CALF"
```

Line 10 is a simple comment to identify what the program does. It is usually advisable to begin a new program with some form of identification like this. Line 20 then uses CLS to remove any previous display. Line 30 asks for an animal's name to be typed and whatever the user enters is assigned to the string variable, A$, by line 40. Line 50 then begins the sentence which will be displayed whichever animal has been typed.

After this are a series of five IF-THEN conditions between lines 60-100. Each will identify a particular animal. Thus if the user has typed CAT, this string of three letters C, A, T is assigned to the string variable, A$. In line 60 the condition A$="CAT" will be true and so the action following the BASIC word THEN will be carried out. The word KITTEN will be printed on the screen. In a similar way lines 70, 80, 90 and 100 will identify DOG, BEAR, HORSE and COW and print PUPPY, CUB, FOAL or CALF accordingly.

Naturally the program does not respond very effectively if the user is awkward and types BABOON or HAIRY NOSED WOMBAT, but even the most cleverly written program can be tricked by somebody with sufficient insight. This, after all, is the *raison d'etre* of computer hackers. Nevertheless, it is remarkable just how much can be achieved by simple IF-THEN statements in a program.

The name of the young animal appears on the same line of the Notepad's display as the rest of the sentence as a result of the semicolon after the second pair of quotes at line 50. A semicolon can be used like this to merge two printed items together on the

Decisions and Loops

screen even if they have been printed by different lines of the program. Note also how a space has been left in front of the quotes. This ensures that the display is correctly shown with the usual gap between all words.

Extending a decision – ELSE

The simple IF-THEN condition can be extended to include an alternative action if the condition after the IF is not satisfied. This is by including the extra word ELSE, as shown in this example:

```
10 PRINT "Type name"
20 INPUT name$
30 IF name$="POLLY" THEN PRINT "Tea please" ELSE PRINT "A coke!"
```

The convenience of this program structure will be obvious if the above listing is tested and contrasted with the following:

```
10 PRINT "Type name"
20 INPUT name$
30 IF name$="POLLY" THEN PRINT "Tea please"
40 IF name$<>"POLLY" THEN PRINT "A coke!"
```

The symbol <> (shifted <comma> followed by shifted <full stop>) is the way of writing 'does not equal' in BASIC.

Including program blocks – GOSUB, RETURN

There is a limit to the amount of text, or other BASIC statements, that can be placed after the THEN of a conditional statement. One possible solution to this is the use of a 'subroutine'. This is a block of program code to which the execution of a program can be temporarily transferred by the use of the BASIC word GOSUB, followed by the line number at which the additional code begins. The end of the block of code is marked by the word RETURN. When this is reached, the execution of the program jumps back to the next statement after the original GOSUB. The earlier program can now be modified to illustrate the use of subroutines:

```
10 REM A decision using subroutines
20 CLS
30 PRINT "Type name of animal"
40 INPUT A$
50 IF A$="CAT" THEN GOSUB 140
60 IF A$="DOG" THEN GOSUB 200
70 IF A$="BEAR" THEN GOSUB 220
80 IF A$="HORSE" THEN GOSUB 240
90 IF A$="COW" THEN GOSUB 260
100 PRINT
110 REM And now the naughty statement...
120 GOTO 30
130 END
```

```
140 PRINT "Cats are really fun animals. They are prepared"
150 PRINT "to live in moderate luxury, only insisting upon"
160 PRINT "100% attention, condensed milk and tins of tuna."
170 PRINT "Most of the time they either sleep or meditate."
180 PRINT "They understand T.S.Eliot and tensor calculus."
190 RETURN
200 PRINT "Dogs are O.K."
210 RETURN
220 PRINT "Bears are also O.K."
230 RETURN
240 PRINT "See details on dogs or bears."
250 RETURN
260 PRINT "Cats think highly of cows."
270 RETURN
```

With this modified program, typing in the names of the five different animals will cause the execution of five different subroutines. For example, if CAT is typed in, line 50 uses GOSUB 140 to execute the subroutine between lines 140-190. Similarly the other subroutines can be 'called' by the appropriate animal name.

A statement to avoid – GOTO

The program above does not end until the <Stop> key is pressed. This is because line 120 always redirects program execution back to line 30. This continues indefinitely in a continuous loop. Using the GOTO statement to achieve a repeated loop within a program is not regarded as good programming technique and there are other ways in which code can be repeated.

Selecting a subroutine – ON GOSUB

IF-THEN conditions are not the only way in which a decision can be made to jump to a subroutine. Another possibility is the ON GOSUB structure. This takes the general form:

ON [variable name] GOSUB [sequence of line numbers]

A variable has to follow the ON. It will have possible values 1, 2, 3... which then call the subroutine at the 1st, 2nd, 3rd... line number specified after the GOSUB. This is illustrated by this short program:

```
10 REM Selecting a subroutine
20 CLS
30 PRINT "Type 1, 2 or 3"
40 INPUT N
50 ON N GOSUB 70,90,110
60 END
70 PRINT "You typed 1"
80 RETURN
90 PRINT "You typed 2"
```

```
100 RETURN
110 PRINT "You typed 3"
120 RETURN
```

Subroutines do not have to follow conditions, as in the two examples given above. It is quite acceptable to have an unconditional call to a subroutine. For example, GOSUB 500, could be a program line which always deflected program execution to a subroutine. However, although this is possible it is not very sensible programming technique.

Unconditional loops – FOR, TO, NEXT

One way in which program code can be repeated without employing GOTO is to use a FOR-NEXT loop. This begins with a FOR statement, which determines the range of values through which the loop's 'control variable' will repeat. It ends with a NEXT statement which marks the end of the loop. All lines between the two statements are repeated the number of times specified at the beginning of the loop. For example, type in and run this listing:

```
10 FOR I=1 TO 5
20    PRINT; I
30 NEXT I
```

The loop prints out the value of the control variable I at each repeat of the loop. First I is 1, then it is 2, then 3, 4 and finally 5. At this point the loop stops. Contrast this first example with the alternative loop:

```
10 FOR I=6 TO 10
20    PRINT; I
30 NEXT I
```

Again the loop repeats five times but this time the value of I is 6, 7, 8, 9 and 10. A FOR-NEXT loop can be used to repeat anything. Try:

```
10 FOR I=1 TO 35
20    PRINT "..PHILIP GLASS.."
30 NEXT I
```

Any variable can be used to control the loop. In the examples in this book the convention of using I and J will be adopted most of the time, but not always. The Notepad automatically indents the lines inside a loop, as shown in the examples above. FOR-NEXT loops are a very powerful programming technique, as will be appreciated as successive examples are encountered. The tern 'unconditional loop' is used because a FOR-NEXT loop specifies in advance how many times the repeat will take place. It does not depend upon any condition being evaluated, as occurs with the other type of loop structure available in the Notepad's BASIC. This is described below.

Modifying a loop with STEP

A FOR-NEXT loop does not have to follow all the values within the range stated in the initial FOR statement. The use of STEP allows regular intervals to be imposed on to the range. For example, this loop will count in 2s:

```
10 CLS
20 PRINT ' '
30 FOR I=1 TO 55 STEP 2
40   PRINT; I " ";
50 NEXT I
60 PRINT
```

This example also shows how the display can be controlled by the use of extra PRINT statements, even if these place nothing on the screen. Line 20 moves the cursor three lines down the screen, once for the initial PRINT and once for each of the single quote marks (two keys to the right of <L>) following it. The empty space between the normal quotes at line 40 spaces out the numbers being displayed.

The addition of a minus sign to the number following STEP allows a loop to count backwards. Try this example:

```
10 CLS
20 PRINT ' '
30 FOR I=55 TO 1 STEP -2
40   PRINT; I " ";
50 NEXT I
60 PRINT
```

Creating a delay with a loop

The Notepad operates so quickly that it is often quite difficult for the human user to adjust to what is happening. When a message appears on the screen, for example, time is needed to read it and assimilate its meaning. This can be hard if the program is determined to get on with something else. One method to tackle this problem is the inclusion of a strategically placed FOR-NEXT loop which does nothing at all, except to count up to a suitably large number. While the Notepad is thus preoccupied, the user can study the display. The technique is demonstrated by this program:

```
10 REM Delay loop using FOR-NEXT
20 CLS
30 PRINT "This program has a delay which"
40 PRINT "makes it easier to read the display."
50 FOR T=1 TO 3000
60 NEXT T
70 PRINT "This is the next part of the message."
```

After the screen has been cleared, lines 30 and 40 place the initial text on the screen. The FOR-NEXT loop between lines 50-60 then assigns values to the variable T from 1 to 3000. This has to be completed before line 70 can be executed. Then the rest of the text is displayed. The loop could use any variable, of course. The choice of T is made here to stress the fact that all the loop does is mark time.

Nested FOR-NEXT loops

One FOR-NEXT loop can be placed, or 'nested' inside another. Although this might first appear a rather artificial structure to introduce, there are many occasions when nested loops are an essential programming technique. The following example demonstrates the way the J FOR-NEXT loop has been nested inside the I FOR-NEXT loop. While I counts from 1 to 7, the value of J keeps cycling more rapidly from 1 to 10:

```
10 REM Demonstrating nested loops
20 CLS
30 FOR I=1 TO 7
40   PRINT "I = "; I " AND";
50   FOR J=1 TO 10
60     PRINT " J = "; J;
70     IF J<>10 THEN PRINT ","; ELSE PRINT "."
80   NEXT J
90 NEXT I
```

The order in which the two loop variables appear in the NEXT statements must be the reverse of their order in the FOR statements.

The program uses semicolons in a fairly involved way in order to place all the numbers on the display. Note also how an IF-THEN-ELSE is used at line 70 to provide correct punctuation in the list of J values displayed.

Conditional loops – REPEAT, UNTIL

The second way in which the Notepad can set up a program loop is with a 'conditional' loop using the BASIC words REPEAT and UNTIL. The loop begins with REPEAT. Then follow the program lines which are intended to be executed more than once. At the end of this block of code is UNTIL. It must be followed on the same line by a conditional expression. This needs to be satisfied in order for the loop to stop. Here is a simple example of a REPEAT-UNTIL loop:

```
10 REPEAT
20   PRINT "Type a name"
30   INPUT N$
40 UNTIL N$="Alan Sugar"
```

The user will be constantly asked to enter a name and the Notepad will not be satisfied until it recognises its creator:

```
Type a name
? Alan Turing
Type a name
? Clive Sinclair
Type a name
? Alan Sugar
>
```

In contrast with the unconditional FOR-NEXT structure, REPEAT-UNTIL loops can add great complexity to a program. Their versatility depends solely upon the programmer's ingenuity in designing suitable 'exit' conditions to follow the UNTIL.

Coding letters – ASC and CHR$

Indeed, the addition of REPEAT-UNTIL loops to programming techniques marks the point where code can begins to be ambitious! Reviewers of early dialects of BASIC rightly bewailed the absence of conditional loop structure. For example, a REPEAT-UNTIL loop can make it easy to identify which key is pressed on the Notepad's keyboard. The letters, numbers and other keys are all identified by a unique number called the 'ASCII' code. This is an acronym for 'American Standard Code for Information Interchange', adopted by computer manufacturers in 1963 in order to make their equipment compatible. In ASCII code, the capital letter A has code 65. The code runs sequentially through to a value of 90 for capital Z. You can check A's code using the BASIC word ASC by typing:

```
PRINT ASC "A"
```

Similarly the conversion can be made the other way with the BASIC word CHR$. To see a letter Z appear on the screen, type:

```
PRINT CHR$ 90
```

It can be seen that this FOR-NEXT loop will print the alphabet:

```
10 CLS
20 FOR I=65 to 90
30   PRINT CHR$ I;
40 NEXT I
50 PRINT
```

Detecting a keypress – GET

ASCII values can now be combined with a REPEAT-UNTIL loop to detect which key has been pressed by the user. The program below requires the additional BASIC word GET, which delays program execution until a key is pressed. GET then has a value equal to the ASCII code for that key. A statement like K=GET assigns this ASCII value to a variable, here assumed to be 'K' for 'Key':

```
10 CLS
20 REPEAT
30   PRINT "Press a key"
40   K=GET
50 UNTIL K>64 AND K<91
60 PRINT "You chose the letter " CHR$ K
```

At line 40 the ASCII value of the key pressed by the user is given to K. The value is checked at line 50 to see if it lies in the range 65-90, corresponding to the capital letters of the alphabet. Note how the usual arithmetical signs for greater than and less than can be employed in BASIC. If the value of K does not match the values for the alphabet, the loop repeats. When an appropriate key has been pressed the loop will exit. The relevant letter is then identified by the program, which prints the character using CHR$.

A program routine like this is very convenient because it permits the user to express a choice without the need to press the <Enter> key.

Detecting a keypress – INKEY

Another way of detecting the key pressed by the user is to employ the INKEY instruction. This is like GET, because it returns the ASCII value of the first key selected. However, unlike GET it does not wait indefinitely. GET will stop a program from doing anything until a key is pressed. INKEY just waits until a set time has elapsed. Then it has either adopted the ASCII value of the key, or a value of -1 if no key at all has been pressed. The time that INKEY should wait is placed in brackets. It is measured in one hundredths of a second. Thus INKEY(100) will pause for a second, INKEY(200) for two seconds and INKEY(50) for half a second.

The usefulness of INKEY will be seen later in games programs where, obviously, action must not stop completely every time the player is faced with a decision. In the short example below, INKEY allows doodling on the screen. A trail of lower case letter 'o' is drawn, the direction determined by the cursor key pressed:

```
10 REM Detecting the cursor
20 CLS
30 X=40 : Y=3
40 REPEAT
50    K=INKEY(100)
60    IF K=243 THEN X=X+1
70    IF K=242 THEN X=X-1
80    IF K=241 THEN Y=Y+1
90    IF K=240 THEN Y=Y-1
100   PRINT TAB(X,Y) CHR$ 111
110 UNTIL K=81
120 PRINT "Exit from loop"
```

Line 30 is an example of a 'multistatement' line. Values are assigned to both X and Y, with the two statements separated by a colon. These variables are the coordinates of the letter o. This is printed on the screen by line 100 using the ASCII value of 111. Before this, the user can adjust the coordinates by pressing the cursor keys. The ASCII value of the key selected is assigned by INKEY to the variable K at line 50. The conditions between lines 60-90 then increase or decrease the value of X and Y to match the cursor key pressed.

The ASCII values of the cursor are: cursor up – 240, cursor down – 241, cursor left – 242, cursor right – 243. If the letter Q (for 'quit') is pressed instead of a cursor key, the REPEAT-UNTIL loop will end because of the condition, UNTIL K=81, at line 110. Pressing other keys does not affect the display. The program is not intended to be regarded too seriously and it crashes when the edge of the display is reached.

Nested REPEAT-UNTIL loops

Complicated program structure can involve a series of nested REPEAT-UNTIL loops, just as it can use nested FOR-NEXT loops. A short program is shown below which employs three levels of such nesting. The program allows a series of numbers to be added quickly. They must be digits between 0 and 9. Their total is displayed continuously on the screen. When a new series has to be added, the current total is reset to zero by pressing N. The next digit pressed is then the first number in the new sequence being summed. The object of this program is simply to demonstrate the loop structure involved. It is not intended to rival the excellent calculator available on the Notepad.

```
10 REM Counter
20 REPEAT
30    CLS
40    PRINT "Press a digit."
50    total=0
60    REPEAT
70       REPEAT
80          K=GET
90       UNTIL K>47 AND K<58 OR K=78
100      A=K-48
110      IF A<10 THEN total=total+A :
            PRINT "The number pressed was "; A "."
120      PRINT "Total is now "; total ".";
130      PRINT " Press a digit"
140      PRINT "or  to add a fresh total."
150      PRINT
160   UNTIL K=78
170 UNTIL FALSE
```

The key pressed is detected by the REPEAT-UNTIL loop between lines 70-90. The exit condition used at line 90 ignores all keys except the digits 0-9, which have ASCII value 48 to 57, or the <N> key, which has ASCII value 78. The value assigned to K then has to be reduced by 48 in order to be the actual numerical value selected. This correction is made by line 100 and the number assigned to the variable A. Provided that A is a digit, and not the accidental value acquired when is pressed, it is added to the running total at line 110. This line also confirms the key pressed, employing another example of a multistatement after the THEN.

Line 120 displays the total and lines 130, 140 add further prompts. Then the REPEAT-UNTIL loop between lines 60-160 continues the addition until the <N> key causes exit at line 160. A further addition is then possible as a result of the third REPEAT-UNTIL loop between lines 20-170. The 'FALSE' condition is explained below.

Arithmetic in exit conditions – MOD, DIV

Two further arithmetic operators, MOD and DIV, are often useful when writing the exit condition for a REPEAT-UNTIL loop. MOD gives the remainder of a division. Thus 17 MOD 5 is 2 and 30 MOD 8 is 6. DIV gives the result of integral division, ignoring any remainder. So 17 DIV 5 is 3 and 30 DIV 8 is also 3. Here for example is MOD used to test whether one number is a factor of another:

```
10 REPEAT
20   PRINT "Type a number which is a factor of 24"
30   INPUT N
40 UNTIL 24 MOD N=0
```

Multiple exit conditions – AND, OR, NOT

The logical operators AND, OR and NOT can also be useful in designing exit conditions. This loop repeats until a multiple of 3 bigger than 20 is entered:

```
10 REPEAT
20   INPUT "Type a number:", N
30 UNTIL N>20 AND N MOD 3=0
```

Note the variation used above on the INPUT statement. In the next example numbers are requested until either a multiple of 4 is entered or a number which is not bigger than 10:

```
10 REPEAT
20   INPUT "Type a number ", N
30 UNTIL N MOD 4=0 OR NOT (N>10)
```

Boolean values – TRUE, FALSE

The concept of satisfying conditions, introduced first with IF-THEN and continued with REPEAT-UNTIL program structure, leads to the general idea of expressions being 'true' or 'false'. In BBC BASIC, expressions can have a truth value of 0 for false or (a little strangely) -1 for true. Test this by entering:

```
PRINT 6*5 > 20
```

Here you are not asking the Notepad to calculate an expression for you. Instead you are simply asking it for its opinion as to whether six multiplied by five is bigger than 20. The Notepad will politely print -1, which is its value for true. Now try:

```
PRINT 7 > 8
```

The Notepad now prints 0 because 'Seven is greater than eight' is false. Improbable as it first seems, being able to use these Boolean values of true and false offers a way of improving programs. TRUE and FALSE even exist as BBC BASIC words. Since FALSE is never true, this loop will repeat indefinitely:

```
10 REPEAT
20   PRINT "Press <Stop>...."
30   FOR T=1 TO 1500
40   NEXT T
50 UNTIL FALSE
```

This is a convenient method for obtaining indefinite repeating of a body of code. Any other false condition could be used, of course, like UNTIL 0>1.

The term 'Boolean' is derived from George Boole, a 19th Century mathematician whose work, like Charles Babbage's, aided the later development of computers.

Simplifying conditions with Boolean expressions

It can now be shown how the use of Boolean logic extends beyond designing exit conditions for REPEAT-UNTIL loops. A hypothetical, and quite unlikely, situation is considered in which four numbered trays are placed in two rows and two columns:

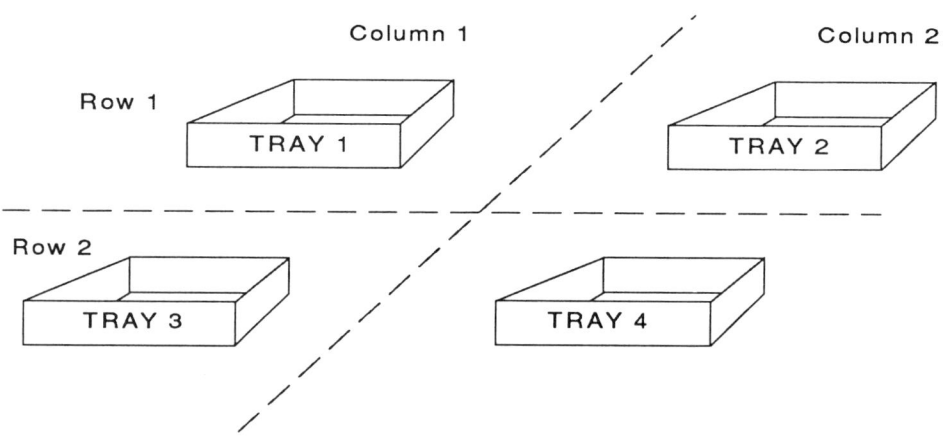

Decisions and Loops

A program has to be written which will calculate the number of a tray, given its row and column. It should be obvious that there are four possible conditions to code into the program:

- If the column is 1 and the row is 1, then the tray is 1.
- If the column is 1 and the row is 2, then the tray is 3.
- If the column is 2 and the row is 1, then the tray is 2.
- If the column is 2 and the row is 2, then the tray is 4.

A simple way of writing the program is therefore:

```
10 REM Processing input - Version 1
20 CLS
30 REPEAT
40    REM Obtain inputs
50    INPUT "Type column...1 or 2", A
60    INPUT "Type row......1 or 2", B
70    REM Calculate output
80    IF A=1 AND B=1 THEN C=1
90    IF A=1 AND B=2 THEN C=3
100   IF A=2 AND B=1 THEN C=2
110   IF A=2 AND B=2 THEN C=4
120   REM Display result
130   PRINT
140   PRINT "The tray is number...."; C
150   PRINT
160 UNTIL FALSE
```

A is the column number, B the row number and C the tray. Studying the combination of values, though, will show that the four conditions between lines 80-110 can be simplified. When B is 1, C has the same value as A. When B is 2, C has the value A+2. A single condition could therefore be adopted:

```
IF B=1 THEN C=A ELSE C=A+2
```

This gives the program listing:

```
10 REM Processing input - Version 2
20 CLS
30 REPEAT
40    REM Obtain inputs
50    INPUT "Type column...1 or 2", A
60    INPUT "Type row......1 or 2", B
70    REM Calculate output
80    IF B=1 THEN C=A ELSE C=A+2
90    REM Display result
100   PRINT
110   PRINT "The tray is number...."; C
```

```
120    PRINT
130 UNTIL FALSE
```

The condition at line 80 can be simplified still further to remove the IF-THEN-ELSE structure. C always has at least the value of A, but when B is 2 a further 2 has to be added to C. The Boolean value of (B=2) is 0 when B is 1 and -1 when B is 2. Extending this, the value of -2*(B=2) is either 0, or 2 when B is 2. The value of C is thus always given by:

```
C=A-2*(B=2)
```

This single Boolean expression has replaced the entire set of conditions.

Structured Programming

The Notepad is capable of storing and running programs of considerable complexity. Nevertheless this can be a disadvantage as well as an advantage. The sheer length of the programs possible can tempt you into constructing vast structures of inpenetrable complexity. Frequently these are liable to behave oddly when confronted with an unusual set of inputs. Removing errors from them becomes extremely tedious and even understanding how they manage to work at all can be very frustrating.

Critics of BASIC often speak disparagingly of the spaghetti code that can be created using it. It is a particular fault to which this language is prone. Fortunately, the dialect implemented on the Notepad is one of the better versions of BASIC and, if some care is exercised by the programmer, it is possible to produce elegant and understandable code.

In order to write coherent large-scale programs it is vital to think through a given problem very carefully before beginning to write any code at all. An 'algorithm' must be devised. This is a concise set of explicit instructions which can be followed without ambiguity and which will provide the required solution.

The first recorded example of a useful working algorithm appears in Euclid's Elements. It shows how to find the greatest divisor that two numbers have in common. (For example, the largest number which divides without remainder into 24, and which also divides into 40, is 8.) Euclid's algorithm dates to at least 300 BC and could, of course, have been discovered by an earlier Greek mathematician. Euclid complied existing mathematical wisdom into his comprehensive work.

The term 'algorithm' itself is derived from the Persian mathematician Mohammed al-Khowarizmi. He explained the rules of arithmetic for the decimal number system and the Latinised version of his name, Algorismus, therefore passed into the language.

Planning an algorithm

It is always hard to describe, or rather prescribe, a creative process. So often the essential idea occurs quite unconsciously. Oblivious to exhortation or exercise, the final solution pops unprompted into the mind at an unexpected moment. Everybody knows the traditional stories: how Kekulé elucidated the structure of the benzene molecule in a dream about a snake biting its tail, or how Stravinsky claimed that he was only the instrument through which The Rite of Spring wrote itself. Nevertheless, the programmer has to train this creative instinct. Somehow a productive idea has to be forced from the unconscious spring.

There does seem to be a methodology which helps. First, the problem to be solved must be made quite explicit. Usually in life we grasp only the outlines of an overall situation and let intuition hover vaguely about the details. This vagueness must not satisfy the programmer. All minutiae of the problem must be exposed to view.

Next, each stage of the solution must be thought through in detail, noting all the steps that would need to be performed if the problem were tackled practically by the programmer.

Finally these stages must be reviewed and checked to see whether they are as obvious and obligatory as first assumed. Perhaps instead they can be simplified. Specifically, the computer might be able to attempt processes which would be unrealistic for a human being. Repetitive number crunching is the obvious candidate here.

As a practical example of algorithm design, the issue tackled by Euclid's algorithm can be attempted. How, in practice, would you find the largest factor which divides without remainder into any pair of given numbers? We all know that, provided the two numbers are small enough, the solution will present itself without any logical thought at all. The answer will just appear. Alternatively if the two numbers are quite large we might start making a mental list of factors of each, quite randomly as they occur to us. Simultaneously we compare the two lists for a match. Such an imprecise process will not be satisfactory for a computer program. A more formal algorithm is essential.

Perhaps an orderly list of factors of one of the numbers can be constructed. Each time a new factor is added to this list we check to see if it divides as well into the other number. This is more promising, but is it better to begin with the smallest divisor of one of the numbers or the largest?

Obviously the latter is the correct approach, as the largest common divisor needs to be found. This rudimentary algorithm thus suggests that one of the two numbers should be selected and its largest divisor found, which will be the number itself. One way of then finding further factors is to decrease this initial divisor by 1 to see if the new number is a factor. Although this is a tedious method for the human calculator,

Structured Programming 31

computers can handle this arithmetic very quickly. A list of divisors of the number, decreasing in size, can therefore be established. Each in turn can be checked to see if it is also a divisor of the other number.

Finally, one last decision is made. Is this list of divisors compiled for the larger or smaller of the two numbers? Clearly the list should be generated for the smaller. The larger number will probably have divisors that are too big to divide into the smaller.

Pseudocode

After informal thought like the preceding section, the tentative algorithm must be established as a series of precise stages. These will still be written in ordinary English, but because they resemble the formal statements of a computer language they are referred to as 'pseudocode'. It is convenient to number these stages. They must be quite pedantic and state the completely obvious. The pseudocode for solving Euclid's problem is therefore:

i) Input both numbers.

ii) If the first number is the larger, exchange them.

iii) Initialise a divisor equal to the first number.

iv) Output the divisor if it divides into the second number and then stop.

v) Reduce the divisor by 1 and continue from stage iv)

Note that Euclid's 'problem' is referred to here, rather than Euclid's 'algorithm'. There are frequently different solutions to the same problem and without doing some research there can be no guarantee that your thought processes have matched Euclid's!

Flowcharts

A numbered pseudocode solution is one way in which an algorithm can be represented. Another method is to draw a flowchart. This represents each stage of an algorithm as a box of a particular shape. The beginning and end of the algorithm are shown as rectangles with curved ends. Input and output of data is indicated by a parallelogram. Any decision that has to be made is shown by another parallelogram, but in the 'diamond' orientation, with routes clearly marked 'yes' and 'no' leading from it. All operations are represented by rectangles. All these are illustrated in this flowchart which shows the same algorithm as indicated by the pseudocode above:

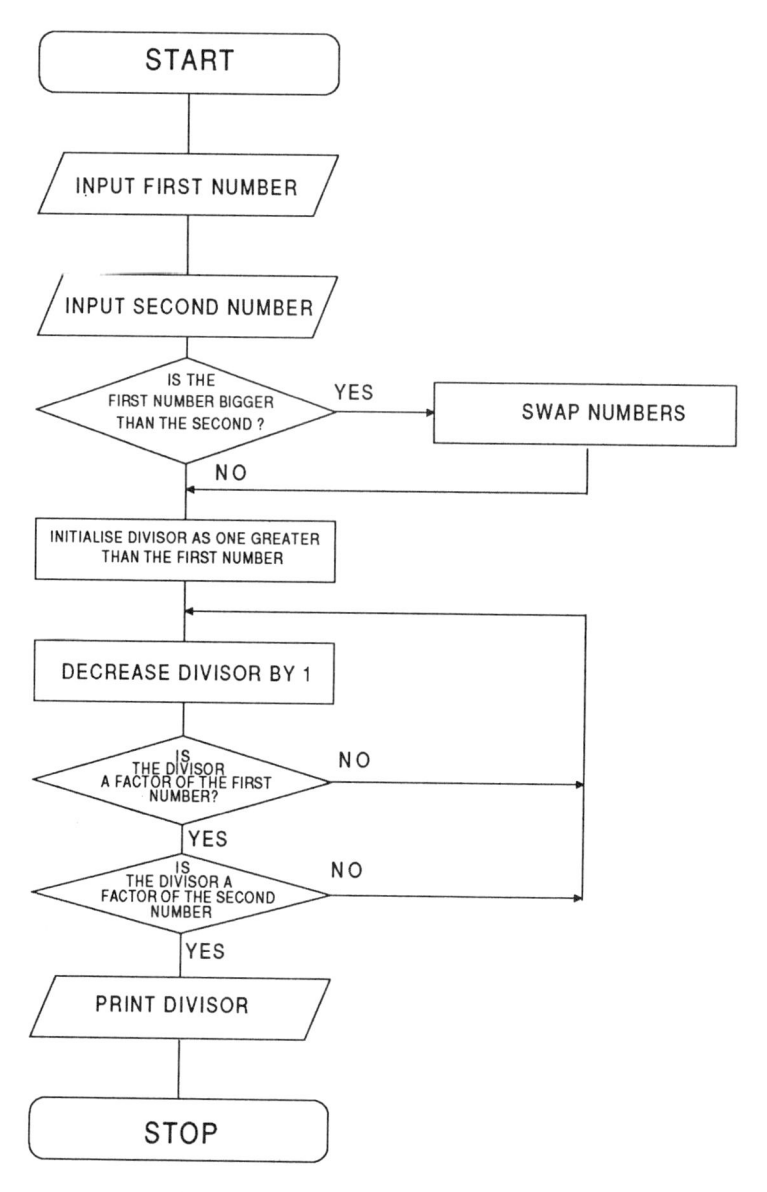

```
                    ┌─────────┐
                    │  START  │
                    └────┬────┘
                         │
              ┌──────────┴──────────┐
              │ INPUT FIRST NUMBER  │
              └──────────┬──────────┘
                         │
              ┌──────────┴──────────┐
              │ INPUT SECOND NUMBER │
              └──────────┬──────────┘
                         │
                    ╱ IS THE ╲       YES    ┌──────────────┐
                   ╱ FIRST NUM╲────────────▶│ SWAP NUMBERS │
                   ╲ BIGGER  ╱              └──────┬───────┘
                    ╲ THAN  ╱                      │
                         │ NO                      │
                         │◀────────────────────────┘
                         │
          ┌──────────────┴──────────────┐
          │ INITIALISE DIVISOR AS ONE   │
          │ GREATER THAN THE FIRST NUM  │
          └──────────────┬──────────────┘
                         │
                         │◀────────────────────┐
          ┌──────────────┴──────────────┐      │
          │    DECREASE DIVISOR BY 1    │      │
          └──────────────┬──────────────┘      │
                         │                     │
                    ╱IS THE  ╲     NO          │
                   ╱ DIVISOR  ╲────────────────┤
                   ╲ FACTOR   ╱                │
                    ╲ OF 1ST ╱                 │
                         │ YES                 │
                    ╱IS THE  ╲     NO          │
                   ╱ DIVISOR  ╲────────────────┘
                   ╲ FACTOR   ╱
                    ╲ OF 2ND ╱
                         │ YES
              ┌──────────┴──────────┐
              │    PRINT DIVISOR    │
              └──────────┬──────────┘
                         │
                    ┌────┴────┐
                    │  STOP   │
                    └─────────┘
```

A flowchart for Euchlid's problem

Note how a clear, unambiguous route is indicated through the flowchart by straight lines. Where a junction could make the direction undecided, for example when routes merge again after a decision, an arrow head is added. Sometimes a flowchart can become so complicated that different sections have to be joined together by an imaginary line. The ends of this are shown by the connector symbol, a circle with an inscribed letter indicating the other connector with which it is paired.

Coding an algorithm

Once the algorithm for a computer solution has been established, it can be coded into the computer language used. Up to this point no assumption has been made about the language available. Pseudocode and flowcharts should not really include chunks of BASIC because ideally they can be coded by another programmer who prefers Pascal, C or some other favoured language. However, here is a listing in BBC BASIC for the Notepad:

```
 10 REM Notepad's attempt at Euclid's problem
 20 CLS
 30 INPUT "Type first number ", A
 40 INPUT "Type second number ", B
 50 REM Rearrange to make A smaller of two
 60 IF A>B THEN C=A : A=B : B=C
 70 REM Initialise divisor variable, N
 80 N=A+1
 90 REM Loop tests whether N is common divisor
100 REPEAT
110    N=N-1
120 UNTIL A MOD N=0 AND B MOD N=0
130 PRINT "The greatest common divisor is "; N
```

Typical output from the program is:

```
>RUN
Type first number 40
Type second number 24
The greatest common divisor is 8
>RUN
Type first number 15
Type second number 60
The greatest common divisor is 15
>RUN
Type first number 35
Type second number 49
The greatest common divisor is 7
```

Lines 30 and 40 prompt the user to enter the two numbers and these are assigned to the variables A and B. The algorithm assumes that A will not be larger than B and so line 60 checks that this is so. If A is larger than B the two values are exchanged, employing a third variable, C, to help shuffle the two numbers past each other. (This technique will be used in the program, Bubble, in Chapter 13.)

The divisor, N, is initialised at line 80 as being 1 greater than A. This is necessary because the loop between lines 100-120 immediately decreases N by 1. The loop continues to reduce N until the exit condition at line 120 detects that it is a factor of both A and B. The loop then ends and the final value of N is identified as the greatest common divisor at line 130.

Structured programming

A program as short as the example above can be left quite safely in this form. In contrast, when programs grow to greater complexity, it becomes advisable to impose a formal structure upon them in order to emphasise how they work. Each separate operation performed by the program, or set of operations with a common goal, is regarded as forming a distinct block of code. These blocks are given an individual identity to distinguish them from the other blocks. If a program is written in this way it is 'structured'.

Writing a structured program with such distinct modules has certain advantages. The way in which the algorithm operates is usually far easier to envisage when a listing is presented in modular form. Writing the program in modules will impose a degree of logic upon the programmer and reduce the risk of those errors which tend to arise from careless thinking. In addition the modules developed for one program can often be adapted for insertion into another program altogether.

Control routine and subroutines

The same program is now rewritten in a modular form using subroutines:

```
10 REM 'Euclid's problem' using subroutines
20 CLS
30 GOSUB 80 : REM Input numbers
40 IF A>B THEN GOSUB 110 : REM Swap numbers
50 GOSUB 150 : REM Find divisor
60 PRINT "The greatest common divisor is "; N
70 END
80 INPUT "Type first number ", A
90 INPUT "Type second number ", B
100 RETURN
110 C=A
120 A=B
130 B=C
140 RETURN
150 N=A+1
160 REPEAT
170    N=N-1
180 UNTIL A MOD N=0 AND B MOD N=0
190 RETURN
```

Running the program will give precisely the screen display as before. Examining the listing, though, shows how three major operations of the program have been separately coded as three distinct subroutines. The input of the two numbers is handled by the subroutine between lines 80-100. Exchanging the order of the numbers is performed when necessary by the subroutine between lines 110-140. Determining the greatest common divisor is achieved by the subroutine between lines 150-190.

These subroutines are called by the code at the beginning of the program. This forms the 'control routine'. (This is also variously referred to as 'supervisor', 'monitor' or 'executive' routine.) The division of a program into a control routine and separate modules called by it is the distinguishing feature of a structured program.

Global and local variables – LOCAL

It is quite possible to write well structured programs using subroutines as in this example. In some dialects of BASIC this is the only way to produce a modular program. The method does have one disadvantage, though, because it does not allow the programmer to distinguish easily between 'global' and 'local' variables.

A global variable will have the same value throughout the entire program, whereas a local variable can have one value in one module of the program and another value in a different module. This can be extremely useful in some circumstances. For example, the use of local variables makes it easier to include modules from one program as part of another listing.

The two examples which follow will illustrate the way a 'procedure' permits the use of local variables but a subroutine will not. The first listing uses a procedure. The new BASIC words introduced here are explained in the next section and should just be accepted at this point:

```
 10 REM Global and local values
 20 CLS
 30 FOR I=1 TO 7
 40   PRINT "In the main routine, I="; I;
 50   PROCcount
 60 NEXT I
 70 END
 80 REM
 90 DEF PROCcount
100 LOCAL I
110 PRINT ", but in the procedure I=";
120 FOR I=1 TO 5
130   PRINT; I;
140   IF I<>5 THEN PRINT CHR$ 44;
150 NEXT I
160 PRINT CHR$ 46
170 ENDPROC
```

When this program is run the display will be:

```
In the main routine, I=1, but in the procedure I=1,2,3,4,5.
In the main routine, I=2, but in the procedure I=1,2,3,4,5.
In the main routine, I=3, but in the procedure I=1,2,3,4,5.
In the main routine, I=4, but in the procedure I=1,2,3,4,5.
In the main routine, I=5, but in the procedure I=1,2,3,4,5.
In the main routine, I=6, but in the procedure I=1,2,3,4,5.
In the main routine, I=7, but in the procedure I=1,2,3,4,5.
```

The precise details of the code do not matter in the context of this example. Instead it should be noted that the variable I has managed to count smoothly from 1 to 7 in the main FOR-NEXT loop between lines 30-60, while at the same time, as a local variable in the procedure between lines 90-170, the value of I has simultaneously cycled repeatedly from 1 to 5.

Now the same process is attempted using a subroutine:

```
10 REM Caution. This is a deliberate mistake!
20 CLS
30 FOR I=1 TO 7
40   PRINT "In the main routine, I="; I;
50   GOSUB 80
60 NEXT I
70 END
80 PRINT ", but in the subroutine I=";
90 FOR I=1 TO 5
100   PRINT; I;
110   IF I<>5 THEN PRINT CHR$ 44;
120 NEXT I
130 PRINT CHR$ 46
140 RETURN
```

The only way to stop this program when it is running is to press <Stop>. The values of I in the main FOR-NEXT loop do not follow the order that naively one might expect. The contrast between the two programs should indicate why in structured programming it is more convenient to use procedures. The BASIC required will now be introduced formally.

Structured programs with procedures – PROC, DEF PROC, ENDPROC

Three further BBC BASIC words are needed when defining and using procedures: PROC, DEF PROC and ENDPROC. DEF PROC is usually written with the space between the two words, although this is not essential. ENDPROC does not have a space.

A given program module which is going to be written as as procedure first has to be given a name. Reserved BASIC words should be avoided, but using lower case for procedure names circumvents this possible source of error. Suppose 'procname' has been chosen as the name. The procedure can then be called by the control routine with:

```
PROCprocname
```

Again, there should be no gap between the word PROC and the procedure's name. The program code making up the procedure 'procname' has to be placed at the end of the program. DEF PROCprocname is placed at the beginning of the procedure's code and ENDPROC at the end:

```
DEF PROCprocname
    [ Code defining the procedure ]
    ENDPROC
```

It is important to make sure that the execution of the control routine does not extend into the procedure definitions. The END statement is used to prevent this from happening. As a further example of how procedures are included in a program, here is the original program in a third version:

```
 10 REM 'Euclid's problem' using procedures
 20 REM Control routine
 30 CLS
 40 PROCinput
 50 IF A>B THEN PROCswap
 60 PROCdivisor
 70 PRINT "The greatest common divisor is "; N
 80 END
 90 DEF PROCinput
100 INPUT "Type first number ", A
110 INPUT "Type second number ", B
120 ENDPROC
130 REM
140 DEF PROCswap
150 C=A
160 A=B
170 B=C
180 ENDPROC
190 REM
200 DEF PROCdivisor
210 N=A+1
220 REPEAT
230    N=N-1
240 UNTIL A MOD N=0 AND B MOD N=0
250 ENDPROC
```

For extra clarity, blank REM statements have been inserted between the procedures. This is a convenient way of highlighting the structure of the program. Structured programming does occupy more space in memory, and in hard copy, than a compact, unstructured program but this is usually regarded as a minor disadvantage.

Calling a procedure with a parameter

Sometimes it can be appropriate to call a procedure with a particular value given to a variable, or variables, needed by it. Calling a procedure with a 'parameter' will be used in later examples in this book. Here is a simple example in which a line of dashes is drawn by a procedure, PROCline(L). Brackets are used to indicate the parameter in both the call to the procedure and in its definition:

```
 10 REM Procedure called with parameter
 20 PRINT "Type length of line, 1-60"
 30 INPUT L
 40 PROCline(L)
 50 END
 60 DEF PROCline(L)
 70 CLS
 80 FOR I=1 TO L
 90    PRINT TAB(I,3) CHR$ 45
100 NEXT I
110 ENDPROC
```

Variables

So far variables have been used in examples, but not investigated in detail themselves. BBC BASIC does contain many instructions which permit different operations upon string and numeric variables. Although, when considered in an abstract way these can appear rather trite or academic, they do all play an important role in coding algorithms into feasible programs. This will become apparent in the later chapters of this book.

As an initial example of handling strings, two can be joined together or 'concatenated'. This can apply to string variables, as shown at line 30 below, or to string constants, as at line 40:

```
10 A$="LIGHT"
20 B$="HOUSE"
30 PRINT A$ + B$
40 PRINT "KEEP" + "ER"
```

Finding the length of a string – LEN

Often it is important to know how many characters are present in a string. This is achieved with the BASIC statement LEN:

```
10 REPEAT
20 INPUT "Type a string ", A$
30 PRINT "The number of characters is ";
40 PRINT; LEN A$
50 UNTIL FALSE
```

Manipulating strings – LEFT$, RIGHT$, MID$

Parts of a string can be separated off to form separate strings. This is done with the functions LEFT$, RIGHT$ and MID$. LEFT$ identifies characters at the beginning of a string. It is followed by brackets containing first the string and then the number of characters to be separated. The new string can be assigned to a variable and the original string left intact:

```
10 A$ = "SATURNINE"
20 B$ = LEFT$(A$,6)
30 C$ = LEFT$(A$,3)
40 PRINT C$
50 PRINT B$
60 PRINT A$
```

RIGHT$ behaves in a very similar way, except that the characters are removed from the end of the string:

```
10 A$ = "TREASONABLE"
20 B$ = RIGHT$(A$,10)
30 C$ = RIGHT$(A$,4)
40 PRINT C$
50 PRINT B$
60 PRINT A$
```

MID$ can extract characters from any part of a string. It requires two numbers, the starting location for the extracted string and the number of characters that it should contain:

```
10 A$ = "INTERPLANETARY"
20 B$ = MID$(A$,6,5)
30 C$ = MID$(A$,9,3)
40 D$ = MID$(A$,11,3)
50 PRINT D$
60 PRINT C$
70 PRINT B$
80 PRINT A$
```

Formal practice with LEFT$, RIGHT$ and MID$ does not indicate just how indispensable these functions are in practical programming.

Interchanging numerics and strings – STR$, VAL

A numeric can be turned into a string with STR$. The reverse is achieved with VAL. In the following program STR$ and VAL are illustrated helping to translate numerical input into English words:

```
10 REM Number conversion using STR$ and VAL
20 CLS
30 REPEAT
40    PRINT "Enter a 3-digit number"
50    INPUT N
60    N$=STR$ N
70    H=VAL( LEFT$(N$,1) )
```

```
 80    T = VAL( MID$(N$,2,1) )
 90    U = VAL( RIGHT$(N$,1) )
100    REM Translate hundreds
110    ON H GOSUB 200,210,220,230,240,250,260,270,280
120    PRINT "HUNDRED AND ";
130    REM Translate tens
140    ON T GOSUB 290,300,310,320,330,340,350,360,370
150    REM Translate units
160    ON U GOSUB 200,210,220,230,240,250,260,270,280
170    PRINT
180 UNTIL FALSE
190 END
200 PRINT "ONE "; : RETURN
210 PRINT "TWO "; : RETURN
220 PRINT "THREE "; : RETURN
230 PRINT "FOUR "; : RETURN
240 PRINT "FIVE "; : RETURN
250 PRINT "SIX "; : RETURN
260 PRINT "SEVEN "; : RETURN
270 PRINT "EIGHT "; : RETURN
280 PRINT "NINE "; : RETURN
290 PRINT "TEN" : RETURN
300 PRINT "TWENTY "; : RETURN
310 PRINT "THIRTY "; : RETURN
320 PRINT "FORTY "; : RETURN
330 PRINT "FIFTY "; : RETURN
340 PRINT "SIXTY "; : RETURN
350 PRINT "SEVENTY "; : RETURN
360 PRINT "EIGHTY "; : RETURN
370 PRINT "NINETY "; : RETURN
```

Line 40 requests a number. This must have just three digits, otherwise the program will not work. The number is assigned to the numeric variable N at line 50 and then converted to the string variable, N$, by line 60. After this, LEFT$, MID$ and RIGHT$, identify each of the digits of the number at lines 70, 80 and 90. They are extracted, of course, as strings and so VAL is employed to restore their numeric value. These are then assigned to the obviously named numeric variables H, T and U.

An ON GOSUB structure can then be used to call appropriate subroutines which print out the number in words. (A better way of doing this will be apparent after 'arrays' are introduced in the next chapter.) A REPEAT-UNTIL FALSE loop between lines 30-180 indefinitely requests further numbers for conversion. Typical output from this program is:

```
Enter a 3-digit number
?.872
EIGHT HUNDRED AND SEVENTY TWO
? 395
THREE HUNDRED AND NINETY FIVE
```

The program should not be considered as a finished exercise. Note what occurs when numbers involving teens are entered!

Adding spaces – SPC

Sometimes adding blank spaces to the display is a good way of removing a few unwanted characters or adding a gap. SPC, followed by the number of spaces required, can do this.

Telling the time – TIME$

The instruction TIME$ provides information from the Notepad's internal clock about the date and time. This is made available as a string, which can then be manipulated to provide data which can be inserted into a program. This example just extracts and displays the seconds, but other parts of the overall string could appear instead:

```
10 REPEAT
20    T$=TIME$
30    S=VAL(RIGHT$(TIME$,2))
40    PRINT TAB(40,3) SPC (2)
50    PRINT TAB(40,3); S
60    K=INKEY(100)
70 UNTIL FALSE
```

Line 60 here incorporates INKEY(100) as a pause for one second rather than to request input from the user.

Removing a decimal – INT

Various functions can be used to manipulate a numeric variable. For example, the fractional part of a decimal number can be removed with INT:

```
10 PRINT "Enter a number"
20 INPUT N
30 A=INT N
40 PRINT "The number was "; N
50 PRINT "The whole number part was "; A;
60 PRINT " and the decimal fraction was "; N-A "."
```

Removing a minus sign – ABS

Similarly, ABS returns the 'absolute' value of a number. It removes the minus sign, if present:

```
10 PRINT "Enter a number"
20 INPUT N
30 A=ABS N
40 PRINT A
```

Finding a square root – SQR

Another useful function is SQR, which obtains the square root of a number:

```
10 PRINT "Enter a number"
20 INPUT N
30 A=SQR N
40 PRINT A
```

Random numbers – RND

The Notepad will generate apparently random numbers with the RND function. The most convenient use of this is with a number in brackets specifying the range over which the numbers should appear. This program will print numbers between 1 and 10:

```
10 FOR I=1 TO 200
20    PRINT; RND(10) " ";
30 NEXT I
```

RND has an obvious application in games. It can assign locations on the screen, for example, or call different procedures to elaborate the action taking place.

Error trapping input

It is essential that the person using a program is prevented from entering values for variables which will cause the program to crash. How this is achieved will depend upon individual circumstances, but usually a REPEAT-UNTIL loop with a suitable exit condition is appropriate. This, for example, only permits entry of a whole number:

```
10 REPEAT
20    PRINT "Enter number"
30    INPUT N
40 UNTIL N = INT N
```

This loop only permits the values 1, 2 or 3:

```
10 REPEAT
20    PRINT "Enter number"
30    K=GET
40 UNTIL K>48 AND K<52
```

Using flags

'Flag' is the name given to a variable which is used internally in a program to indicate the status of some particularly important situation. Here is an example of the use of a flag, F, in a quarter-hearted attempt at developing an adventure game. Apologies are offered to those addicted to the genre.

```
10 REM Role playing game to demonstrate flags
20 CLS
30 REM Set flag's initial value
40 F=0
50 PROCcharacter
60 FOR T=1 TO 3000
70 NEXT T
80 CLS
90 IF F=1 THEN GOSUB 330
100 PRINT
110 PRINT "GAME OVER"
120 END
130 DEF PROCcharacter
140 PRINT "Choose your role:"
150 PRINT "Wise magician............Press 1"
160 PRINT "Ugly, deformed dwarf.....Press 2"
170 PRINT "Chartered accountant.....Press 3"
180 REPEAT
190    K=GET
200 UNTIL K>48 AND K<52
210 CLS
220 K=K-48
230 PRINT "Okay you are a ";
240 ON K GOSUB 260,280,300
250 ENDPROC
260 PRINT "really enlightened, intellectual magician."
270 RETURN
280 PRINT "ugly little thing, but loyal and cute."
290 RETURN
300 PRINT "chartered accountant."
310 F=1
320 RETURN
330 PRINT "Oh dear. A rampaging horde of demented"
340 PRINT "locusts is descending amidst blasts"
350 PRINT "of lightning and thunderbolts. Sorry!"
360 RETURN
```

The way in which this program works should be fairly obvious. The behaviour of the flag F should be considered carefully, though, because it illustrates the general use of flags. F is initialised at line 40, where it assigned a value of 0. It retains this value unless the subroutine between lines 300-320 is called. It then becomes equal to 1. It has been 'reset' to this new value. Line 90 detects the altered value of F and calls the subroutine between lines 330-360. The flag has played a significant part in the program's operation.

5

Arrays and Data

There are many occasions in writing a program where it is necessary to refer back to the value of a certain variable. This variable can be numeric, integer or string. As an example of the last, consider a situation where a list of five names is typed into a program. Afterwards it must be possible to recall any one of the names just by typing in its position in the list. The initial input and possible output of the program will be like this:

```
Enter name
? ANDREW
Enter name
? BARBARA
Enter name
? CHARLES
Enter name
? DEBORAH
Enter name
? EDWARD
Type entry 1-5
? 3
That person was CHARLES

Type entry 1-5
? 1
That person was ANDREW

Type entry 1-5
? 4
That person was DEBORAH
```

Storing names in a program

It is not difficult to write a program to achieve this:

```
10 REM Storing names
20 CLS
30 PRINT "Enter name"
40 INPUT A$
```

```
 50 PRINT "Enter name"
 60 INPUT B$
 70 PRINT "Enter name"
 80 INPUT C$
 90 PRINT "Enter name"
100 INPUT D$
110 PRINT "Enter name"
120 INPUT E$
130 REPEAT
140   PRINT "Type entry 1-5"
150   INPUT E
160   PRINT "That person was ";
170   IF E=1 THEN PRINT A$
180   IF E=2 THEN PRINT B$
190   IF E=3 THEN PRINT C$
200   IF E=4 THEN PRINT D$
210   IF E=5 THEN PRINT E$
220   PRINT
230 UNTIL FALSE
```

The screen is cleared by line 20. Then the user is prompted to type the first name and the input is assigned to the variable A$ at line 40. Whatever is entered by the user will be represented in the program from this point on by A$. As five names have to be stored altogether, this routine has to be repeated four more times, from line 50 to line 120. The distinct variables used are B$, C$, D$ and E$.

Once all the entry is complete the program enters a loop between lines 130-230 which allows all the names to be recalled as required. Here the user is asked to type in a number between 1 and 5. This is assigned to the variable E at line 150. Five conditional statements then follow which allow the value of E to select and display the appropriate name.

This program achieves all that is required. Naturally, as is so often the case with programming, there is a choice of methods that can be used to produce the same output. Here, for example, the conditional statements of the first program could be replaced with an ON GOSUB structure. This second program is identical as far as the user is concerned:

```
 10 REM Storing names with subroutines
 20 CLS
 30 PRINT "Enter name"
 40 INPUT A$
 50 PRINT "Enter name"
 60 INPUT B$
 70 PRINT "Enter name"
 80 INPUT C$
 90 PRINT "Enter name"
100 INPUT D$
110 PRINT "Enter name"
120 INPUT E$
130 REPEAT
140   PRINT "Type entry 1-5"
150   INPUT E
160   PRINT "That person was ";
```

Arrays and Data

```
170   ON E GOSUB 200,220,240,260,280
180     PRINT
190 UNTIL FALSE
200 PRINT A$
210 RETURN
220 PRINT B$
230 RETURN
240 PRINT C$
250 RETURN
260 PRINT D$
270 RETURN
280 PRINT E$
290 RETURN
```

The five conditions of the previous example have been replaced by the single ON GOSUB at line 170, together with the five subroutines between lines 200-290.

Introducing arrays – DIM

Neither of the program versions above manages the compact code possible if the concept of an 'array' is introduced. Arrays are a vital part of BASIC and allow a very convenient way of referring to a set of variables.

The great disadvantage of the example in its present form is the way the five similar items, the names entered by the user, have each been given distinct variable names, A$, B$, C$, D$ and E$. This has made it inevitable that specific code has been required to deal with each variable in turn. If the names could be assigned instead to a variable which recognised their similar role in the program, and distinguished between them in a more subtle way, the overall code would become briefer and more elegant.

An array allows this concise reference to the separate names. They are assigned to the five similar variables N$(1), N$(2), N$(3), N$(4) and N$(5). Collectively these form the N$ array. One way of visualising the way in which an array works is to think of it as a set of numbered boxes:

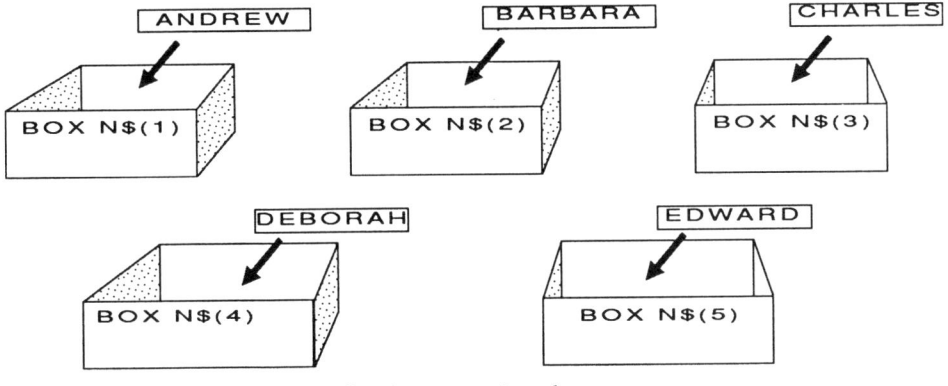

Putting paper into boxes

The names entered into the program are then like pieces of paper dropped into each box. To retrieve a name again, all that is needed is the number on the box.

An array variable, like the N$(1) here, is sometimes called a 'subscripted' variable and the number in brackets is the 'subscript'. Before an array is going to be used in a program it has to be initialised or 'dimensioned'. This means that the Notepad needs to know what type of variable is going to be used – numeric, integer or string – and how many 'locations' are needed in the array. In the example here the variables are strings and there are five of them. So the array is dimensioned by the statement:

```
DIM N$(5)
```

This statement actually sets up six locations, because there is a zeroth, N$(0), as well. Usually, it is convenient to ignore this location for most programming purposes. The name chosen for the array is a matter of choice. Here for example the array could have been NAME$(1), NAME$(2)... NAME$(5). It is sensible to use an array name which makes its role in a program clear, like ROAD$(4) or price(10). Reserved BBC BASIC words must be avoided, or put in lower case.

BBC BASIC does not allow an array to be dimensioned again in a program. It is, therefore, important to keep the DIM statement well clear of loops or procedures which are called more than once. A sensible place is at the beginning of a program or in an initialisation procedure which is going to be called only once. Some dialects of BASIC do allow redimensioning of an array to be used, in order to re-initialise the array locations. In BBC BASIC one way to do this is with a loop:

```
FOR I=1 TO 5
  N$(I)=""
NEXT I
```

As the variable I takes the values 1, 2, 3, 4 and 5, it identifies each of the array locations in turn: N$(1), N$(2), N$(3), N$(4) and N$(5). These are then assigned the empty string, "", to erase their previous content.

Using an array

The original program can now be rewritten to take advantage of the array structure. The names input by the user could be assigned to the N$ locations in the same way as in the original version:

```
 30 PRINT "Enter name"
 40 INPUT N$(1)
 50 PRINT "Enter name"
 60 INPUT N$(2)
 70 PRINT "Enter name"
 80 INPUT N$(3)
 90 PRINT "Enter name"
100 INPUT N$(4)
110 PRINT "Enter name"
120 INPUT N$(5)
```

Arrays and Data   49

This would work, but it loses the whole advantage of using an array in the program. Instead, a FOR-NEXT loop is employed to assign the name entered to each of the locations. As the loop repeats, it automatically identifies the location needed:

```
40 FOR I=1 TO 5
50    PRINT "Enter name"
60    INPUT N$(I)
70 NEXT I
```

Similarly the original set of conditions can be replaced. Previously, this code was used to display the name requested:

```
140    PRINT "Type entry 1-5"
150    INPUT E
160    PRINT "That person was ";
170    IF E=1 THEN PRINT A$
180    IF E=2 THEN PRINT B$
190    IF E=3 THEN PRINT C$
200    IF E=4 THEN PRINT D$
210    IF E=5 THEN PRINT E$
220    PRINT
```

Instead of this, all that is needed is to identify the N$ array location directly by the value of E that has been entered:

```
90     PRINT "Type entry 1-5"
100    INPUT E
110    PRINT "That person was ";
120    PRINT N$(E)
130    PRINT
```

These modifications lead to this final version of the program:

```
10 REM Storing names with an array
20 DIM N$(5)
30 CLS
40 FOR I=1 TO 5
50    PRINT "Enter name"
60    INPUT N$(I)
70 NEXT I
80 REPEAT
90    PRINT "Type entry 1-5"
100   INPUT E
110   PRINT "That person was ";
120   PRINT N$(E)
130   PRINT
140 UNTIL FALSE
```

Two-dimensional arrays

The concept of an array can be extended to allow for cases where the variables stored fit more appropriately into a table, rather than a single row of locations like the simple box representation assumed above. The program at this point assumes that only Christian names are being held in the array. However, if surnames are held in the array as well, it is plausible to have a structure like the one shown in the diagram:

N$(1,1) stores the FIRST CHRISTIAN NAME	N$(1,2) stores the FIRST SURNAME
N$(2,1) stores the SECOND CHRISTIAN NAME	N$(2,2) stores the SECOND SURNAME
N$(3,1) stores the THIRD CHRISTIAN NAME	N$(3,2) stores the THIRD SURNAME
N$(4,1) stores the FOURTH CHRISTIAN NAME	N$(4,2) stores the FOURTH SURNAME
N$(5,1) stores the FIFTH CHRISTIAN NAME	N$(5,2) stores the FIFTH SURNAME

A two-dimensional array

The array is now two dimensional. An alternative name used for a two-dimensional array is 'matrix'. Two subscripts are needed to identify each location and the array has to be dimensioned with two numbers as well. In the case of five Christian and surnames this will be by the statement:
DIM N$(5,2)

The program can be extended to incorporate a two-dimensional array:

```
 10 REM Storing names with a
 20 REM two dimensional array
 30 DIM N$(5,2)
 40 CLS
 50 FOR I=1 TO 5
 60    PRINT "Enter Christian name"
 70    INPUT N$(I,1)
 80    PRINT "Enter surname"
 90    INPUT N$(I,2)
100 NEXT I
110 REPEAT
120    PRINT "Type entry 1-5"
130    INPUT E
140    PRINT "Type 1-Christian name"
```

Arrays and Data

```
150    PRINT "Type 2 - Surname"
160    INPUT F
170    PRINT "That person was ";
180    PRINT N$(E,F)
190    PRINT
200 UNTIL FALSE
```

Line 30 dimensions the array. A FOR-NEXT loop is used to request the information placed into the array locations. This loop determines which of the five names is being entered. At line 70 the Christian name is assigned to the first array location for the Ith value. Line 90 assigns the surname to the second location for the Ith value. This matches the locations shown in the diagram. A REPEAT-UNTIL loop allows a particular name to be chosen at lines 130 and 160. The values entered for the variables E and F will select first a pair of related Christian and surnames and then either the first or second of the pair.

Higher dimensional arrays are also possible in BBC BASIC. In practice, though, one and two dimensions are usually sufficient.

Storing data in programs – READ, DATA, RESTORE

The data held in an array does not have to be typed in by the user when the program is run. Instead it can be stored in the program itself, in 'data statements'. These are lines beginning with the BASIC word DATA followed by data items which can be numeric, integer or string in type. This data is accessed via the instruction READ. For example, here is a rather involved way of putting 'HI!' on the screen:

```
10 READ A$
20 PRINT A$
30 DATA HI!
```

Line 10 reads the single data item and assigns it to the variable A$. This is then printed on the screen.

The items in a data statement are separated by commas. There is no comma after the last item. Although it might be necessary to place large quantities of data into successive data statements, the Notepad just reads everything as one long list. As far as the computer is concerned, the two following examples of data are completely equivalent:

```
100 DATA ALWYN,BIRTWISTLE,CROSSE,DAVIES,ELGAR,FERNEYHOUGH

100 DATA ALWYN
110 DATA BIRTWISTLE
120 DATA CROSSE
130 DATA DAVIES
140 DATA ELGAR
150 DATA FERNEYHOUGH
```

When the data items are read, a 'data pointer' starts at the first item and moves one place along the list every time the READ instruction is encountered. The data pointer is placed back at the first item whenever the program is run. It can also be reset to the beginning of the data items by the command RESTORE. This is illustrated by the program which follows. RESTORE can also reset the data pointer to a given program line containing a data statement with, for example, RESTORE 500.

Launching the Shuttle

An example is given now of READ, DATA and RESTORE in a short program which should entertain Cape Canaveral enthusiasts. It provides the opportunity to practice countdown for a Shuttle launch. Pressing any key except <R> on the Notepad will advance the count by one second. The <R> key, in contrast, takes the count back to 10 again, as shown by this typical output:

```
TEN Press a key to continue or <R> to restart sequence.
NINE Press a key to continue or <R> to restart sequence.
EIGHT Press a key to continue or <R> to restart sequence.
SEVEN Press a key to continue or <R> to restart sequence.
SIX Press a key to continue or <R> to restart sequence.
FIVE Press a key to continue or <R> to restart sequence.
FOUR Press a key to continue or <R> to restart sequence.
TEN Press a key to continue or <R> to restart sequence.
NINE Press a key to continue or <R> to restart sequence.
EIGHT Press a key to continue or <R> to restart sequence.
SEVEN Press a key to continue or <R> to restart sequence.
SIX Press a key to continue or <R> to restart sequence.
FIVE Press a key to continue or <R> to restart sequence.
FOUR Press a key to continue or <R> to restart sequence.
THREE Press a key to continue or <R> to restart sequence.
TWO Press a key to continue or <R> to restart sequence.
ONE Press a key to continue or <R> to restart sequence.
We have IGNITION!
```

The listing for the program is:

```
10 REM Countdown using READ, DATA and RESTORE
20 ON ERROR PRINT "We have IGNITION!" : END
30 REPEAT
40    READ A$
50    PRINT A$;
60    PRINT " Press a key to continue";
70    PRINT " or <R> to restart sequence."
80    K=GET
90    IF K=82 THEN RESTORE
100 UNTIL FALSE
110 DATA TEN,NINE,EIGHT,SEVEN,SIX,FIVE,FOUR,THREE,TWO,ONE
```

The numbers to be used in the countdown are held as a data statement at line 110. When the program is first run, the data pointer is at the first data item, the word TEN.

Arrays and Data

Line 40 reads the value and assigns it to the variable A$. Line 50 prints A$ on the display. The word *TEN* therefore appears, followed by the prompt: *Press a key to continue or <R> to restart sequence*. The prompt appears on the same line as a result of the semicolon after the A$ in line 50. Nothing further will happen until a key is pressed because line 80 is waiting to assign the ASCII code of a keypress to the variable K.

If the key pressed is not R, the data pointer moves to the next number in the data statement, NINE, and this is displayed. If R is pressed, though, line 90 uses RESTORE to place the data pointer back at the first item and so the countdown reverts to TEN. In this way the user can pretend to be a liquid oxygen leak in one of the Shuttle's main engines, strong winds off the Cape or an unsympathetic Congressional funding committee.

Avoiding an error message – ON ERROR

When the countdown does, however, reach the final zero the Notepad has a problem. The data pointer has now reached the end of the data statement and has nowhere to go. Normally a program stops at this point with an *Out of data* error. Line 20 avoids this happening by using the cheerful 'ON ERROR' escape route. Instead of the error message appearing, a jaunty *We have ignition* is displayed instead. The program then ends. ON ERROR is a very useful way of preventing a program from crashing. The line:

```
ON ERROR OLD : RUN
```

is quite a useful catch-all, though some might feel it was cheating and that your programs ought to work properly!

Searching through an array

A development of the earlier program which stored names in an array is now possible. This new program places names from data lines into an array and then allows a simple searching routine to take place:

```
10 REM Storing names as data
20 DIM N$(5,2)
30 CLS
40 REM Place names in array
50 FOR I=1 TO 5
60    FOR J=1 TO 2
70       READ N$(I,J)
80    NEXT J
90 NEXT I
100 REM Identify user
110 REPEAT
120    PRINT "Type your surname"
130    INPUT SN$
```

```
140    FOR I=1 TO 5
150       IF SN$=N$(I,2) THEN PRINT "Hello " N$(I,1)
160    NEXT I
170    PRINT
180 UNTIL FALSE
190 DATA JEREMY,FISHER
200 DATA BASIL,BRUSH
210 DATA PUSSYCAT,WILLUM
220 DATA PADDINGTON,BEAR
230 DATA ANDY,PANDY
```

When the program is run, a surname can be identified and the corresponding Christian name displayed:

```
Type your surname
? FISHER
Hello JEREMY

Type your surname
? BEAR
Hello PADDINGTON

Type your surname
? WILLUM
Hello PUSSYCAT
```

Five pairs of Christian and surnames are held as data between lines 190-230. These are read and assigned to locations in the N$ array by the nested FOR-NEXT loops between lines 50-90. The user can then enter a surname, which is assigned to the variable SN$ at line 130. A further FOR-NEXT loop between lines 140-160 then compares SN$ with each surname in the array. If a match is found, line 150 prints the corresponding Christian name.

Monitoring user interaction in a program

There are occasions when a number of different responses might be required from the person using a program. Each response has to be detected by the use of INKEY or GET during the program's execution. Recall that this is to make the program convenient to use and to avoid the need to press <Enter>.

Various ways are possible to write a routine which detects particular keypresses. Two contrasted methods will be illustrated in this section. Both are designed to identify one of the five keys selected by the user: A, Z, N, M and Q. You could, perhaps, imagine that this routine was intended for an animated game in which keys A and Z controlled the vertical position of an object on the screen, N and M its horizontal position and in which pressing Q caused the game to stop. Alternatively the keys might represent the five choices of a menu displayed on the screen.

Choosing between GET and INKEY

In both methods developed, GET is used to assign the ASCII value of the key pressed to a variable K. This means of course that the program's execution will halt at this point until a key is chosen. The alternative, INKEY, would just pause the program briefly while the keyboard was being checked. If the user did not react in time, the program would move on.

Which of these should be used in a particular program will depend upon the context in which the keyboard is being scanned. A game would probably need INKEY, in order to punish the waverer, while a menu which required some thought before a decision could be made would be better served by GET. In the program examples shown below this distinction is a little academic. All that matters is that the keyboard does return an ASCII value.

Scanning the keyboard

In the first approach, a series of IF-THEN conditions are used to respond to the user's choice of key. It is important that one of the five predetermined keys is pressed and so a REPEAT-UNTIL loop keeps placing the prompt *Press a key* on the screen until the user cooperates with the correct choice. The ASCII value of the keypress is assigned to the variable K. The ASCII codes for A, Z, N, M and Q are 65, 90, 78, 77 and 81 and so the value K has acquired can be used in this condition permitting the loop to exit.

```
UNTIL K=65 OR K=90 OR K=78 OR K=77 OR K=81
```

Once a relevant key has been chosen, this response can be confirmed by one of a sequence of conditions. Each merely calls a subroutine which echoes the letter which the user pressed. In a serious application of a routine like this, various code could be summoned to achieve some previously decided task.

The routine written in full is as follows:

```
10 REPEAT
20   PRINT "Press a key"
30   K=GET
40 UNTIL K=65 OR K=90 OR K=78 OR K=77 OR K=81
50 IF K=65 THEN GOSUB 110
60 IF K=90 THEN GOSUB 130
70 IF K=78 THEN GOSUB 150
80 IF K=77 THEN GOSUB 170
90 IF K=81 THEN GOSUB 190
100 END
110 PRINT "You pressed A"
120 RETURN
130 PRINT "You pressed Z"
140 RETURN
```

```
150 PRINT "You pressed N"
160 RETURN
170 PRINT "You pressed M"
180 RETURN
190 PRINT "You pressed Q"
RETURN
```

When this program is typed in and run on the Notepad, the prompt *Press a key* will be repeated on the display every time a key is pressed until one of the specific keys, A, Z, N, M or Q is pressed. Then the further text *You pressed...* appears.

Defining hot-keys with an array

The method above is quite adequate when only a limited choice of keys is involved. However, there are occasions when several 'hot-keys' need to be checked. (In the program Tangrams in Chapter 20, 14 separate possible keypresses have to be identified.) When the user interaction reaches this level of complexity, the method above is inappropriate. The exit condition from the REPEAT-UNTIL loop becomes hopelessly unwieldy and a long series of IF-THEN conditions is inelegant.

An alternative method, avoiding these two disadvantages, is illustrated below. It involves the use of an array, K(5), in which all possible keypresses are stored as their ASCII values. The values required for the array locations are held in a data statement at the end of the program. This is the BASIC required to intialise the array and fill it with the ASCII codes:

```
10 DIM K(5)
20 FOR I=1 TO 5
30    READ K(I)
40 NEXT I
[Program code]
250 DATA 65,90,78,77,81
```

The K(5) array can now be used to identify keypresses. As before, a REPEAT-UNTIL loop presents the user with the prompt *Press a key* and assigns the ASCII value of the key pressed to K. However, now the exit condition for the loop does not look directly at the value of K itself. Instead, an embedded FOR-NEXT loop compares K's value with each of the K(5) array locations in turn. If a match is found, the current value of the loop variable is assigned to the further variable, CH (for 'CHoice'), which has been initialised as zero within the outer loop.

A little thought will show that, if an appropriate key is pressed, CH will have the sequential value of this key as stored in the data statement. If another key is selected, CH will remain zero and the exit condition for the outer loop, CH<>0, is not satisfied. The nested loops ensure that program execution is halted until a relevant key is chosen. The value then assigned to CH is ideal for inclusion in an ON-GOSUB condition and the long list of IF-THEN conditions has been avoided, as well as the

Arrays and Data

clumsy UNTIL condition of the previous method. Here is the complete version of the code:

```
 10 DIM K(5)
 20 FOR I=1 TO 5
 30    READ K(I)
 40 NEXT I
 50 REPEAT
 60    PRINT "Press a key"
 70    CH=0
 80    K=GET
 90    FOR I=1 TO 5
100       IF K=K(I) THEN CH=I
110    NEXT I
120 UNTIL CH<>0
130 ON CH GOSUB 150,170,190,210,230
140 END
150 PRINT "You pressed A"
160 RETURN
170 PRINT "You pressed Z"
180 RETURN
190 PRINT "You pressed N"
200 RETURN
210 PRINT "You pressed M"
220 RETURN
230 PRINT "You pressed Q"
240 RETURN
250 DATA 65,90,78,77,81
```

6

Display and Graphics

Despite the relatively small size of the Notepad's screen, it is possible to produce quite impressive displays. This is mainly because the BBC BASIC implemented on the Notepad was one of the earliest to permit versatile graphics on a home machine. Although the Notepad's display is only a fraction of the size of the original BBC Microcomputer's, the majority of the screen-handling commands have been retained in its BASIC. A simple way of putting a display on the Notepad's screen is to use the PRINT TAB statement. An effective 'chunky' screen picture can be created in this way, like the one in the diagram:

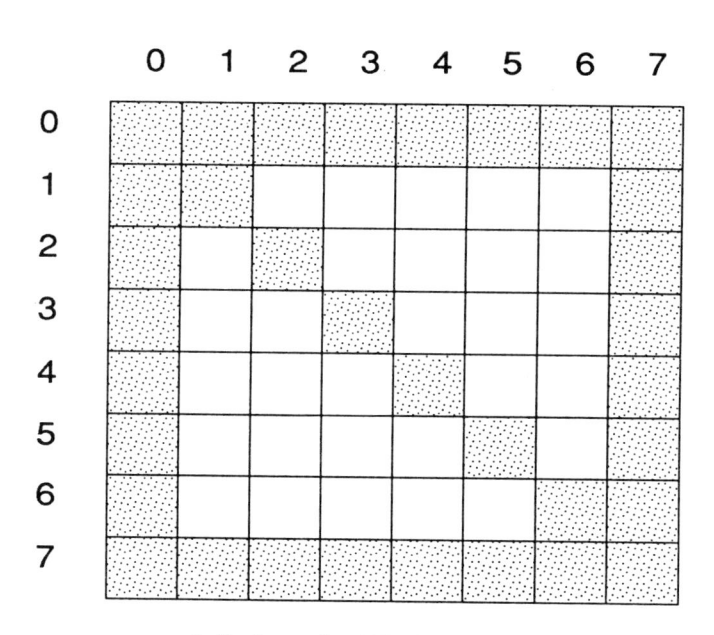

A display using PRINT TAB

Display and Graphics

This is an outlined square filling the whole height of the screen and placed on the far left hand side. One diagonal is also shaded to give the impression of a capital letter N superimposed on to the square. This display, of course, is only meant as a simple illustration of the methods to employ. Each of the filled squares can be placed on the screen as the character CHR$ 219. PRINT TAB, combined with the appropriate coordinates, locates the character in the correct place. The BASIC required to create the top line of the display is like this:

```
10 CLS
20 PRINT TAB(0,0) CHR$ 219
30 PRINT TAB(1,0) CHR$ 219
40 PRINT TAB(2,0) CHR$ 219
50 PRINT TAB(3,0) CHR$ 219
60 PRINT TAB(4,0) CHR$ 219
70 PRINT TAB(5,0) CHR$ 219
80 PRINT TAB(6,0) CHR$ 219
90 PRINT TAB(7,0) CHR$ 219
```

This short program is not the best way to proceed. If a separate PRINT TAB statement is written for every character position, the program will be far too long. Too much memory will be used and the program listing will appear silly and inelegant. The repetitive use of the PRINT TAB suggests that a program loop is required. The coordinates for the character position have to be included in this loop and there are two ways in which this can be done. The first method is to read the coordinates from data lines. The alternative is to find a way of calculating the coordinates within the loop, so that it generates the character positions required automatically as it repeats.

Holding display coordinates as data statements

This is the first method. The coordinates required for the top line of the display are: (0,0), (1,0), (2,0), (3,0), (4,0), (5,0), (6,0), and (7,0). These are placed in a data statement without brackets like this:

```
DATA 0,0,1,0,2,0,3,0,4,0,5,0,6,0,7,0
```

The program then becomes:

```
10 CLS
20 FOR I=1 TO 8
30    READ X,Y
40    PRINT TAB(X,Y) CHR$ 219
50 NEXT I
60 DATA 0,0,1,0,2,0,3,0,4,0,5,0,6,0,7,0
```

As the loop repeats, the relevant coordinates are assigned in turn to the variables X and Y by the READ statement at line 30. They are then used with the PRINT TAB at line 40 to locate the correct position for each character on the Notepad's display.

Although this is a very simple and direct way of creating a display, it has the disadvantage of involving a large number of data statements. In order to generate the whole of the diagram, including all four sides of the square and the diagonal, 34 pairs of numbers would have to be stored. The possibility of error when typing in 68 numbers in order is obvious. More realistic displays, occupying a far greater area of the Notepad's screen, will be at even greater risk. This is why it is preferable, where possible, to find an arithmetical method for creating a display.

Generating a display by arithmetic

When a display is fairly regular, like this example, it is quite straightforward to use the regularity to calculate all the coordinates required. For example the coordinates of the top line of the display all have the form (X,0), where X is the horizontal displacement ranging from 0 to 7. Clearly these X-values can be generated by a FOR-NEXT loop like this:

```
10 CLS
20 FOR X=0 TO 7
30   PRINT TAB(X,0) CHR$ 219
40 NEXT X
```

The advantage of calculating coordinates in this manner is seen immediately, because with only simple additions to the initial loop, further parts of the display can be added. For example the coordinates of the bottom line of the diagram have the form (X,7). The addition of one program line inside the loop creates both top and bottom of the display:

```
10 CLS
20 FOR X=0 TO 7
30   PRINT TAB(X,0) CHR$ 219
40   PRINT TAB(X,7) CHR$ 219
50 NEXT X
```

A loop can also be used to print the two sides of the square. The coordinates of the character positions remaining unfilled on the left hand side have the general form (0,Y), where Y is the vertical displacement down the screen. The unfilled positions on the right have the form (7,Y). This means that an additional FOR-NEXT loop, with Y ranging from 1 to 6, can fill in both sides. The program now becomes:

```
10 CLS
20 FOR X=0 TO 7
30   PRINT TAB(X,0) CHR$ 219
40   PRINT TAB(X,7) CHR$ 219
50 NEXT X
60 FOR Y=1 TO 6
70   PRINT TAB(0,Y) CHR$ 219
80   PRINT TAB(7,Y) CHR$ 219
90 NEXT Y
```

Display and Graphics

A little thought will show that the program can be simpler than this. There is, after all, no reason why the four corners of the square should not be filled in twice. The second loop could have just the same range of values as the first, 0-7. This means that all four PRINT TAB statements can be placed within the same loop. It now makes more sense to use a different variable, not X or Y, for the loop because both horizontal and vertical sides are being generated. The code could therefore become:

```
10 CLS
20 FOR I=0 TO 7
30   PRINT TAB(I,0) CHR$ 219
40   PRINT TAB(I,7) CHR$ 219
50   PRINT TAB(0,I) CHR$ 219
60   PRINT TAB(7,I) CHR$ 219
70 NEXT I
```

A further refinement to the FOR-NEXT loop is the addition of the diagonal. This has the coordinates (0,0), (1,1), (2,2), (3,3), (4,4), (5,5), (6,6), (7,7). In terms of the loop variable, each character position in the diagonal has the coordinates (I,I) and so a final version of the program is:

```
10 CLS
20 FOR I=0 TO 7
30   PRINT TAB(I,0) CHR$ 219
40   PRINT TAB(I,7) CHR$ 219
50   PRINT TAB(0,I) CHR$ 219
60   PRINT TAB(7,I) CHR$ 219
70   PRINT TAB(I,I) CHR$ 219
80 NEXT I
```

This will produce the entire display and can be easily seen to be much simpler and more elegant than the alternative method of storing large quantities of data.

Producing a display with nested loops

Similar techniques can be devised for any screen display which has sufficient regularity. Sometimes nested FOR-NEXT loops will be needed. For example the labyrinth in the program Maze in Chapter 17 is generated by nested loops. The arithmetic becomes a little more complicated in such a situation and how quickly the necessary expressions in the FOR-NEXT loops can be devised is mainly a matter of experience. A useful approach is to sketch the display, note the range of coordinates required and jot down the values of loop variables that match these coordinates. Listing numbers alongside each other in columns often helps in spotting arithmetical patterns.

Suppose, for example, this display is needed:

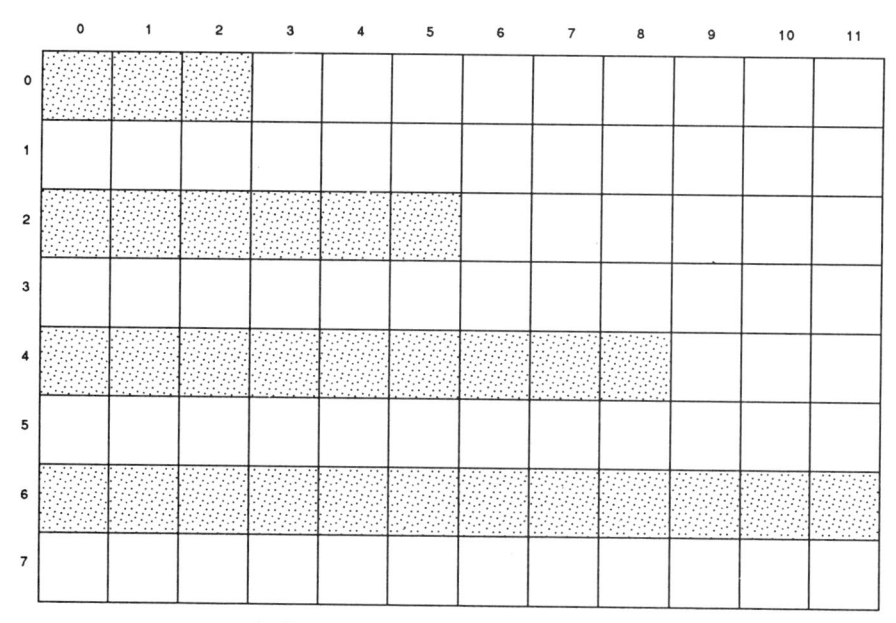

A display produced by nested loops

Four alternate rows of the display are filled in, with an increasing number of character positions in each row. As with the previous display example, a deliberately simple design has been chosen here. In practice a far more complicated display is likely, but the method of devising a solution will remain the same. The first step in analysing the pattern might be to note down this relationship, in tabular form:

Coordinate of row, Y	X coordinate of final position, P
0	2
2	5
4	8
6	11

It is immediately obvious how BASIC code can be used to generate the values in the left hand column. It simply requires a FOR-NEXT loop which increases in steps of 2. This short routine will print out the values:

```
10 FOR Y=0 TO 6 STEP 2
20    PRINT Y
30 NEXT Y
```

The next stage is to break down the relation between the two columns into one which can be as easily coded into BASIC. Clearly the final X-coordinate, P, is determined by the value of Y, but this relationship has to be specified precisely as an arithmetic expression. Some people will see this expression immediately. Others, more distant from their secondary school maths, will need to follow a laborious number-crunching method, perhaps similar to the following.

Analysing the arithmetic

Reduce the Y sequence of numbers, 0, 2, 4, 6, to the simpler sequence 1, 2, 3, 4. This can be done by taking one half of each number in the sequence and then adding 1, like the values in this table:

Y	Y/2	(Y/2)+1
0	0	1
2	1	2
4	2	3
6	3	4

Next reduce the P sequence of numbers in the second column of the original table to an identical series: 1, 2, 3, 4. This is achieved by adding 1 to each number and then dividing by 3. A third table is therefore:

P	P+1	(P+1)/3
2	3	1
5	6	2
8	9	3
11	12	4

Once the same series has been worked out for each table, the algebraic expression relating Y and P can be deduced. This is done by reversing the two arithmetic expressions operating upon P. Instead of adding 1 and dividing by 3, you must take the value of (Y/2)+1 and multiply by 3 and then subtract 1. This should give the value of P in the first column. Interpreting this in symbols gives:

```
P = ( (Y/2+1) * 3 ) - 1
```

Working out the content of the brackets leads to:

```
P = ( Y*3/2 + 3 ) - 1
```

Simplifying further yields:

```
P = Y*3/2+2
```

This can be checked by writing out a further table, in which the values of Y and P are written down:

Y	P = Y*3/2+2
0	2
2	5
4	8
6	11

It can be seen that this matches the original table of Y and P exactly. The correct expression has been found.

Completing the nested loops

The new expression will now give the upper range of the nested loop which will calculate the X-coordinate of each filled character position in the array. The loop variable is X and the loop is nested inside the outer Y-loop. The combination of values generated by both loops working together will produce exactly those positions required to reproduce the original diagram on the Notepad's display. As in the previous example, CHR$ 219 is used to print a filled space:

```
10 CLS
20 FOR Y=0 TO 6 STEP 2
30   FOR X=0 TO Y*3/2+2
40     PRINT TAB(X,Y) CHR$ 32
50   NEXT X
60 NEXT Y
```

A similar process to the one just explained will help in many cases where a regular screen display is needed. There is never any need to resort to three levels of nesting, unless a three dimensional screen display with perspective effects is to be attempted. This would exceed in any case the definition possible with character positions.

Storing display coordinates in an array

So far it has been assumed that a screen display is being produced just once, with character positions being printed on to the screen as soon as they are calculated, or read from data. There will be occasions, though, when a screen display needs to be created again later in the execution of the program. It would be unwise to go through the entire process of recalculation. Instead the coordinate positions should be stored into a two dimensional array so that they can be used again as required.

This can be done by using two procedures. One will calculate the coordinate positions and place them into the array. The other will use these array values to create the screen display. This is illustrated here using the previous program as its starting point.

The first procedure, PROCinit, initialises the array and places the coordinates into the appropriate array locations. The array is dimensioned as DIM D(11,6). This will waste memory in the specific case of this program's display. The blank lines of the display need not be stored. However, it is simpler to have a direct correlation between the PRINT TAB coordinates and the array locations, using the same subscripts for each. The modified code, without line numbers is:

Display and Graphics 65

```
DEF PROCinit
DIM D(11,6)
FOR Y=0 TO 6 STEP 2
  FOR X=0 TO Y*3/2+2
    D(X,Y)=219
  NEXT X
NEXT Y
ENDPROC
```

The relevant array locations are identified with the ASCII code of the character that will build up the display. The other locations remain zero and will not contribute to the display.

The procedure which uses the array to create the screen is PROCdisplay. This just uses two further nested loops to scan the D array and print out the characters represented by the ASCII codes stored at each location. Rather than have ranges for the loop variables that reflect those locations known to be non-zero (mirroring the way the array was initially filled), it is simpler to inspect the entire array with loop variables that extend to every location. This will be be vital if the display has to be altered at some point in the program and the array values are adjusted as a consequence. The code, again ignoring line numbers, for the procedure is:

```
DEF PROCdisplay
CLS
FOR Y=0 TO 6
  FOR X=0 TO 11
    PRINT TAB(X,Y) CHR$ D(X,Y)
  NEXT X
NEXT Y
ENDPROC
```

Using two procedures for the display, one to calculate it and the other to draw it on screen, leads to an overall program which at its simplest will be:

```
 10 REM Control routine
 20 PROCinit
 30 PROCdisplay
 40 END
 50 REM
 60 DEF PROCinit
 70 DIM D(11,6)
 80 FOR Y=0 TO 6 STEP 2
 90   FOR X=0 TO Y*3/2+2
100     D((X,Y)=219
110   NEXT X
120 NEXT Y
130 ENDPROC
140 REM
150 DEF PROCdisplay
160 CLS
170 FOR Y=0 TO 6
```

```
180   FOR X=0 TO 11
190     PRINT TAB(X,Y) CHR$ D(X,Y)
200   NEXT X
210 NEXT Y
220 ENDPROC
```

Like all structured programs, the listing is much longer than the simplest way of solving the problem but is clearer to follow in its logic.

Producing a bar chart

Similar display techniques to those already described can be used in programs which produce graphical output on the Notepad. The program below creates a simple bar chart. Six numbers are entered. A horizontal chart is then displayed, the length of the separate bars proportional to the size of each number in turn:

```
10 REM Bar chart
20 DIM N(6)
30 MAX=0
40 FOR I=1 TO 6
50   PRINT "Type number ";I
60   INPUT N(I)
70   IF N(I)>MAX THEN MAX=N(I)
80 NEXT I
90 CLS
100 FOR I=1 TO 6
110   PRINT TAB(0,I); I
120   FOR J=2 TO 70*N(I)/MAX
130     IF N(I)>0 THEN PRINT TAB(J,I) CHR$ 220
140   NEXT J
150 NEXT I
```

Line 20 initialises the N(6) array to accept the numbers entered by the user in the FOR-NEXT loop between lines 40-80. There is no way of telling in advance what the range of these numbers will be. A variable, MAX, is therefore introduced which detects, by the end of the input loop, what the largest number is. At line 30, MAX is initialised as 0. Line 70 then reassigns it the value of the input, whenever this is larger. At the end of the loop, MAX has the maximum value of the numbers in the N array. It can then be used, in the two nested loops which follow, to scale the bar chart drawn.

The two variables of the loops at lines 100-150 generate the text coordinates for a character, CHR$ 220, which builds up each bar of the graph as a thick, solid line. The outer I loop determines the Y-coordinate of this character. The J loop decides how many of the characters will be drawn in each bar by controlling the X-coordinate. The J value begins at 2 and continues up to the scaled value of 70*N(I)/MAX at line 120. This means that the longest bar will always be (70-2) characters long, irrespective of the actual size of the numbers entered by the user.

Line 110 partially calibrates the chart by placing the number of the entry at the beginning of each bar.

Using graphics coordinates

The text coordinates used up to this point inevitably create rather heavy-handed graphics effects. Far finer scale is possible using a separate set of coordinates on the Notepad's display. These graphics coordinates treat the screen as if it were a piece of graph paper, numbered along the horizontal X-axis from 0 to 479 and up the vertical Y-axis from 0 to 63. This means that the bottom left hand corner has the coordinates (0,0), the top left hand corner (0,63), the top right corner (479,63) and the bottom right hand corner has coordinates (479,0). Note that brackets are not used in the BASIC code referring to any graphics points.

The individual points that can be added to the display using graphics coordinates are called 'pixels'. This is an American abbreviation of 'picture element' which seemed to enter colloquial language about the time that NASA probes were sending back photographs of the moon and Mars as streams of telemetered bits. The pixels on the Notepad's screen are small enough to permit finely-detailed screen display.

Adding lines with MOVE and DRAW

Many commands exist to allow points, lines and areas of a screen display to be highlighted In its original version BBC BASIC allowed colour as well, but the Notepad is restricted to just two. These will be referred to here as black and white, although the screen is really grey with dark blue pixels. Normally it will be assumed that black is used for all drawing on the white background although in the next chapter it will be explained how drawing in white permits animation effects.

Two commands are particularly useful in creating a display. MOVE X,Y places the graphics cursor at the point X pixels across the screen and Y pixels up. This is like shifting a pencil above a sheet of paper to the point where you wish to begin drawing. DRAW X,Y displays a line from the current position of the graphics cursor to the new point (X,Y). This program will therefore draw two diagonal lines across the screen:

```
10 CLS
20 MOVE 0,63
30 DRAW 479,0
40 MOVE 0,0
50 DRAW 479,63
```

Outlined shapes from coordinate data

The versatility of MOVE and DRAW is enhanced if the two commands are combined with coordinates held as data. The following short routine draws a square, but is sufficiently general to be adapted to any outlined shape:

```
 10 REM Drawing an outline from data
 20 CLS
 30 READ N,X,Y
 40 MOVE X,Y
 50 FOR I=1 TO N
 60    READ X,Y
 70    DRAW X,Y
 80 NEXT I
 90 REM Data for outline
100 DATA 4,10,10
110 DATA 60,10,60,60,10,60,10,10
```

Line 30 reads three numbers. The first, N, is the number of points that will draw a shape. The next two, X, Y, are the coordinates of the point where the shape will begin. After this the loop repeats N times, reading the coordinates of a fresh point at each repeat and drawing a line to it. The data here will draw a square 50 X 50 pixels in size. Different data can be constructed to draw a shape with any number of straight sides.

Drawing a circle – SIN, COS, DEG and RAD

The Notepad does not have a circle command, but it is easy to use a little trigonometry to write a short routine that will draw a circle. This listing could be included as a procedure in another program which required circles to be drawn:

```
 10 REM Drawing a circle
 20 CLS
 30 REM Obtain values
 40 INPUT "Type the X-coordinate of centre", XC
 50 INPUT "Type the Y-coordinate of centre", YC
 60 INPUT "Type the radius required", R
 70 CLS
 80 REM Draw circle
 90 MOVE XC+R,YC
100 FOR I=0 TO 2*PI STEP PI/8
110    X=XC+R*COS I
120    Y=YC+R*SIN I
130    DRAW X,Y
140 NEXT I
```

The diagram will help to illustrate how this program works:

Display and Graphics 69

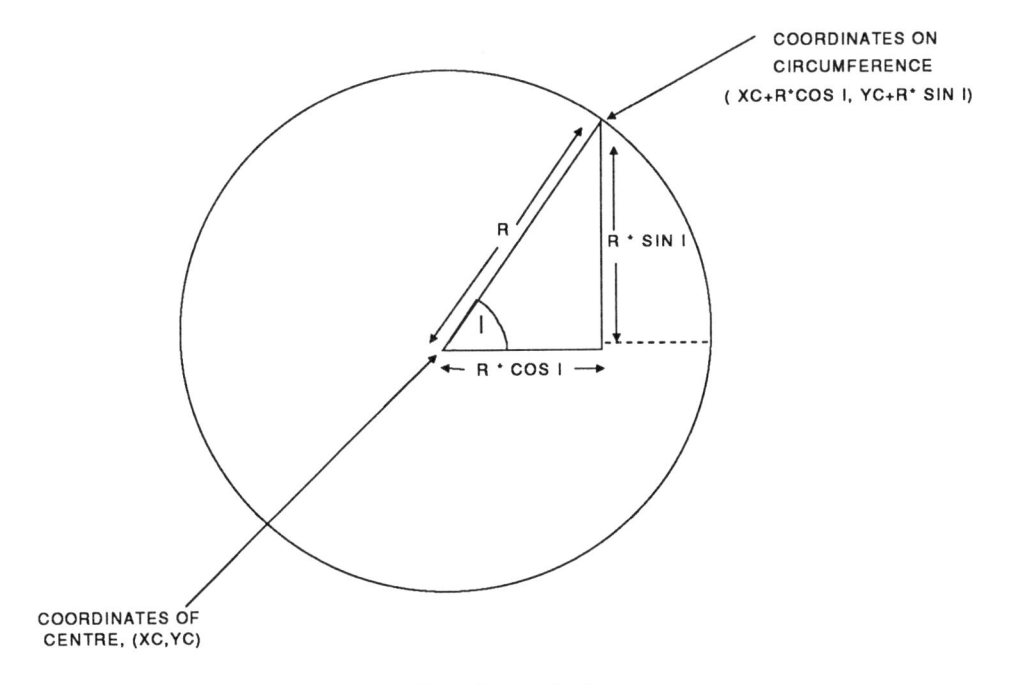

Drawing a circle

Lines 40-60 obtain the necessary data to draw the circle. The centre has coordinates (XC,YC). The circle's radius is R. The triangle in the diagram shows that the point indicated on the circumference has an X-coordinate equal to XC plus the horizontal side, R*COS I. Its Y-coordinate is YC plus the vertical side, R*SIN I. Lines 110 and 120 of the program calculate these coordinates.

The graphics cursor first has to be moved to the point (XC+R,YC) at the extreme right of the horizontal radius. After this, the loop repeatedly draws short lines to the points calculated on the circumference. The range of the loop is from 0 to 2*PI because a whole circle contains 2*PI radians, the equivalent of 360 degrees.

Although this program uses angles measured in radians, conversion to and from the more familiar degrees can be made with the DEG and RAD instructions. This is shown in a later example.

Creating a pie chart

The circle drawing routine can be extended further to give a program which will draw pie charts. The example developed here will accept five numbers entered by the user and display them as scaled sectors of a circle which fills nearly the full height of the screen.

```
10 REM Pie chart
20 DIM N(5)
30 T=0 : B=0
40 REM Input data
50 CLS
60 FOR I=1 TO 5
70   PRINT "Type number ";I
80   INPUT N(I)
90   T=T+N(I)
100 NEXT I
110 CLS
120 REM Show title
130 PRINT TAB(40,0) "PIE CHART"
140 REM Draw circle
150 MOVE 230,30
160 FOR I=0 TO 2*PI STEP PI/8
170   X=200+30*COS I
180   Y=30+30*SIN I
190   DRAW X,Y
200 NEXT I
210 REM Calibrate circle
220 A=2*PI/T
230 FOR I=1 TO 5
240   B=B+N(I)
250   MOVE 200,30
260   REM Draw division
270   DRAW 200+30*COS (A*B), 30+30*SIN (A*B)
280   REM Add values
290   PRINT TAB(40,I+1); I "......." N(I)
300 NEXT I
```

The loop between lines 60-100 accepts the five numbers typed by the user and assigns them to locations in the N array initialised at line 20. It also adds the running total of the numbers and stores this as the value of the variable T. This value is required later to calculate what fraction of the circle each of the numbers is.

Line 130 then prints the title, Pie Chart, on the display. A circle is added by the loop between lines 160-200. It uses the same routine as already explained. The centre of the circle is at (200,30) and its radius is 30 pixels.

The divisions of the pie chart are added by the final FOR-NEXT loop at lines 230-300. The angle of each of the five lines has to be calculated first. The variable B adds the running total of all the numbers, N(I), as the loop repeats. Multiplying this number by 2*PI and dividing by the overall total, T, gives the relevant angle in radian. Part of this calculation is performed outside the loop, leading to the variable A becoming a multiplying factor of 2*PI/T. The angle inside the loop is therefore A*B.

Inserting this into the same equation as before for calculating points on the circumference of the circle permits MOVE and DRAW to add the five radii that mark

Display and Graphics

off the divisions of the circle. Finally the values typed in are repeated beside the pie chart by line 290.

Producing a tabular display – TAN

Output from a program will sometimes consist of values which are best represented in tabular form. Designing a screen display to show regular columns and rows can require some thought. An example is given here of the type of problem encountered. The trigonometric functions that have just been introduced together with the further ration, TAN, are used as a convenient source of data for the table. A complete set of trigonometric values for these three ratios is produced at five degree intervals up to an angle of 90 degrees. Although the listing is included here as a programming example, it is quite a useful utility to add to a Notepad library.

The program emphasises the way in which a screen display has to be planned carefully in advance of any actual programming. This is always important with a computer program, but it becomes especially so with the long, narrow display on the Notepad. The listing is:

```
10 REM Trigonometric functions
20 CLS
30 REM Headings
40 FOR I=5 TO 57 STEP 26
50    PRINT TAB(I,0) "SIN    COS    TAN"
60 NEXT I
70 REM Display table
80 FOR I=1 TO 18
90    REM Calculate angle
100   A=I*5.
110   REM Calculate coordinates
120   X=-26*(I>6)-26*(I>12)
130   Y=I MOD 6 - 6*(I MOD 6=0)
140   REM Determine functions
150   S$=LEFT$( STR$( SIN (RAD A)),4)
160   C$=LEFT$( STR$( COS (RAD A)),4)
170   T$=LEFT$( STR$( TAN (RAD A)),4)
180   REM Display functions
190   X=X-(I=1)
200   PRINT TAB(X,Y); A "..."
210   X=X+(I=1)
220   PRINT TAB(X+5,Y) S$
230   PRINT TAB(X+11,Y) C$
240   PRINT TAB(X+17,Y) T$
250 NEXT I
260 REM Corrections
270 PRINT TAB(5,1) "0.09"
280 PRINT TAB(17,1) "0.09"
290 PRINT TAB(63,5) "0.09"
300 PRINT TAB(63,6) "0   "
310 PRINT TAB(69,6) "inf."
```

The diagram indicates how three columns can be fitted on to the display to permit angles from 5 to 90 degrees to be shown. Only the number of each entry is shown, not the angle that will be displayed on the screen. The six rows in each column lead to 18 entries conveniently matching the range of angles to be displayed. As the first angle shown is 5 degrees, and the interval between angles is also 5 degrees, the final value displayed will be (18 x 5) or 90 degrees.

Text coordinates for table

The 18 angles require a loop that will repeat this number of times. In the program this is the main FOR-NEXT loop between lines 80-250. Showing the values calculated would be easy if a standard computer monitor were available. Long columns of figures could be displayed, with 18 rows reflecting the information available for the 18 angles. With the Notepad's screen, a little more work needs to be put into organising the display, because everything has to be fitted into the three separate columns available. This can be done, but some arithmetic, and Boolean thinking, is required.

Calculating the table's coordinates

First the X-coordinates for the screen items will be considered. These depend upon the value of the control variable for the loop, I, in a regular way. When I is less than 7, the angles need to be shown on the left of the display. An X-coordinate of 0 is required. When I is between 7 and 12, the angles need to be placed one third of the way across the screen. An X-coordinate of 26 is then needed. Finally, when I is greater than 12, the display must take place two thirds of the way across the screen. This is an X-coordinate of 52. The calculation of X-values can be summarised as an informal algorithm:

❏ Initially assume the X-coordinate is zero

❏ When the value of I exceeds 6, add 26 to the X-coordinate

❏ When the value exceeds 12, add another 26

The algorithm can be coded into BASIC with the use of Boolean conditions. The expression which shows that I is greater than 6 is, simply, (I>6). Until I is greater than 6 the Boolean value of this expression will be 0. However as soon as I passes 6, the expression's value becomes true, or -1. At first this seems unhelpful, but multiplying by -26 will give precisely the value then required for the X-coordinate. This leads to:

```
X = -26 * (I>6)
```

Now all the correct values for the X-coordinate are given up to 12. It is clear that an expression involving the Boolean value of (I>12) will similarly augment the X-coordinate for the third column on the display. This leads to the BASIC code at line 120 of the program.

The Y-coordinates also need to be calculated for the diagram. They depend upon the value of the loop variable, I, but not in the way that the X-coordinates alter. Once the X-coordinates increase in value the increment is retained. The Y-coordinates in contrast cycle three times between 0 and 6. This pattern indicates the values generated by I MOD 6:

I	I MOD 6
1	1
2	2
3	3
4	4
5	5
6	0
7	1

I MOD 6 gives exactly the Y-coordinate required except that values of 0 need to be replaced by the screen coordinate of 6. This, too, can be achieved with a Boolean expression. This time it is (I MOD 6=0). When this is true, Y needs to be increased from 0 to 6. The value of (I MOD 6=0) will then be -1 and so multiplying by -6 and adding back on to the value I MOD 6 creates exactly the correction required. This is the expression at line 130:

```
Y=I MOD 6 - 6*(I MOD 6=0)
```

Calculating the table's values

Calculating these coordinates is probably the most complicated part of the program. After this, all that has to be done is the evaluation and display of the angles and their sine, cosine and tangent at the coordinate positions that have been determined. Line 100 calculates the angle in degrees by multiplying the loop variable, I, by 5. The angle is then displayed on the screen at the coordinates calculated. This is at line 200.

As so many trigonometric values are going to be shown on the screen, it is necessary to truncate the number of decimal places displayed. Including a routine that would do this accurately, rounding up where necessary, would complicate this version of the program and so is left as an exercise for the enthusiast. Instead, a simpler method is adopted.

Each function is converted into a string and then shortened to the first four characters by using LEFT$. When looking at the lines that perform this task, 150-180, it must be appreciated that the evaluation of each expression always begins with the lowest level of nesting of the brackets. For example, line 150 first converts the angle A to radians, as RAD A. It then calculates the sine. This is SIN (RAD A).

Next a string is produced, STR$(SIN (RAD A)). Finally the first four characters are obtained by LEFT$(STR$(SIN (RAD A)),4). These are assigned to the string variable, S$, and represent the value of the sine that will be displayed on the screen. In a similar fashion, values for cosine and tangent are assigned to C$ and T$. All three values are then appended to the angle already shown on the screen by the appropriate coordinates in the PRINT TAB statements between lines 220-240.

Acknowledging an algorithm's weakness

At this point the program is almost finished, but still needs some modifications. The quick and easy way in which the trigonometric functions have been calculated has led to unavoidable errors in a few of the values. Very small numbers, and very large, are calculated by the Notepad in standard scientific notation rather than simple decimal fractions. Taking the first four characters of a number like this ignores the trailing power of 10 which is essential to give the real value. In this program lines 270-310 provide the 'fudge factor' that overprints the incorrect parts of the display.

A further minor adjustment is added by lines 190 and 200. These use another Boolean condition to shift the X-coordinate one place to the right and back. This means that the single digit 5 is printed in line with the other two digit angles.

Drawing a graph

MOVE and DRAW can be used to draw graphs on the Notepad's display. Input could be typed in by the user, or perhaps read from a data file using techniques that will be introduced in Chapter 8. For the graphical demonstration program here, though, the

Display and Graphics

Notepad's trigonometric ability is used again in a routine which produces a sine curve. This shows the values of sine from 0 to 360 degrees.

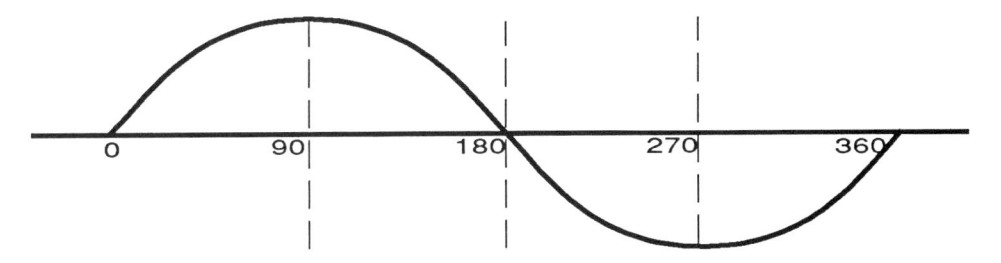

Producing a graph with MOVE and DRAW

The listing is as follows:

```
 10 REM Sine curve
 20 CLS
 30 REM Draw X-axis
 40 MOVE 120,32
 50 DRAW 360,32
 60 REM Draw dotted lines
 70 FOR I=0 TO 60 STEP 4
 80    FOR J=180 TO 300 STEP 60
 90       MOVE J,I : DRAW J,I+2
100    NEXT J
110 NEXT I
120 REM Add angles
130 PRINT TAB(20,5) "0"
140 PRINT TAB(27,5) "90"
150 PRINT TAB(36,5) "180"
160 PRINT TAB(46,5) "270"
170 PRINT TAB(59,5) "360"
180 REM Draw sine curve
190 MOVE 120,32
200 FOR I=0 TO 360 STEP 5
210    X=120+I*2/3
220    Y=32+30*SIN(RAD I)
230    DRAW X,Y
240 NEXT I
```

Line 40 moves the graphics cursor to the left hand end of the X-axis at point 120,32. Line 50 then draws a horizontal line 240 pixels long to 360,32. This line represents angles from 0 to 360 degrees, or four complete right angles making up a whole circle. The axis is placed halfway up the display because the values of sine of an angle range from -1 to 1.

To make the graph easier to follow, each right angle is indicated by a vertical dotted line. These four lines are drawn by two nested FOR-NEXT loops, controlled by variables I and J. I represents Y-coordinates and J represents X-coordinates of the points making up the lines. The range of each loop has to be defined carefully. The quarter divisions along the axis will be at X-coordinates 180, 240 and 300. This is achieved by the use of STEP 60 for the J value at line 80. The I loop has to create a dotted effect. It does this with STEP 4 at line 70. This is exactly twice the width of the dotted line created by the loop. Line 90 then moves to the point J,I and draws a short vertical line to J,I+2. This line is repeated by the nested loops to create the pattern required.

Lines 130-170 then add the appropriate angles, in degrees, for each of the dotted lines and also the 0 and 360 which indicate the extent of the graph. After this the graph itself can be drawn. Line 190 moves the graphics cursor to the zero on the axis. The FOR-NEXT loop which follows then calculates the value of the sine in 5 degree intervals up to the final angle of 360 degrees.

The X- and Y-coordinate for each point of the graph is calculated separately at lines 210, 220 before line 230 draws a line to this new point from the previous one. The calculation of the X-value is quite straightforward. The total range of the loop variable, I, is 360, but the range for X is two thirds of this, or 240. The I value therefore has to be multiplied by 2 and divided by 3 before 120 is added. The start of the axis is, of course, at X=120. The Y-coordinate is calculated by using SIN. The value of I is in degrees and so RAD is required. The sine then has to be multiplied by 30 to extend the maximum value from 1 to a number large enough to fill the display. Finally 32 must be added as this is the Y-coordinate of the axis.

Drawing a filled triangle – PLOT 85,X,Y

The Notepad can cover areas of the screen with solid blocks of pixels. This is convenient for drawing large, filled-in shapes. A triangle can be drawn with PLOT 85,X,Y. The instruction constructs a triangle from the point (X,Y) to the last two graphics points 'visited' by another command, like MOVE or DRAW. Triangles are demonstrated by this program:

```
 10 REM Filled triangle
 20 CLS
 30 INPUT "Type 1st X-coordinate", X1
 40 INPUT "Type 1st Y-coordinate", Y1
 50 INPUT "Type 2nd X-coordinate", X2
 60 INPUT "Type 2nd Y-coordinate", Y2
 70 INPUT "Type 3rd X-coordinate", X3
 80 INPUT "Type 3rd Y-coordinate", Y3
 90 CLS
100 MOVE X1,Y1
110 MOVE X2,Y2
120 PLOT 85,X3,Y3
```

Drawing a filled rectangle – PLOT 101,X,Y

Filled rectangles can be drawn with PLOT 101,X,Y. This draws a rectangle from the point (X,Y) to the last point visited, putting the two points at opposite ends of a diagonal of the shape. This is illustrated by the following program:

```
10 REM Filled rectangle
20 CLS
30 INPUT "Type X-coordinate",X
40 INPUT "Type Y-coordinate", Y
50 INPUT "Type length", L
60 INPUT "Type width", W
70 CLS
80 MOVE X,Y
90 PLOT 101,X+L,Y+W
```

Drawing a filled circle

The Notepad's version of BBC BASIC does not have a filled circle command. However circles can be drawn quite easily as a series of thin triangles rotated about the centre. The following program does this. Points on the circumference of the circle are calculated by SIN and COS, as in the earlier example that drew an outlined circle. Triangles can be drawn by alternately moving to the centre of the circle and then applying PLOT 85 to the next point on the circumference. The circle is really a filled polygon. This becomes apparent if the value of the step at line 80 is made larger.

```
10  REM Filled circle
20  CLS
30  INPUT "Type X-coordinate",X
40  INPUT "Type Y-coordinate", Y
50  INPUT "Type radius", R
60  CLS
70  MOVE X,Y
80  FOR I=0 TO 2*PI STEP PI/8
90     MOVE X,Y
100    PLOT 85, X+R*COS I, Y+R*SIN I
110 NEXT I
```

Filled shapes from coordinate data

When a complicated filled shape is required on the display, an efficient way of creating it is to use PLOT 101 and PLOT 85 within separate FOR-NEXT loops to build it up as a series of filled rectangles and triangles. The graphics coordinates required are held in lines of data and read as required. The principle is similar to the technique used earlier to draw an outline with DRAW combined with coordinate data.

The technique is illustrated here with a program which draws a picture of a three-stage rocket:

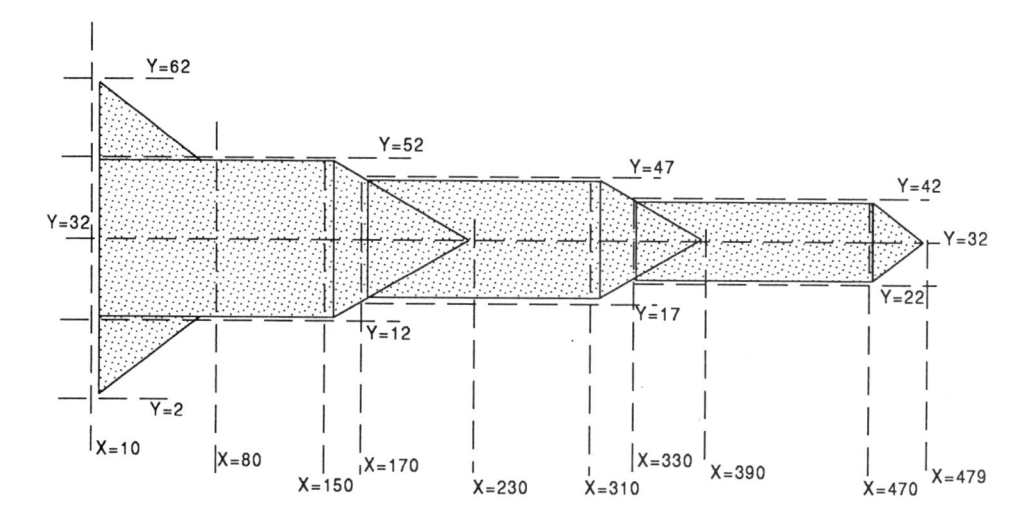

Drawing with filled rectangles and triangles

The dotted lines indicate the coordinates of the vertices of all the component rectangles and triangles creating the picture. For example, the bottom left hand corner of the first stage of the rocket has coordinates (10,2) and the top of the nose cone is at (479,32). Using two sets of perpendicular coordinate lines like this makes labelling the vertices far easier than writing down the pair of coordinates for each point required. Initial preparation of the coordinate data is obviously made easier if graph paper is used.

A picture of a rocket has been chosen as this example because it is long and thin and conveniently fills the full length of the Notepad's screen. Naturally the program could be adapted to draw smaller pictures. Only the data needs to be altered. Here is the listing:

```
10 REM Drawing filled shapes
20 CLS
30 REM Number of each shape
40 READ R,T
50 REM Draw rectangles
60 FOR I=1 TO R
70    READ A,B,C,D
80    MOVE A,B
90    PLOT 101,C,D
100 NEXT I
110 REM Draw triangles
120 FOR I=1 TO T
130    READ A,B,C,D,E,F
```

```
140    MOVE A,B
150    MOVE C,D
160    PLOT 85,E,F
170 NEXT I
180 PRINT TAB(33,7) "3-STAGE ROCKET";
190 REM Numbers of shapes
200 DATA 3,5
210 REM Data for rectangles
220 DATA 10,12,150,52
230 DATA 170,17,310,47
240 DATA 330,22,470,42
250 REM Data for triangles
260 DATA 10,2,10,12,80,12
270 DATA 10,52,10,62,80,52
280 DATA 150,12,150,52,230,32
290 DATA 310,17,310,47,390,32
300 DATA 470,22,470,42,479,32
```

The program can be seen to consist of two loops, between lines 60-100 and lines 120-170. The first loop draws the three rectangles representing the stages of the rocket and the second adds the five triangles forming the fins, nose cone and inter-stage fairing.

As well as the coordinates for the rectangles and triangles, the program requires the total numbers of each shape to be held as data. This is so that the two loops can repeat the correct number of times. The two numbers – 3 rectangles and 5 triangles – are placed in the data statement at line 200. They are then assigned to the two variables, R and T, by the READ statement at line 40. The value of R makes the first loop repeat three times. This loop uses line 70 to read the rectangle coordinate data between lines 220-240. The coordinates of the bottom left hand corners of each rectangle are assigned at each execution of the loop to the variables A and B. Similarly the coordinates of the top right hand corners are assigned to the variables C and D. Line 80 then moves the graphics cursor to the point (A,B) and line 90 employs PLOT 101 to fill in a rectangle to the point (C,D).

The triangles are added in an analogous way. The value of T makes the second loop repeat five times. On each execution of the loop the coordinates of the vertices of one of the triangles are read from the data stored between lines 260-300 and assigned to the pairs of variables (A,B), (C,D) and (E,F). The graphics cursor is moved to (A,B) by line 140 and to (C,D) by line 150. The PLOT 85 statement at line 160 then fills in a triangle between these two vertices and point (E,F).

Although this drawing routine is shown here as a separate short program, it is more likely to be of use as a procedure held within a larger program that requires a method for creating a screen display for some other purpose.

Drawing with repeated triangles

The picture of the rocket has been created by the use of both filled rectangles and triangles. This has required quite a large amount of data because two points, or four coordinate numbers, have been needed for each rectangle and six coordinate numbers for each triangle. It is not possible to avoid storing this amount of data in a program which is going to produce a generalised screen display. If there is no pattern to the distribution of the rectangles and triangles, each has to be located precisely with its whole complement of numbers. However, when a shape has a great deal of regularity it is possible to reduce the amount of data that has to be stored.

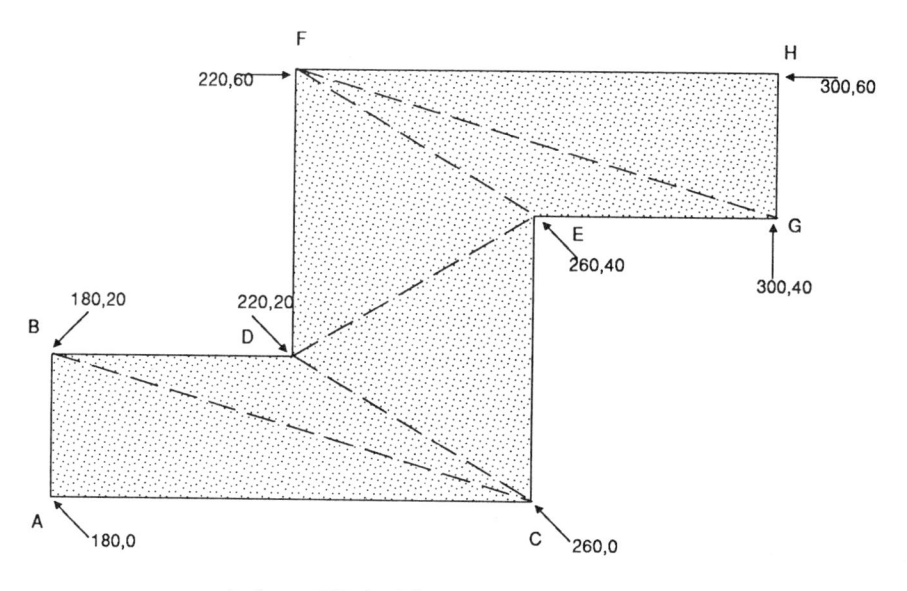

A shape filled with repeated PLOT85,X,Y

For example the diagram shows a pattern which can be filled quite easily just using triangles alone. Furthermore, by drawing the triangles in a carefully selected order, each only requires the coordinates of one vertex to be held as data. The other two vertices are already present on the shape from the previous triangles that have been drawn.

In order to fill in the shape shown, the graphics cursor first needs to be moved to the point A, coordinates (180,0), and then to point B, coordinates (180,20). This is done by lines 30 and 40 of the program below. After this, the whole shape can be filled by using PLOT 85, with the appropriate coordinates for points C, D, E, F, G and H. Each time a triangle is filled back to the previous two points visited. The order of the points has been arranged so that this will fill the shape. Here is the listing of the program required:

Display and Graphics

```
 10 REM Repeated triangle fill
 20 CLS
 30 MOVE 180,0
 40 MOVE 180,20
 50 FOR I=1 TO 6
 60    READ X,Y
 70    PLOT 85,X,Y
 80    K=GET
 90 NEXT I
100 DATA 260,0,220,20,260,40
110 DATA 220,60,300,40,300,60
```

The loop between lines 50-90 reads the coordinates of points C to H at line 60 and adds the appropriate triangle at line 70. Line 80 prevents further execution of the loop until a key is pressed. This allows the sequential addition of the triangles to be seen clearly.

7

Animation and Sound

Many programs can be improved with the inclusion of animated graphics and sound effects. Fortunately it is easy to add both of these to programs written for the Notepad. It is capable of all of the graphics effects possible in BBC BASIC, except those which involve 'colour switching' animation and which are therefore impossible with a monochrome display. The sound produced by the Notepad is also limited compared with the techniques available on an Acorn machine, but it is still versatile enough to be worth exploiting at a relevant point in a program.

The basic principles of animation

Animation on the screen of a computer depends upon the same concepts as animation on a TV or cinema screen. Fundamentally the technique relies upon the finite time the human brain takes to process signals sent by the eye. If a series of separate images, each slightly different from the one before, is presented on a display screen, the brain will assume that it is being confronted with the same object moving rather than the sequence of distinct items really present.

A typical computer program for moving graphics will depend upon this very informal algorithm:

i) Present an image on the screen

ii) Pause long enough for it to register on the visual cortex, but no longer

iii) Calculate the details required for the next image

iv) Erase the previous image

v) Display the new one

vi) Repeat this routine as long as required

Animation and Sound 83

This can be demonstrated very easily with an extremely brief program that moves a capital letter A across the Notepad's screen:

```
10 REM Simple character animation
20 CLS
30 FOR X=1 TO 78
40    PRINT TAB(X,3) " A"
50    FOR T=1 TO 300
60    NEXT T
70 NEXT X
```

Here the outer FOR-NEXT loop selects character positions from the left of the Notepad's display to the right. The final value given to the X-coordinate is 78 rather than 79 because two character positions are printed at line 40. These are the letter A itself together with a 'trailing' empty space. This is essential for stage iv) of the algorithm above. If the previous position of the letter is not overwritten by this blank character, a trail of letters will be left across the screen and the animation effect is lost.

Stage ii) of the general algorithm is achieved with the inclusion of the nested FOR-NEXT loop at lines 50 and 60. The number of times the additional loop repeats will control the speed of the letter A.

An animated title

Although this simple example of animation is not very exciting, it can be extended quite easily to create a reasonably amusing effect. In the following, longer, example the same technique is used to decorate the title of a program displayed on the screen.

The program title, in this case simply 'Program name', is surrounded by a rectangular box of asterisks. A lower case letter 'o' then races around the inside of this boundary. It continues until any key is pressed. The screen display then clears to permit the main part of the program to be executed. Here it is just the appearance of *Program now begins...* on the screen, but, if this program were to be modified and incorporated into a serious piece of software, at this point the real code would commence. The listing is as follows:

```
10 REM Animating a title sequence
20 A=0
30 CLS
40 PRINT TAB(34,3) "PROGRAM NAME"
50 REM Place box around title
60 FOR X=31 TO 48
70    PRINT TAB(X,0) CHR$ 42
80    PRINT TAB(X,6) CHR$ 42
90 NEXT X
100 FOR Y=1 TO 5
110    PRINT TAB(31,Y) CHR$ 42
120    PRINT TAB(48,Y) CHR$ 42
```

```
130 NEXT Y
140 PRINT TAB(55,3) "< Press a key >"
150 REM Animation loop
160 REPEAT
170   REM Animate top
180   FOR X=32 TO 47
190     PRINT TAB(X,1) CHR$ 111
200     PROCpause
210     PRINT TAB(X,1) CHR$32
220   NEXT X
230   REM Animate right
240   FOR Y=2 TO 4
250     PRINT TAB(47,Y) CHR$ 111
260     PROCpause
270     PRINT TAB(47,Y) CHR$ 32
280   NEXT Y
290   REM Animate bottom
300   FOR X=47 TO 32 STEP -1
310     PRINT TAB(X,5) CHR$ 111
320     PROCpause
330     PRINT TAB(X,5) CHR$ 32
340   NEXT X
350   REM Animate left
360   FOR Y=4 TO 2 STEP -1
370     PRINT TAB(32,Y) CHR$ 111
380     PROCpause
390     PRINT TAB(32,Y) CHR$ 32
400   NEXT Y
410 UNTIL A=1
420 CLS
430 PRINT "Program now begins..."
440 END
450 DEF PROCpause
460 K=INKEY(20)
470 IF K<>-1 THEN A=1
480 ENDPROC
```

The name of the program is placed at the centre of the display by:

```
PRINT TAB(34,3) "PROGRAM NAME"
```

at line 40. The Y-coordinate of 3 is clearly close enough to the centre of the screen and the X-coordinate is deduced from the number of characters in the title and the width of the Notepad's display. The title then has to be enclosed in a box of asterisks. This is done by two FOR-NEXT loops. The one between lines 60-90 adds the top and bottom of the box. Both of these extend from an X-coordinate of 31 to 48. These values are deduced from the length and position of the title, bearing in mind that the box must be spaced symmetrically about it. In a similar way the FOR-NEXT loop between lines 100-130 adds the left and right sides to the box. The asterisk is printed by using its ASCII value, 42.

Animation and Sound 85

After this, four separate loops move the letter 'o' along the inside of the top of the box from left to right, down its right hand side, then from the bottom right hand corner to the bottom left and finally up the left hand side. The technique is almost the same as the simpler example above, but does differ in two ways. First the letter is displayed by its ASCII code of 111 and erased by the ASCII code of a blank space, 32. Secondly the delay required is produced by a call to a separate procedure, PROCpause.

Using PROCpause has two advantages. It avoids the need for four additional nested loops to create each delay. In addition it permits the keyboard to be scanned to detect when the user grows tired of admiring the animation and wants to start the program proper! This is done by assigning the value of INKEY(20) to the variable K. Most of the time K will have the value of -1, indicating that no key has been pressed. However, as soon as any key at all is chosen, K will cease briefly from being -1 and assume that key's ASCII code. This is immediately detected by line 470, which then reassigns a value of 1 to the flag A.

This flag has initially been assigned the value 0 at line 20. While it remains zero the REPEAT-UNTIL loop between lines 160-410 keeps repeating the four animation loops. However, when A has a value of 1 the main loop will exit as soon as the letter races into the top left hand corner. Then the rest of the program, albeit here fairly vacuous, can continue. Note that the user does not have to press a key when the letter reaches this specific point. Instead the value of A will 'remember' if a key has been pressed at any time.

Using PLOT 5,X,Y and PLOT 7,X,Y

Animating the display using PRINT TAB and text coordinates can produce useful effects, but more precision is possible if animation is created using graphics coordinates. This is an inevitable consequence of the relative size of characters and pixels.

Two commands which are convenient in such animation are PLOT 5,X,Y and PLOT 7,X,Y. The former draws a line in black from the current graphics cursor position to point (X,Y). In contrast the latter command draws the same line in white. It can be appreciated that PLOT 5 is ideal for drawing a shape and PLOT 7 for erasing it again. This provides the essential details of animation.

The two commands can first be illustrated by this short program. It draws a horizontal line across the screen and then, after a screen prompt requesting that a key is pressed, removes it:

```
10 REM Demonstrating PLOT 5,X,Y and PLOT 7,X,Y
20 CLS
30 MOVE 0,32
40 PLOT 5,479,32
```

```
50 PRINT TAB(0,0) "Press any key to make the line vanish..."
60 K=GET
70 PLOT 7,0,32
80 PRINT "Told you!"
```

Line 30 moves the graphics cursor to a middle point on the left hand side of the display. Line 40 then draws a horizontal black line to the right hand side with PLOT 5 followed by the appropriate coordinates. Since the graphics cursor is now at the end of the line, all that is needed in order to erase it is to draw a second line, in white, back to the left. This is done by PLOT 7, with the original coordinates of the left hand point. If this happened immediately there would be no proof that a line had existed at all. To make clear what is happening, line 50 prompts for a keypress and then line 60 uses GET to pause the program until any key is selected. After this PLOT 7 is able to erase the line.

Animating an outlined shape

PLOT 5 and PLOT 7 can now be used to create an outlined shape which can be animated on the display. The program listed below is quite short, but nevertheless illustrates a technique which can be extended to quite subtle animation effects. Use will be made of it in the later chapters of this book, in particular in the Tangrams program in Chapter 20. The example given here moves a large arrow across the screen from left to right:

```
10 REM Animating an outlined shape
20 CLS
30 Y=30
40 FOR I=1 TO 5
50   FOR X=0 TO 400 STEP 20
60     PROCarrow(X,Y,5)
70     FOR T=1 TO 500
80     NEXT T
90     PROCarrow(X,Y,7)
100  NEXT X
110 NEXT I
120 END
130 DEF PROCarrow(X,Y,D)
140 RESTORE
150 MOVE X,Y
160 FOR J=1 TO 7
170   READ A,B
180   PLOT D,X+A,Y+B
190 NEXT J
200 ENDPROC
210 REM
220 REM Data for arrow
230 DATA 30,0,30,-10,50,5,30,20
240 DATA 30,10,0,10,0,0
```

The nested loops between lines 40-110 animate the arrow but it is actually drawn by a separate procedure, PROCarrow(X,Y,D). This is another example of a procedure called with parameters. The X and Y parameters specify the location of the arrow on the screen and the value of the parameter D determines whether the arrow is displayed in black or white. This is needed, of course, to enable the animation effect to take place. This diagram shows how PROCdiagram(X,Y,D) constructs the arrow:

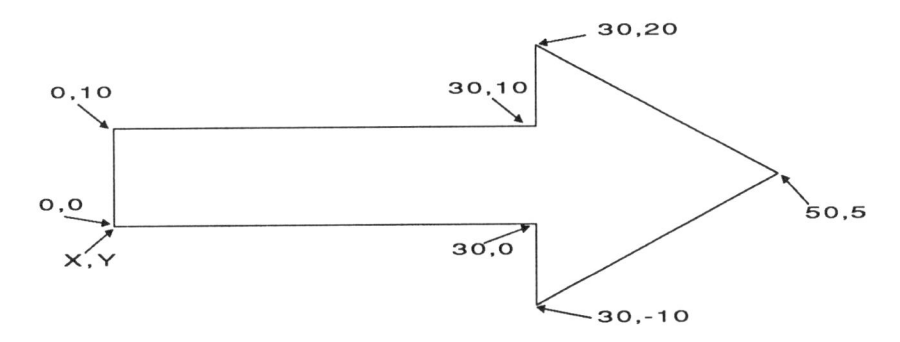

Animating an arrow

The outline is defined with reference to its bottom left hand corner, labelled (0,0) on the diagram. Each time the procedure is called to draw the arrow, the graphics cursor is first moved to this point by line 150. After this the seven short lines needed to produce the outline are drawn by the FOR-NEXT loop between lines 160-190. The variable J is used to control this loop because the whole procedure is called within a loop which uses I as its variable. (An alternative would be to declare I as LOCAL to the procedure.)

Each line drawn is to the point (X+A,Y+B), which is a relative displacement from the starting point, (X,Y). As the loop proceeds, the necessary values for A and B are read from the lines of data, 230,240. For example, the first line drawn is the lower side of the arrow's shaft. This starts on the diagram at (0,0) and reaches the point (30,0). The numbers 30 and 0 are therefore held as the first two data items at line 230. In a similar way all the seven lines can be drawn from the coordinates held in the two data statements. As a result of all the lines being drawn with an explicit reference to X and Y, the arrow can be drawn at any location on the Notepad's display. The lines are drawn by PLOT D, rather than DRAW. Therefore specifying a value for D of 5 or 7 allows the arrow to be shown in black or white. The procedure has the versatility required for producing animation.

Note that one important part of the procedure is line 140, which restores the data pointer to the first item each time PROCarrow(X,Y,D) is called. Without this, an *Out of data* error would appear the second time the procedure was called.

The simpler section of the program is the set of nested loops which call the procedure and move the arrow along the screen. The loop between lines 50-100 increases the X-coordinate from 0 to 400 in steps of 20. Note that the Y-coordinate is fixed as 30 at line 30. Y does not actually need to appear explicitly as a variable in the procedure, but has been included in this example for generality. Line 60 calls PROCarrow with a D value of 5. This makes the arrow appear on the screen. Then, after a short delay created by the empty loop at lines 70,80, PROCarrow is called again with a D value of 7. This erases the arrow before the X loop calculates its new position. Finally, an overall FOR-NEXT loop, the one using I as its control variable, repeats the whole animation five times for illustrative purposes.

Computer simulation and mathematical models

Another example is given now of how PLOT 5,X,Y and PLOT 7,X,Y can create animation. It is a short simulation program, demonstrating the way in which a convex lens forms an image of an object placed in front of it. No background in physics is required to appreciate the effect investigated. Anybody who has picked up a magnifying glass, or squinted at the bar through a glass of lager, will be familiar with the general idea.

Just like any full-scale computer simulation, the program involves a mathematical model. The real situation has to be converted into an idealised and simplified picture, in which variables and equations represent what happens in the physical world. Although the program is brief and only tackles a very simple problem in optics, this reduction of reality into the 'Cartesian dream' does reflect the basic approach of all computer simulation.

The standard diagram used to show ray optics is very simple. The convex lens is represented by the short vertical line at the centre of the diagram. The horizontal line is the axis of the lens. The object in front of the lens is indicated by the vertical arrow. A similar arrow to the right is the image formed by the lens.

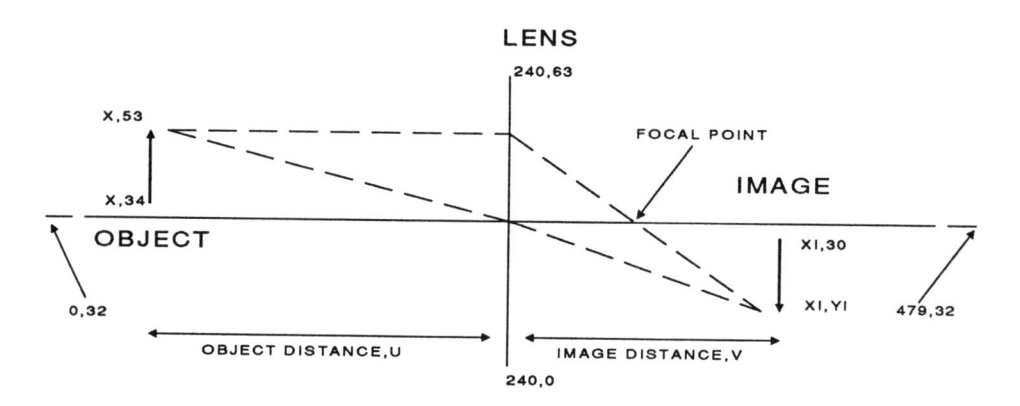

Computer simulation with the Notepad

Animation and Sound

The physics of the situation is introduced by the inclusion of two rays of light. One passes from the top of the object, moves parallel to the axis and is then refracted by the lens to pass through its focal point. The second ray travels from the top of the object, passes undeviated through the centre of the lens and meets the first ray. The top of the image is at this point.

The position of the image could be found in practice by drawing these two rays accurately with pencil and paper. Indeed, this is the impression that the program attempts to create. However the location of the image can also be calculated from two standard equations in optics, which is the method that must be employed by the program. Computers are happier with equations than with pencils!

The two equations form part of the mathematical model. The other part is the variables that describe the lens, object and image. These variables are:

U, the distance of the object from the lens

V, the distance of the image from the lens

F, the distance of the focal point from the lens

Further variables used to draw the graphics of the display are X, the distance of the object from the left hand side of the screen (this is not the same as the object distance!) and the coordinates, (XI,YI), of the head of the arrow forming the image. The image requires two variables to describe it because it will vary in size as well as position. The object is of fixed height and so only needs one variable.

The first equation taken from optics theory and employed in the mathematical model is:

$$1/(\text{object distance}) + 1/(\text{image distance}) = 1/(\text{focal length})$$

Substituting the variables gives:

$$1/U + 1/V = 1/F$$

Subtracting $1/U$ from both sides leads to:

$$1/V = 1/F - 1/U$$

This is a straightforward subtraction of two fractions. The lowest common multiple is $F * U$ and so:

$$1/V = (U - F)/(F*U)$$

Hence the image distance is given by:

$$V = F*U/(U - F)$$

Coded as BASIC this becomes:

```
V=F*U/(U-F)
```

It is in this form that the equation is incorporated into the program. The second equation of the mathematical model is:

Image height/Object Height = Image distance/Object distance

The BASIC variable H is introduced for the image height. The object height is set as 20 pixels on the Notepad's display. The equation therefore becomes the BASIC expression:

```
H=20*V/U
```

After this mathematical diversion, these equations can now be incorporated into the program.

Coding the mathematical model

The program allows the user to adjust the distance of the object from the lens and also the position of the focal point. It calls a procedure, PROCdisplay, which draws the object, image and the two light rays. Additionally the procedure erases the previous positions of the three items to create animation. A further procedure is also called when necessary. This is PROChead, which adds an arrow head to the object if it is large enough. The listing for the program is below, followed by an explanation of the routines used.

```
 10 REM Lens program
 20 X=100 : F=50 : CLS
 30 REM Initial display
 40 MOVE 240,0 : DRAW 240,63
 50 PROCdisplay(5)
 60 REPEAT
 70   REM Scan keyboard
 80   REPEAT
 90     K=GET
100   UNTIL K>64 AND K<69
110   REM Remove object
120   PROCdisplay(7)
130   REM Move object
140   IF K=65 THEN X=X-5
150   IF K=66 THEN X=X+5
160   IF K=67 THEN F=F-2
170   IF K=68 THEN F=F+2
180   IF X>230-F THEN X=X-5
190   REM Show object
200   PROCdisplay(5)
210 UNTIL FALSE
220 END
230 DEF PROCdisplay(D)
240 REM Draw axis
250 MOVE 0,32 : DRAW 479,32
260 REM Draw object
270 MOVE X,34 : PLOT D,X,53
280 MOVE X-5,48 : PLOT D,X,53 : PLOT D,X+5,48
```

```
 290 REM Image parameters
 300 U=240-X
 310 V=F*U/(U-F)
 320 H=20*V/U
 330 XI=240+V : YI=32-H
 340 REM Draw image
 350 MOVE XI,30 : PLOT D,XI,YI
 360 IF H>10 THEN PROChead
 370 REM Draw rays
 380 MOVE X+5,53 : PLOT D,240,53
 390 PLOT D,XI-5,YI
 400 MOVE X+5,53 : PLOT D,XI-5,YI
 410 ENDPROC
 420 DEF PROChead
 430 MOVE XI-5,YI+5 : PLOT D,XI,YI
 440 PLOT D,XI+5,YI+5
 450 ENDPROC
```

The program begins by assigning two values at line 20: X, the initial distance in pixels of the object from the left hand side of the display, and F, the focal length of the lens. Both will be altered by the user. Line 20 also clears the screen, just in case part of some previous display is still present when the program is first run.

After this, line 40 places the lens on the screen as a short vertical line. It does not add the long axis across the display because this will constantly be redrawn by PROCdisplay. The first call to PROCdisplay is made at line 50 and places the object and image on the screen, using the initial values of X and F that have been assigned. PROCdisplay is called with a parameter set to 5 to draw in black.

The loop between lines 60-210 then controls the redrawing of the diagram, according to the current values for X and F selected by the user. The embedded loop at lines 80-100 restricts keypresses to A, B, C or D. These keys increase or decrease X and F at lines 140-170. Line 180 prevents the image from becoming too close to the lens and creating a 'virtual image' which would not fit on to the display.

The current diagram is displayed on the screen until a keypress is detected. Then as soon as one of the appropriate letters has been selected, the diagram is erased by a call to PROCdisplay, with a parameter of 7 to draw in white, before either of the X or F values is adjusted. This procedure call must appear at precisely this point. The display must not be erased until the new values are known for its fresh position. Similarly it should not be erased after the values assigned to X and F are changed because then the overwriting of the previous object and image locations will be in the wrong place and not erase it.

Drawing the diagram

The coordinates for drawing the ray diagram in PROCdisplay can be found on the diagram above. Line 250 draws the axis of the lens between points (0,32) and (479,32). MOVE and DRAW are used because the axis is always shown in black.

However, PLOT D is used at lines 270, 280 to draw the object as this can be in white or black. The X-coordinate of the object is X. The foot of the arrow will therefore be at (X,34), just above the axis, and its top at (X,54). This gives the fixed size of 20 pixels mentioned earlier. Line 280 adds the two short lines representing the arrow's head. At this point the position of the head of the image, (XI,YI), has to be calculated. Line 300 deduces the object distance, U. Line 310 can then employ the first equation of the mathematical model to calculate the image distance, V. Line 320 then uses both of these in the second equation of the model to calculate the image height, H. Knowing V and H permits the coordinates XI and YI to be found at line 330. Line 350 draws the image, with line 360 calling PROChead if the image is big enough. Knowing the values of XI and YI also allows the two light rays to be added by lines 380-400.

Filled shape animation with PLOT 87,X,Y

Animation of outlined, wireframe shapes is quite efficient on the Notepad. The machine is able to update the display quickly enough to create the sensation of continuous motion. It is possible to extend the same animation technique to the movement of filled shapes, and this is illustrated in the listing below, but unfortunately it is not quite so effective. The larger number of pixels that need to be refreshed leads to a moving display which shows a noticeable flicker. In order to avoid this the only real solution is to embed assembly language routines within the BASIC listing. This is too difficult to introduce into the current book. The reader should note Cliff Lawson's warning on page 179 of the Notepad's manual. It is hoped that the topic of developing Z80 assembly code with the Amstrad Notepad will be the subject of a later Sigma book. The program developed here will animate this picture:

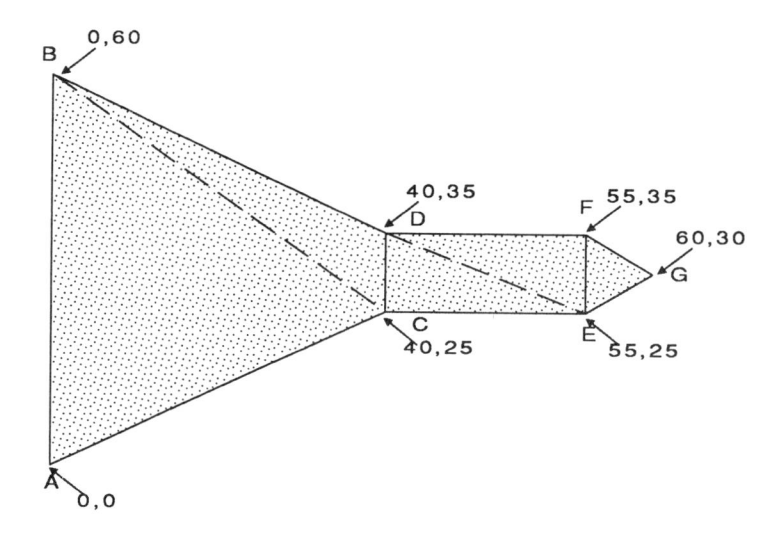

Animating a filled shape

Animation and Sound

It is intended to show an aircraft, either a delta-wing A-bomber or a stealth fighter, depending upon the age of the programmer! Detailed diagrams are not really feasible with this animation technique. The dotted lines show the sections that will comprise the aircraft. The shape is filled by a series of triangles, as in the example in the previous chapter. As before, the order of the triangles is vital if each is to be filled using just the coordinates of one vertex. Again here the letters on the diagram indicate the order in which the points are to be visited by the graphics cursor. The listing for the program is:

```
 10 REM Animating a filled shape
 20 CLS
 30 FOR X=0 TO 400 STEP 20
 40   PROCplane(X,85)
 50   FOR T=1 TO 500
 60   NEXT T
 70   PROCplane(X,87)
 80 NEXT X
 90 END
100 DEF PROCplane(X,D)
110 RESTORE
120 MOVE X,0
130 MOVE X,60
140 FOR I=1 TO 5
150   READ A,B
160   PLOT D,X+A,B
170 NEXT I
180 ENDPROC
190 REM
200 REM Data for plane
210 DATA 40,25,40,35,55,25,55,35,60,30
```

The plane is both drawn and erased by PROCplane(X,D). Two parameters are passed to the procedure. X governs how far across the display the plane will appear. The value assigned to D, 85 or 87, decides whether the plane will be drawn in black or white. PLOT 87,X,Y behaves in just the same way as PLOT 85,X,Y except that the triangle it produces is in white, not black. It can therefore be used for erasing shapes in an animation routine. The Y-coordinate of the plane is not included as a parameter because the plane is drawn at a fixed height up the display. There is no choice in this matter because it is 60 pixels wide.

Lines 120 and 130 move the graphics cursor to the first two points of the shape, A and B. The FOR-NEXT loop between lines 140-170 then draws the five triangles needed to create the plane's shape by reading the coordinates of points C, D, E, F and G in turn and filling in with PLOT D,X,Y. D has the value 85 when the plane is drawn and 87 when it is erased. The data for the points is stored at line 210 and RESTORE at line 110 makes sure that the procedure always has the data pointer in the correct place.

The procedure is called by the main loop between lines 30-80. This assigns values for the X-coordinate passed to PROCplane and also alternates the value of D between 85 and 87. Between the assignment of these two D values the empty FOR-NEXT loop at lines 50, 60 creates the necessary delay for the animation effect.

Including simple sound effects – VDU 7

Sound, as well as animation, will improve programs written for the Notepad. The machine produces a wide range of frequencies on two separate channels and at a respectable volume.

A very convenient way to introduce a brief tone into a program is with the statement VDU 7. This creates one short note. Its great advantage is the brevity of the command, together with the penetrating pitch of the sound produced. It can be included at any point in a program where the user's attention should be drawn back to the display. It can be embarrassing if you use your Notepad in a library. The sound is loud enough to gain other people's attention as well. It is much louder than the ubiquitous beep produced by watches and calculators, which now has become an acceptable background noise.

This short program demonstrates the use of VDU 7. It produces five beeps every time a key is pressed. The <Stop> key is used to exit the program:

```
10  REM Demonstrating beep
20  REPEAT
30    CLS
40    PRINT ' '
50    FOR I=1 TO 5
60      VDU 7
70      PRINT "BEEP...";
80      FOR T=1 TO 1000
90      NEXT T
100   NEXT I
110   PRINT ' '
120   PRINT "Press a key to repeat."
130   K=GET
140 UNTIL FALSE
```

The beep is produced at line 70. The loop between lines 50-100 repeats it five times, with a delay created by the embedded loop at lines 80, 90. The overall REPEAT-UNTIL loop will then produce the five beeps once more when a keypress is detected at line 130. This will continue indefinitely.

Altering the pitch and duration with SOUND

The Notepad inherits the SOUND statement from the original BBC Micro and the command still requires four values to follow it. Originally these were channel, volume, frequency and duration. No alteration of the volume is possible with the

Notepad and so this variable should be set to a constant zero. The remaining parameters can be altered: The channel can be 1 or 2 and the frequency has the effective range 0-255, but actually jumps in multiples of 4. The duration is in units of 1/100 of a second in the range 0-254, but setting it to -1 produces a sound which does not stop until another sound with duration zero stops it. Try this:

```
10 SOUND 1,0,160,-1
20 K=GET
30 SOUND 1,0,0,0
```

Some of the frequencies available are demonstrated in this brief routine which creates an alarm. The program produces a continuous telephone-like warble until any key is pressed:

```
10 REM Alarm
20 PRINT "Press a key to stop"
30 REPEAT
40   FOR I=180 TO 220 STEP 8
50     SOUND 1,0,I,1
60   NEXT I
70   FOR I=220 TO 180 STEP -8
80     SOUND 1,0,I,1
90   NEXT I
100  K=INKEY(20)
110 UNTIL K<>-1
```

The FOR-NEXT loop between lines 40-60 increases the pitch in steps of 8, or two semitones. The second loop, between lines 70-90, similarly decreases the pitch over the same range of frequencies. The overall REPEAT-UNTIL loop continues this until the keypress at line 110.

Note the difference in this use of a keypress to end the program. In the previous listing, the program was halted by K=GET until a key was selected. The sound continued from line 10 and was then switched off at line 30. In the second example, K=GET must not be used because the two FOR-NEXT loops need to repeat without a noticeable delay. The program must not wait indefinitely for a keypress. Instead K=INKEY(20) is used. This means that the program only waits for 1/5 of a second until continuing with a K value of -1. As soon as a key is pressed K is no longer -1 and so line 110 permits the loop to exit.

Playing a chord

Both sound channels can be used simultaneously to produce two note chords, as illustrated here:

```
10 REM Demonstrating chords
20 P=128
30 CLS
40 PRINT TAB(27,3) "Press A to decrease pitch"
```

```
 50 PRINT TAB(27,4) "Press C to increase pitch"
 60 REPEAT
 70    REPEAT
 80       K=GET
 90    UNTIL K=65 OR K=67
100    P=P+8*(K-66)
110    IF P<100 THEN P=100
120    IF P>156 THEN P=156
130    SOUND 1,0,P,-1
140    SOUND 2,0,P+96,5
150    SOUND 1,0,0,0
160 UNTIL FALSE
```

Line 20 initialises the pitch at 128. Screen prompts then instruct the user to press A or C. This is detected by lines 70-90. At line 100 the value of (K-66) will be -1 if A has been pressed and 1 if C was chosen. The expression P=P+8*(K-66) will therefore increase or decrease P by a whole tone. Lines 110, 120 restrict the possible range.

Line 130 plays this tone on channel 1 with unlimited duration. Line 140 superimposes the tone an octave higher on channel 2. After this channel 1 is switched off by line 150, where there is a duration of 0.

Data statements and music

Just as lines of data can be used to hold the X- and Y-coordinates needed to draw a picture on the display, they can also store the pitch and duration of notes that will let the Notepad play a simple tune. A FOR-NEXT loop is then used to read these values and insert them into the sound statement. An example of such a program is this short demonstration:

```
 10 REM Playing a melody from data
 20 REPEAT
 30    CLS
 40    PRINT TAB(29,3) "Fast tempo....Press F"
 50    PRINT TAB(29,4) "Slow tempo....Press S"
 60    REPEAT
 70       K=GET
 80    UNTIL K=70 OR K=83
 90    IF K=70 THEN T=2 ELSE T=3
100    CLS
110    RESTORE
120    FOR I=1 TO 38
130       REM Obtain pitch and duration
140       READ P,D
150       PRINT TAB(P-48) "LA!"
160       REM Play note on channel 1
170       SOUND 1,0,P,-1
180       REM Superimpose higher octave
190       REM on channel 2
200       SOUND 2,0,P+96,D*T
```

```
210    NEXT I
220    REM Switch off channel 1
230    SOUND 1,0,0,0
240 UNTIL FALSE
250 REM
260 DATA 68,4,80,8,88,4,96,8,104,2
270 DATA 96,2,88,2,76,4,60,8,68,2
280 DATA 76,2,80,8,68,4,68,6,64,2
290 DATA 68,4,76,8,64,4,48,8,68,4
300 DATA 80,8,88,4,96,8,104,2,96,2
310 DATA 88,8,76,4,60,8,68,2,76,2
320 DATA 80,4,76,4,68,4,64,4,56,4
330 DATA 64,4,68,8,68,8
```

The data required for the tune is stored between lines 260-330. The organisation of these numbers into pairs is very obvious. The first number is the pitch of the note. For those who are not musical, this can be determined, rather slowly, by trial and error. For those who can read a score, the numbers can be worked out from the value of 100 for middle C and the fact that an increment of 4 represents a semitone. The second number in each pair gives the duration of the note. This is only the ratio of a particular note to the others because the actual length is altered by a further factor, T, in the main loop.

The value of T is determined by the user. After the prompts at lines 40, 50, the REPEAT-UNTIL loop at 60-80 detects either S for slow or F for fast tempo. Line 90 then assigns a value of 2 or 3 accordingly to T. The FOR-NEXT loop between lines 120-210 then reads the pitch and duration from the data. To compensate for the absence of words (which could also be stored as data if required), the Notepad *Lalas* its way through the melody: the pitch determines how far to the right each La is displayed. Lines 170 and 190 generate a two note chord, as above.

The arithmetically minded, who also have perfect pitch, will be able to identify what traditional tune has been chosen just by inspecting the values held in the data statements. Others will have to type in and run the program.

File Handling with the Notepad

Frequently the data required by a program can be held as statements within the program itself. For example all the examples in this book place data at the end of a program, after any procedure definitions. It is also possible to put the data lines in other parts of the listing. Some programmers favour the beginning. Wherever the place, the advantages of using data statements is that they are easy to understand and immediately obvious when examining a listing. They do have one great disadvantage, though, in their inflexibility. Once an item has been included as a data statement, it cannot be altered by the program during its execution. Only the programmer is able to do this when the program is listed on the Notepad's screen and available for editing.

The inadequacy of data statements

Unfortunately there will be occasions when it is necessary to alter data being handled by a program while it is actually running. It might be argued that an array is adequate for this task but of course array contents are erased when a program is no longer in operation. (The exceptional Sinclair ZX81 did, in fact, save its array contents together with the program that established them, but even so the arrays were lost when the computer was switched off.)

What is needed is a method by which data can be made available for the execution of a program, altered if necessary by that program, and then still exist after the computer has been switched off and on again.

Such a technique is possible and involves creating a data file which is independent of the main program. The data present in the file can be accessed and modified as necessary and does not cease to exist until the explicit decision to erase it is made. Using data files extends the possibilities of most programs. To give one, albeit trivial, example, if you have written a really impressive quiz it might be pleasant if the players could record their scores to reappear as a 'hall of fame' the next time the program is run. Without a data file this is not possible. With file handling it becomes extremely easy to include such extra programming refinements.

Using a data file

A simple example is given below of a program which lets the user enter five names. These are stored in a file and can be reproduced on the screen at will. Here is a typical sample run of the program in which five names are entered. A choice of 'writing' or 'reading' the names is made by pressing W or R:

```
>RUN
Press R to read names
Press W to write names
Type a name ? LUCY
Type a name ? SARAH
Type a name ? HEATHER
Type a name ? PAULINE
Type a name ? MICHELLE
>
```

At this point the program could be abandoned. Naturally it has been saved so that it can be reloaded when needed again. Another program could be run, or the Notepad switched off completely. Later, after reloading and running the program once more, the same five names could be retrieved by pressing R:

```
>RUN
Press R to read names
Press W to write names
LUCY
SARAH
HEATHER
PAULINE
MICHELLE
>
```

Alternatively, a new set of five names could be entered instead by running the program and selecting W again:

```
>RUN
Press R to read names
Press W to write names
Type a name ? TOM
Type a name ? WALT
Type a name ? ROBERT
Type a name ? EMILY
Type a name ? SYLVIA
```

If we run the program and press R, the new names replace the previous ones:

```
>RUN
Press R to read names
Press W to write names
TOM
WALT
ROBERT
EMILY
SYLVIA
>
```

The program which achieves this is:

```
10 REM Simple file handling
20 PRINT "Press R to read names"
30 PRINT "Press W to write names"
40 REPEAT
50   K=GET
60 UNTIL K=82 OR K=87
70 IF K=82 THEN PROCread ELSE PROCwrite
80 END
90 DEF PROCread
100 Y=OPENIN "NAMES"
110 FOR I=1 TO 5
120   INPUT #Y,N$
130   PRINT N$
140 NEXT I
150 CLOSE #Y
160 ENDPROC
170 REM
180 DEF PROCwrite
190 X=OPENOUT "NAMES"
200 FOR I=1 TO 5
210   INPUT "Type a name ", N$
220   PRINT #X, N$
230 NEXT I
240 CLOSE #X
250 ENDPROC
```

The file handling is achieved by PROCread and PROCwrite. The former is permissible as a procedure name, of course, only because 'read' is in lower case and so not confused with the BASIC word READ. Either procedure is called when the program is run by the short control routine between lines 20-70. Here the user is prompted to press W to place information in the file or R to inspect the information. The terms 'write' and 'read' are used for this. This is standard terminology used in file handling. The REPEAT-UNTIL loop at lines 40-60 will not exit unless R or W, detected by their ASCII value, is pressed. In the usual way, the ASCII value is assigned to the variable K. Line 70 employs this variable in an IF-THEN-ELSE condition which calls one of the two procedures appropriately.

Writing data to a file – OPENOUT, PRINT # and CLOSE

PROCwrite establishes the file which will be used to store the names. Line 190 opens the file for writing, using the statement OPENOUT. The file is called "NAMES" for clarity. Any name could be used provided that it is adhered to consistently throughout the program. The syntax of the expression is:

```
X=OPENOUT "NAMES"
```

File Handling with the Notepad

The variable X could be replaced by another variable if preferred. A convention is adopted here taken from John Coll's original BBC BASIC manual (1982).

Once the file NAMES has been opened, a FOR-NEXT loop prompts the user to enter each of the five names. They are assigned in turn to the variable N$ at line 210. Then they are written to the file by:

```
PRINT #X, N$
```

At the end of the loop the file must be closed again with:

```
CLOSE #X
```

Reading data from a file – OPENIN and INPUT

The code needed to read data from the NAMES file is located in PROCread. It is analogous to the way in which the file has been set up. First the file is opened for reading by:

```
Y=OPENIN "NAMES"
```

A FOR-NEXT loop then reads each data item from the file with the expression:

```
INPUT #Y,N$
```

After this the value of N$ is printed on the screen. At the end of the loop the file must be closed again with:

```
CLOSE #Y
```

After typing in and practising with this program, it is advisable to experiment further by writing similar routines which save and read data to and from a file.

File handling can be curiously prone to error and so it is a good idea to proceed slowly, gradually extending the complexity of the programs attempted. The similarity of the code used for writing and reading might lead to casual mistake and perhaps this mnemonic could be useful. When writing to a file the initial statement is OPENOUT. 'Write' is linked with 'out', so think of 'outright'!

Detecting the end of file – EOF

In the example program above the assumption has been made that there are only five names present in the file. PROCread has been able to use a FOR-NEXT loop to read these names. With a more realistic example of file handling, though, it is unlikely that the precise number of items present in a file will be known. In the longer example of file handling developed later, the solution to this problem is to specify how many items are being written to a file and to write this number itself to the file as the first item. Another method is to use the end of file function, EOF, to detect the last item in a file. It can be included in the exit condition of a REPEAT-UNTIL loop.

Assuming that the file NAMES is still present on the Notepad, typing in and running this program should display all the entries again:

```
10 REM Using EOF function
20 Y=OPENIN "NAMES"
30 REPEAT
40    INPUT #Y, N$
50    PRINT N$
60 UNTIL EOF #Y
70 CLOSE #Y
```

Line 20 opens NAMES as before. The loop then reads an item from the file as N$ and line 50 prints it on the display. This continues until EOF #Y detects the end of the file at line 60. The file is then closed.

Some file nomenclature

In the next programming example, the file is made up of a number of name/hobby pairs. Separate units within a file like this are usually called 'records'. Each record itself here will just consist of two separate 'fields', the name and the hobby. However, records in a file might each contain several different fields. For ease of programming it is then vital that all the records in a file are organised in the same way. So if the record contains the name, age, address and telephone number of different friends, these have to be written to the file in a consistent order like this:

(Start of file) NAME-1 / AGE-1 / ADDRESS-1 / NUMBER-1 / NAME-2 / AGE-2 / ADDRESS-2 / NUMBER-2 / NAME-3 / AGE-3 / ADDRESS-3 / NUMBER-3 ...(End of file)

A database using file handling

The use of a file is now illustrated on a slightly larger scale than in the first example. The new program is a small database. It sets up a file, called PALS, which allows the names and hobbies of friends to be stored. Three separate file handling operations are available in this program: A new file can be created, an existing file can be viewed and a current record in an exiting file can be updated.

Obviously other options would be included in a large-scale practical database. This example, in contrast, has been kept deliberately short so that it remains easy to understand. Once the program has been typed in and investigated, it should not be too difficult to extend it to involve more features.

File Handling with the Notepad

```
 10 REM File handling mini database
 20 DIM F$(10),H$(10)
 30 REPEAT
 40   PROCmenu
 50 UNTIL K=69
 60 PRINT "You have left the database"
 70 END
 80 REM
 90 DEF PROCmenu
100 CLS
110 PRINT TAB(33) "Mini Database"
120 PRINT TAB(28,2) "Begin new records.....B"
130 PRINT TAB(28,3) "Change a record.......C"
140 PRINT TAB(28,4) "Display all records...D"
150 PRINT TAB(28,5) "Exit the database.....E"
160 REPEAT
170   K=GET
180 UNTIL K>65 AND K<70
190 CLS
200 IF K=66 THEN PROCstart
210 IF K=67 THEN PROCchange
220 IF K=68 THEN PROCdisplay
230 ENDPROC
240 REM
250 DEF PROCstart
260 PRINT "Type number of friends"
270 INPUT N
280 X=OPENOUT "PALS"
290 PRINT #X,N
300 FOR I=1 TO N
310   PRINT "Record number "; I
320   INPUT "Type friend's name", F$
330   INPUT "Type friend's hobby", H$
340   PRINT #X, F$, H$
350 NEXT I
360 CLOSE #X
370 ENDPROC
380 REM
390 DEF PROCdisplay
400 Y=OPENIN "PALS"
410 INPUT #Y,N
420 FOR I=1 TO N
430   PRINT "Record number "; I ": ";
440   INPUT #Y, F$, H$
450   PRINT F$ "'s hobby is " H$
460 NEXT I
470 CLOSE #Y
480 PRINT "Press a key" : K=GET
490 ENDPROC
500 REM
510 DEF PROCchange
520 REM Place data into arrays
530 Y=OPENIN "PALS"
```

```
540 INPUT #Y,N
550 FOR I=1 TO N
560   INPUT #Y, F$(I), H$(I)
570 NEXT I
580 CLOSE #Y
590 INPUT "Type name for alteration", N$
600 F=0
610 FOR I=1 TO N
620   IF F$(I)=N$ THEN F=I
630 NEXT I
640 IF F=0 THEN PRINT "Name not found" ELSE PROCadjust
650 FOR T=1 TO 1000
660 NEXT T
670 ENDPROC
680 REM
690 DEF PROCadjust
700 INPUT "Type new hobby", H$(F)
710 REM Place data in file
720 X=OPENOUT "PALS"
730 PRINT #X,N
740 FOR I=1 TO N
750   PRINT #X, F$(I), H$(I)
760 NEXT I
770 CLOSE #X
780 ENDPROC
```

Line 20 of the program dimensions two arrays which will be needed in two of the procedures of the program. Only 10 array locations (ignoring the zeroth) have been made available. Again this is because the program should be viewed principally as a demonstration. The size of these two arrays can be adjusted as necessary for a large database.

Control with a menu

Although it is a relatively brief program, its nature makes a fully structured approach more necessary than usual. It is vital to have separate procedures to perform the various file handling routines. Ready access to these routines for the user dictates that there is a control routine repeatedly calling PROCmenu, a procedure that lists the possible operations on the screen. The program is therefore menu-driven. After each choice is completed, control returns to the REPEAT-UNTIL loop between lines 30-60.

PROCmenu places the title of the program, 'Mini Database', on the first line of the display. TAB is used to centralise the two words. Then four choices are shown by lines 120-150. The user has to press B to begin new records, C to change a display, D to display all records and E to exit the database.

The choice of wording and the hot keys specified allows a convenient way of checking the user's keypress because all four ASCII codes that will need to be recognised, 66 for B, 67 for C, 68 for D and 69 for E, lie in a continuous range. This permits a relatively uncomplicated exit condition for the loop than scans the keyboard between lines 160-180.

The condition is simply K>65 AND K<70. Lines 200-220 then call the appropriate procedures: PROCstart if B has been pressed, PROCchange if the key was C and PROCdisplay for D. Pressing E does not call a procedure but instead lets the main loop exit at line 50.

Creating a new file

PROCstart creates the file. Each record consists of just two fields: the name of the friend and the single hobby permitted. Once more it must be stressed that the program has been restricted to the simplest possible. Adding more than one hobby would not be a difficult modification to make.

The number of friends is requested at line 260 and assigned to the variable N at line 270. This is needed to control subsequent FOR-NEXT loops. The number will have to be held in the file itself so that when it is displayed the number of records present is known. Obviously the number is the first item required in the file. It is written to the file, therefore, by PRINT #X,N at line 290 immediately after the file is opened for writing at line 280 by X=OPENOUT "PALS".

A FOR-NEXT loop between lines 300-350 then requests each pair of items, name and hobby, in turn. These are assigned to the variables F$ and H$ and written to PALS at line 340 by PRINT #X, F$, H$. Finally the file closed at line 360, immediately after the FOR-NEXT loop ends. Remember that it is important to close a file as soon as possible to avoid error. Program execution then returns to the control routine.

Displaying all the records

PROCdisplay is the next procedure in the program, although apparently not next in the order in which the control routine can call the procedures. Procedures can be appended to a program in any order, though programming etiquette implies some acknowledgement of a systematic order. Here common sense dictates that displaying the existing file is before altering it.

First line 400 opens PALS for reading with the statement Y=OPENIN. The first item obtained is the number of records in the file. This is assigned to the variable N again. N is then used to control the FOR-NEXT loop between lines 420-460. The loop prints out the record number and each friend and hobby. At the end of the loop the file is closed. The remaining records that can still be seen are left on the screen until line 480 detects a keypress. Only then does execution return to the control routine. The user is able to consider the file contents unhurriedly.

Altering a record

The user can alter one of the records by pressing C. The procedure PROCchange is then called. The process of altering a single record can be very complicated, but an easy method is first to place the entire content of the file into the two arrays initialised at the beginning of the program as F$ and H$. The array contents are then altered and after this they are written back into the file.

PROCchange begins this process at line 530, where PALS is opened for reading. Line 540 assigns the number of records to N, which then controls the loop between lines 550-570. This puts all the items in the file into the appropriate array locations of F$(10) and H$(10). Obviously here it is assumed that the file does not contain more than 10 records, but the alteration if needed is simple enough. Line 580 then closes the file.

After this, the arrays have to be searched to locate the record which needs to be altered. At this point clearly the user has to indicate the name of the person who has changed hobby. This is assigned to the variable N$ at line 590.

A loop between lines 610-630 examines all the names in the F$ array. If one of these is the same as N$, its position in the array is recorded as the value assigned to the further variable, F. At the end of the loop F will still have the initial value of 0 given to it by line 600 unless a match with N$ has been achieved. If this is the case, line 640 prints the warning *Name not found*.

After the delay created by the loop at 650, 660 the program returns to the control routine. However, if the name entered by the user has corresponded with one of the names in the F$ array, the value of F will not be 0 and line 640 calls the further procedure, PROCadjust.

The value given to F identifies the record which needs to be changed. The name remains the same, but the hobby has to be altered. The array location involved is therefore H$(F). Line 700 prompts the user to type in a new hobby and assigns it to H$(F). After this, the array contents are correct but the file itself still has to be updated.

Both arrays, F$ and H$, must be written back to PALS. Line 720 opens the file for writing and line 730 writes the number of records. Then the loop, lines 740-760, places the pairs of array locations F$(I) and H$(I), each comprising a single record, into the file. Line 770 closes it once more.

Inspecting a file with the word processor

An interesting feature of the Notepad is that a data file set up by a BASIC program can be viewed directly as a word processor file. After running the database program, enter the word processor, with the yellow and red keys, and view the word processor files. PALS will be present. Select it with the cursor, press Return and the records will be displayed. This does does corrupt the file, unfortunately, and when the program is run again it needs to be retyped.

Using a Printer

For most of the time, the Notepad's screen is perfectly adequate for output from a program. Nevertheless it is likely that the average Notepad user has bought it to use for word processing as well as programming. A printer will therefore be available for use with the machine. It will often be convenient to dump copies of a program listing to the printer. It can then be used as a particularly safe back-up copy should the 'soft' version, electronically stored in the Notepad's memory or on a separate PCMCIA card, be lost. It is always possible, if the final disaster occurs, to type the whole of a listing back in again.

Another use for a printed copy of a listing will be when a program is being written. Often an especially stubborn bug, or hiccough in the flow of creativity, is best tackled by switching a computer off completely and staring at the listing on paper. A third use for a printer in conjunction with the Notepad might also be those programs that actually need to produce printed copy on paper. Chapter 18 gives an example of a program like this.

Output from the Notepad can always be directed towards a suitably connected printer with the BBC BASIC instruction VDU 2. Typing this, then listing the program or running it, will produce a printed copy of everything that has appeared on the display. The output can be directed away from the printer again with the accompanying command, VDU 3. Both of these instructions can also be included as lines of a program itself. Thus at some point in the execution of the program printed copy of the output can be generated and then the printer 'switched off' again. The two commands give great versatility to the way in which the Notepad can be used.

Using the Lapcat

The Notepad is perfectly capable of operating as a stand-alone system, connected to a printer and nothing else. Many users, though, will probably use it in conjunction with another computer and therefore need to transfer files. This can be done with a serial cable, but the easier method is to acquire the Lapcat package from Amor, as detailed on page 102 of the Notepad's manual.

The package includes a disk with conversion software for the second computer specified and a lead which will link the parallel port of the Notepad with the parallel port of the other computer. Hardware details will vary from user to user. However it is quite likely that the Lapcat lead will need to share a port with a printer.

Excessive plug-pulling is tedious and a potential risk to the equipment. One solution is to buy a T-switch, which is a junction box for parallel signals. A 'gender changer' might also be necessary in order to link cables. The first time the Lapcat is used, the Notepad will have to be configured via the systems settings menu. This is explained on page 2 of the Lapcat documentation.

How to prepare a file for transfer via the Lapcat is described in the sections that follow. Here it will be assumed that such a file exists. Suppose it is "FILENAME". Set up the Notepad for file transfer as follows.

Enter the word processor with <Function> and <Word>. List the files with <Calc> and highlight FILENAME. Press <Secret/Menu>, then <T> for transfer functions. Get ready to press <X> for XModem send as soon as the other computer is ready.

The way in which the Lapcat software is loaded on the other computer will vary slightly according to which machine is being used and whether the software is is installed on hard disk or kept on floppy. When using a floppy disk it is important to make sure that a backup of the original software supplied is employed.

The following assumes that an IBM PC compatible machine is the other half of the Notepad combination and that the Lapcat software is on a floppy disk. Type A: <Enter> and then LAPCAT <Enter>. The file transfer screen will appear. Here you should press <F> and then type the name selected, FILENAME. After this press <R> for receive file, <X> for Xmodem and <T> for transfer. Then return to the Notepad and press <X>. After a few seconds the file will be transferred. It is then available on the disk for printing, editing or other use.

Directing program output to a file

As explained at the end of the previous chapter, a file that has been created by a BASIC program can be accessed later by the word processor. There are occasions when this can be used explicitly as one of a program's objectives. This is illustrated here by a program which, it is assumed, is generating anagrams for inclusion in a word processor document. Pretend you are the features editor of a magazine and have to produce yet another quiz! Here you have a program that will automatically do some of your job for you and politely prepare a file for immediate inclusion in your word processor text files.

```
 10 REM Dumping program output to a file
 20 CLS
 30 DIM W$(10),L$(15,2)
 40 PRINT "Press I to input words"
 50 PRINT "Press D to use existing data"
 60 REPEAT
 70 K=GET
 80 UNTIL K=68 OR K=73
 90 CLS
100 IF K=68 PROCdata ELSE PROCinput
110 PROCmuddle
120 PRINT "File complete"
130 END
140 REM
150 DEF PROCdata
160 FOR I=1 TO 10
170 READ W$(I)
180 NEXT I
190 ENDPROC
200 REM
210 DEF PROCinput
220 FOR I=1 TO 10
230 PRINT "Type word number "; I
240 INPUT W$(I)
250 NEXT I
260 ENDPROC
270 REM
280 DEF PROCmuddle
290 X=OPENOUT "JUMBLED"
300 FOR I=1 TO 10
310 PRINT #X, W$(I)
320 PRINT "Now rearranging " W$(I)
330 L=LEN W$(I)
340 REM Insert letters into array
350 FOR J=1 TO L
360 L$(J,1)=MID$(W$(I),J,1)
370 L$(J,2)=""
380 NEXT J
390 REM Generate anagram
400 C=0
410 A$=""
420 REPEAT
430 REPEAT
440 R=RND(L)
450 UNTIL L$(R,2)=""
460 A$=A$+L$(R,1)
470 L$(R,2)="X"
480 C=C+1
490 UNTIL C=L
500 PRINT #X, A$
510 NEXT I
520 CLOSE #X
530 ENDPROC
540 REM
550 REM Data for anagrams
560 DATA ASTEROID,VIOLIN,SIAMESE,NEUTRINO,FROG
570 DATA DAFFODIL,OCEAN,FACSIMILE,MICROWAVE,WITTGENSTEIN
```

Here is how the program works. It gives the user the choice of either entering 10 new words to convert into anagrams or alternatively using the existing data held at lines 560, 570. These 10 words could be altered and the program re-saved to give further possibilities. Alternatively, words could be held in a separate data file. This has been avoided here to prevent confusion with the file, JUMBLED, used to store the anagrams generated.

The program begins with a control routine. The loop between lines 60-80 forces the user to press D or I before the program will continue. These are identified by their ASCII code of 68 or 73. This value then determines whether PROCinput or PROCdata is called by line 100. PROCdata, lines 150-190, reads the words stored as data statements into the W$ array. PROCinput, lines 210-260, prompts the user to type in each of the 10 words in turn. Then, after either PROCdata or PROCinput has been called, program execution returns to the control routine. This then calls PROCmuddle at line 110.

PROCmuddle produces the anagrams of the words now held in the W$ array. The algorithm adopted for producing an anagram consists of these stages:

i) Find the length of the word

ii) Place its letters sequentially into the first locations of a two dimensional array

iii) Set the corresponding second locations, as a set of flags, each to an empty string

iv) Set counter to zero

v) Initialise anagram as an empty string

vi) Select a random number over the range of the word length

vii) If corresponding flag is not an empty string, repeat vi)

viii) Concatenate respective letter on to anagram

ix) Increment counter

x) Repeat steps vi) to ix) until counter equals word length

This algorithm is coded into BBC BASIC by lines 330-490. First line 290 opens the file JUMBLED for writing. This is the file that will contain the data to be used by the word processor. The overall FOR-NEXT loop that turns all the W$ array words into anagrams then begins at line 300. The current word to be jumbled, W$(I), is written to the file by line 310. In addition, line 320 tells the user which word is being tackled by the program.

The length of W$(I) is assigned to the variable, L, at 330. The letters can now be placed into the L$ array. The assumption has been made at line 30 that none of the words has more than 15 letters. The FOR-NEXT loop at lines 350-380 uses MID$ to extract each letter in turn from W$(I) and places it into the first location of the pair of L$ locations identified by the value of the loop variable, J. This is done by line 360. The following line assigns an empty string to the second location identified by J. This is to flush such locations of any data possibly left over from an earlier word.

Lines 400,410 initialise the counter and the anagram string, A$. Two nested REPEAT-UNTIL loops between lines 420-490 now construct the anagram. A random value is assigned to R which will correspond with one of the letters in the L$ array. The condition at 450 ensures that no letters are repeated.

Line 460 then concatenates the letter on to A$ and 470 reassigns a letter X to the second location of the L$ array, thus resetting the flag. Line 480 increments the counter, C, and the value of this is used to control exit from the loop at line 490. Now line 500 can write the completed anagram to the file. The overall loop ends at line 510. At this point the file JUMBLED can be closed by line 520. The control routine resumes with the prompt *File complete* and the program ends.

The user now leaves BASIC by pressing <Function> and <Word> (or yellow and red). Selecting green/<Calc> shows the files available for the word processor. One of these will be JUMBLED. It can be selected with the cursor in the usual way. Pressing <Enter> then places the list of 20 words, the original and its anagram in alternating pairs, on the screen.

Only the top of this list can be seen at first, of course, as it is vertical rather than horizontal. All the text is available to the normal word processing operations and can be edited and modified, inserted into another document, transferred to another computer with the Lapcat or printed.

Documenting a BASIC listing – *SPOOL

Sometimes, after a program has been completed, it is necessary to explain how it works to somebody else. You might even need to produce notes to explain the program to yourself at a later date. It is remarkably easy to forget how a neat algorithm, devised in the early hours of the morning a few weeks previously, actually achieves what so obviously it does.

Alternatively it might be important to provide clear instructions, explaining to a potential user how to run the program. These two types of explanation, the *How it works* and *What to do with it*, are referred to officially as technical documentation and user documentation. They normally form an essential feature of an overall software package. A complicated program without the user guide is not very useful.

One way in which such documentation can be written is the difficult approach, dumping a listing to the printer and then having the hard copy beside you as you begin a fresh document. The other method is easier. A copy of the listing itself is converted into a word processor file and then used as the initial working copy for the documentation. It can be expanded and modified as necessary.

In BBC BASIC there is a very simple way in which a listed program can be turned into an ordinary ASCII file and then used as the basis for word processing. When you have completed a program to your satisfaction, and saved it as a normal BASIC file, select a new name for the ASCII version. Perhaps this is "DOCUMENT". Now enter:

```
*SPOOL "DOCUMENT"
```

After this enter:

```
LIST
```

The program will scroll up the screen in the usual fashion. Finally enter:

```
*SPOOL
```

Now enter the word processor with the yellow and red keys and press green to see the files. Document will be one of them. Highlight it and press <Enter> again. The listing will appear on the screen once more. At first you might think that you have simply gone back into BASIC and are looking at the original listing. There are, though, extra lines at the beginning and end of the listing, LIST and *SPOOL. More importantly you can scroll the listing up and down using the cursor keys in a way which unfortunately you cannot in BASIC.

With this ASCII file you can now write the documentation for the program and then print it out, either directly from the Notepad or indirectly after downloading your completed file to another computer via the serial port, or by using the parallel port and Lapcat software.

Editing a program with the word processor – *EXEC

The use of the Notepad's word processor is not limited to producing the documentation of a finished program. It can even be used in the development of a program itself. This is because the ability to scroll up and down the ASCII file is a rather useful addition to your range of programming tools.

When you are programming in the conventional way it can be a little frustrating that you can only see a few lines of a long program at a time on the Notepad's screen. With some computers you can scroll to another section of code to check what you have written, but BBC BASIC does not allow this.

However, if you obtain an ASCII version of the program as explained above, you can employ all the standard word processing techniques to examine and modify the program as much as you like. When you have completed your changes, and want to know whether the program still works, press <Function> and <B> to re-enter BASIC. Now type:

```
*EXEC "FILENAME"
```

using the name you have given to this file of course.

The modified listing of the program will be displayed. Type RUN and the program will be executed. When you are really confident about your programming skills you could even write a program entirely with the word processor and just use *EXEC to transfer it to BASIC when you have finished. This technique can be extended to running a Notepad program on another computer, like an Acorn machine, using BBC BASIC. Transfer the ASCII file and convert it to a working program with *EXEC.

Obtaining a screen dump

Cliff Lawson (of Amstrad) has very generously made available instructions for obtaining a screen dump to a printer from the Notepad. A 386 PC with Windows 3.0/3.1 is needed as a second machine. The routine will produce an exact reproduction of a Notepad screen display and was used to generate the illustrations used in the manual.

The method is as follows:

❑ Prepare the Notepad screen you wish to copy.

❑ Press <Control>, <Shift> and <S> simultaneously.

❑ After about 10 seconds, press <Function> and <L>. This will show stored documents. A screen file will be present called "s.a". Subsequent screens will be "s.b", "s.c" etc.

❑ Now connect a null modem to the PC and run communications software, like the Terminal program in Windows 3.0/3.1.

❑ On the Notepad select Xmodem send, as described above, and Xmodem receive on the PC with a filename you have chosen.

❑ With Windows 3.0/3.1 (enhanced mode) running use DISPLRAW "FILENAME" to display the picture of the Notepad's display.

❑ Pressing <Print Screen> on the PC will capture it to the Windows Clipboard.

❑ Now run Paint Brush and select Image Attributes from the Options Menu.

❑ Set units in 'Pels', width 480, height 64 (the dimensions of the Notepad display) and colours black and white.

❑ Use the Paste command from the Edit Menu to paste the Clipboard on to the blank image.

❑ Use Save As to save the file with Save file as Type set to PCX files (*.PCX). This file can then be used in a DTP package, like Ventura.

10

Troubleshooting

This chapter is intended as a brief guide to removing errors from the programs that you write. It is very easy to include mistakes and they divide roughly into two types. 'Syntax' errors result when you accidentally type in something that does not make sense in BBC BASIC. This is quite likely to happen, either because an instruction does not work in quite the way you expect, or simply because you have made a typing mistake. 'Logical errors' arise as a result of not thinking through a problem correctly at the algorithm stage. Computers are quite naive. They cannot anticipate what you really mean and hence make allowances for the cutting of logical corners. This was once summarised by a wistful programmer:

This computer is no good.
They really ought not sell it.
It never does quite what I want,
But only what I tell it.

The expression 'debugging' a program has now become so familiar that it is surprising to be reminded of the term's origin...

A moth enters the vocabulary

It is encouraging when an apocryphal story can be nailed to documented truth. The accepted term for removing errors from a program, 'debugging', does indeed relate to an actual insect.

In 1936 a Harvard scientist, Howard Aiken, studied the early theoretical work into computing carried out by the Victorian mathematician, Charles Babbage. Aiken realised that with current engineering techniques Babbage's dream could be realised. Although the project would be too costly for the university, International Business Machine's owner, Thomas Watson, agreed to fund the machine's construction.

Subsequently the 'Automatic Sequence Controlled Calculator' was completed at Endicott in 1943.

Soon rechristened the Harvard Mark 1, it began computing ballistics firing tables for the U.S. Navy. One of its 'coders' (the British term 'programmer' not then widely adopted) was Grace Hopper. One day in 1945 the Harvard Mark 1 stopped. Hopper used tweezers to remove a moth squashed beneath electromechanical relay number 70 on panel F and selotaped it into her log book. Thereafter, whenever her team was queried about the progress of its work, the standard reply was that they were about to debug the machine again.

It is unlikely that an insect would find the patience to clamber into a Notepad. It does not provide the warm environment of the old electronic valve machines. Such an adventurous insect could, in any case, wander in and out again without affecting the performance of the computer. Sadly, bugs in a modern program remain the sole responsibility of the programmer.

Dry running a program

When a program contains a logical error it probably will not stop with an error code. Instead, you will only realise that something is not correct with your work when the wrong results appear on the screen. The only way to proceed at this point is to take out pencil and paper, pretend to be the computer and follow exactly the steps you have prescribed in the program.

Do not write down what you want to happen at each point, but only what the instructions make explicit. In this way you will eventually see what is going wrong. With experience, this process of 'dry running' a program speeds up as intuition helps you to attack the likeliest sections of code first.

Tracing errors

It also will help in finding an error if you insert additional PRINT statements into a program. These should display the intermediate results of important variables in the program's operation. Often you can then see very quickly that a particular number is not following the pattern that you anticipate. This will allow you to narrow down the section of code causing the error.

Programs operate very quickly. Frequently you will find that you have rushed past the place where the error is occurring. One solution to this is to keep adding, then removing, STOP statements at strategic points. You will then know for example, that the program was still functioning properly at line 265, but had definitely gone astray by line 375.

Obviously you do not want to put the extra statements at a 'normal' line number because this will remove part of the program! Alternatively renumbering the program is also silly because it will only confuse you still further. Errors will then be bound not to occur at their real place.

Instead of STOP, the line K=GET is a useful way of temporarily halting a program while you think carefully about the display and whether anything incorrect has yet occurred. The program will not continue until you press a key. Alternatively an 'empty' input, like INPUT Z, will halt the program until <Enter> is pressed.

Using the BASIC trace – TRACE ON, TRACE OFF

The Notepad has a built-in instruction to help you to locate errors in a program. Often it will help you to know exactly what line is being executed at any given instant. Typing TRACE ON as a direct command will then lead to all line numbers being printed out on the display, between square brackets, in addition to anything else that the program is designed to do. Suppose you put a trace into this program:

```
10 REM Illustrating a trace
20 FOR I=1 TO 5
30 PRINT; I
40 NEXT I
```

The screen display will then be like this:

```
[10] [20] [30] 1
[40] [30] 2
[40] [30] 3
[40] [30] 4
[40] [30] 5
[40]
```

It is very clear how program execution has alternated between lines 30 and 40 as the FOR-NEXT loop has calculated and displayed the value of I. This can be a powerful technique for discovering errors. The trace is switched off again with TRACE OFF.

The remaining chapters of this book do not introduce any further BASIC. Instead they develop further the concepts introduced so far in a series of large-scale programs. Each is accompanied by detailed documentation and should help to reinforce understanding of the Notepad and of BBC BASIC.

11

A Shopping Utility

In this chapter the first long program example is presented. It draws upon the BASIC already explained in the earlier chapters of the book, but applies it on a much larger scale than any of the brief programs introduced before this point. The program is written in a highly structured way, with a control routine calling procedures and these procedures calling others. It should not be too difficult to understand the algorithms and their coding. Internal documentation is provided in the form of frequent REM statements. All of the code is then explained in full in the external documentation which follows the program listing. This approach will be adopted for all the long programs which feature in the remaining chapters.

The program developed, Shopper, is designed to help with writing and then using a shopping list. Various commodities, and their price, are held as data by the program. When it is run, each of these is displayed in turn on the screen. The user can choose to include the item on a shopping list, or to ignore it. This is done by pressing the Y and N keys. When all the possible purchases have been considered in this way, the shopping list that has been compiled is displayed as a series of numbered items in three columns on the screen. The first item is highlighted in inverse text. The user can alter the item highlighted by pressing the cursor keys to move the highlighting up or down the list. When an appropriate item has been selected, it is 'bought' by pressing the <Enter> key. The item is then removed from the list and its price is added to a running total at the top of the screen.

It is hoped that this is quite a useful program to store on the Notepad as a helpful utility. The computer is, perhaps, a little too large to carry while shopping is done at the same time. Another member of the family, perhaps a small daughter or son, could be assigned the role of Amstrad-bearer. Alternatively, the pull-out seat supermarket trolleys provide for tired toddlers is just about the right size. As Alan Sugar's colossal advertising campaign for the machine ensures that most people in the country will soon own one, there is little need to fear that your Notepad might be purloined!

Program listing – SHOPPER

```
 10 REM SHOPPER
 20 REM Control routine
 30 PROCinit
 40 PROCcompile
 50 PROCdisplay
 60 PROCshop
 70 CLS
 80 PRINT "Shopping finished"
 90 END
100 DEF PROCinit
110 REM Commodities
120 DIM C$(25),C(25)
130 FOR I=1 TO 25
140    READ C$(I),C(I)
150 NEXT I
160 REM List
170 DIM L$(15),L(15),B(15)
180 REM List coordinates
190 DIM CX(15),CY(15)
200 FOR I=1 TO 15
210    X=1 : Y=I+1
220    IF I>5 THEN X=27 : Y=I-4
230    IF I>10 THEN X=53 : Y=I-9
240    CX(I)=X
250    CY(I)=Y
260 NEXT I
270 T=0
280 bill=0
290 ENDPROC
300 REM
310 DEF PROCcompile
320 CLS
330 I=0
340 REPEAT
350    I=I+1
360    PRINT "Do you want to add "; C$(I);
370    PRINT " to the shopping list?"
380    PRINT "Press Y or N"
390    REPEAT
400       K=GET
410 UNTIL K=78 OR K=89
420 IF K=89 THEN T=T+1 : L$(T)=C$(I) : L(T)=C(I)
430 UNTIL T=15 OR I=25
440 ENDPROC
450 REM
460 DEF PROCdisplay
470 CLS
480 PRINT "Shopping list:";
490 PRINT " Choose item with cursor.";
500 PRINT " Buy with <Enter>.";
510 PRINT " Bill is"
```

A Shopping Utility

```
520 FOR I=1 TO T
530   PRINT TAB(CX(I),CY(I)); I; CHR$ 32; L$(I)
540 NEXT I
550 ENDPROC
560 REM
570 DEF PROCshop
580 REM Initialise items bought
590 basket=0
600 REM Initialise pointer
610 P=1
620 REM Highlight first item
630 VDU 14
640 PRINT TAB(CX(1),CY(1)); 1; CHR$ 32; L$(1)
650 VDU 15
660 REPEAT
670   REM Scan list
680   REPEAT
690     K=GET
700   UNTIL K=240 OR K=241 OR K=13 OR K=81
710   IF K=240 THEN D=-1 : PROChunt
720   IF K=241 THEN D=1 : PROChunt
730   IF K=13 THEN PROCbuy
740   IF basket=T THEN
      PRINT "Everything bought. Press Q to exit."
750 UNTIL K=81
760 ENDPROC
770 REM
780 DEF PROChunt
790 REM Remove highlighting of current item
800 IF B(P)=0 PRINT TAB(CX(P),CY(P)); P; CHR$ 32; L$(P)
810 REM Search for next item
820 REPEAT
830   P=P+D
840   REM Wrap around
850   IF P=0 THEN P=T
860   IF P=T+1 THEN P=1
870 UNTIL B(P)=0
880 REM Highlight new item
890 VDU 14
900 PRINT TAB(CX(P),CY(P)); P; CHR$ 32; L$(P)
910 VDU 15
920 ENDPROC
930 REM
940 DEF PROCbuy
950 REM Count item
960 basket=basket+1
970 REM Remove item from list
980 PRINT TAB(CX(P),CY(P)); SPC(3+LEN L$(P))
990 B(P)=1
1000 REM Add price to bill
1010 bill=bill+L(P)
1020 PRINT TAB(66,0); bill/100
1030 ENDPROC
```

```
1040 REM
1050 REM Data for shopping list
1060 DATA Granary loaf,79
1070 DATA 1lb Apples,39
1080 DATA 1lb Pears,59
1090 DATA 1lb Satsumas,49
1100 DATA Grapefruit,35
1110 DATA Mango,99
1120 DATA Honeydew melon,135
1130 DATA Dates,99
1140 DATA Tinned mackerel,45
1150 DATA Tinned salmon,79
1160 DATA Tuna,45
1170 DATA 1lb Mature cheddar,245
1180 DATA Tinned milk,44
1190 DATA Sunflower margarine,63
1200 DATA Oat biscuits,48
1210 DATA 1 pack razors,69
1220 DATA Soap,24
1230 DATA Toothpaste,99
1240 DATA Deodorant,65
1250 DATA Shampoo,115
1260 DATA 1 pack toilet tissue,89
1270 DATA Detergent,135
1280 DATA Thick bleach,75
1290 DATA Cats' tuna,30
1300 DATA Cats' crunchies,65
```

Storing commodities and their prices

The program assumes that the user will select a specific shopping list from a range of 25 items. This number could easily be adjusted to match personal needs. (A large family is going to require more varied items than a sub-nuclear family of one bachelor and two cats!) The possible products are held as data at the end of the program. The items given here are meant to be merely illustrative, but, as a historical note, the prices are correct according to a visit made to Tescos (Portsmouth) while the program was being written:

```
1050 REM Data for shopping list
1060 DATA Granary loaf,79
1070 DATA 1lb Apples,39
1080 DATA 1lb Pears,59
1090 DATA 1lb Satsumas,49
1100 DATA Grapefruit,35
1110 DATA Mango,99
1120 DATA Honeydew melon,135
1130 DATA Dates,99
1140 DATA Tinned mackerel,45
1150 DATA Tinned salmon,79
1160 DATA Tuna,45
1170 DATA 1lb Mature cheddar,245
```

A Shopping Utility

```
1180 DATA Tinned milk,44
1190 DATA Sunflower margarine,63
1200 DATA Oat biscuits,48
1210 DATA 1 pack razors,69
1220 DATA Soap,24
1230 DATA Toothpaste,99
1240 DATA Deodorant,65
1250 DATA Shampoo,115
1260 DATA 1 pack toilet tissue,89
1270 DATA Detergent,135
1280 DATA Thick bleach,75
1290 DATA Cats' tuna,30
1300 DATA Cats' crunchies,65
```

The regularity of the data is vital. Each commodity is followed by its price and then by the next commodity. This matches the way the data is subsequently read into two arrays. The price is always expressed in pence, even for those items costing over 99p. In this way the calculation of the final bill is made easier. A separate data statement has been used for each pair of data items. This is intended to make it simpler to amend the program when shopping requirements alter.

All of the items are placed into a 'commodity' array, C$(25), by a FOR-NEXT loop in the first procedure called by the control routine, PROCinit. The array has, of course, to be able to store strings. A second array, C(25), is numeric and holds the prices of the items:

```
110 REM Commodities
120 DIM C$(25),C(25)
130 FOR I=1 TO 25
140    READ C$(I),C(I)
150 NEXT I
```

Writing the shopping list

The second procedure called by the control routine, PROCcompile, allows the user to select items from the C$ array and place them into a separate shopping list. Further arrays are required for this. A string array, L$(15), is used to hold the names of the items on the shopping list. A numeric array, L(15) stores their prices. Another numeric array, B(15), is used later to indicate whether a particular item has been bought or not. The three arrays are initialised in PROCinit:

```
160 REM List
170 DIM L$(15),L(15),B(15)
```

Limiting the number of items on the list to 15 is not wholly arbitrary. A maximum of 15 items fits very conveniently into three columns on the Notepad's display. For those who wish to have a longer list, the text coordinates used in PROCdisplay and

PROCshop will have to be calculated to allow more closely spaced columns on the screen. The general technique for this is described below.

PROCinit also initialises the number of items on the shopping list, T. This will be zero at this stage in the program's execution:

```
270 T=0
```

A REPEAT-UNTIL loop is used to let the user copy items from the C$ array into the L$ array. A counter, I, is employed by this loop, initialised as zero outside it and then immediately incremented by 1 after the REPEAT. The value of this counter allows successive items in the C$ array to be displayed on the screen. The user is prompted to press either Y or N according to whether this item should be added to the shopping list. A further REPEAT-UNTIL loop uses the ASCII value of the keypress to halt program execution unless one of these choices is made.

If Y is pressed, the ASCII value of the variable K will be 89. This is used as a condition in a statement which increments the value of T and then copies the current item and its price into this location of the shopping list arrays.

The loop continues to repeat until either the value of T indicates that the shopping list has reached its maximum of 15 items, or all 25 possible items from the commodities array have been considered. The code for this compilation of the shopping list is:

```
330 I=0
340 REPEAT
350    I=I+1
360    PRINT "Do you want to add "; C$(I);
370    PRINT " to the shopping list?"
380    PRINT "Press Y or N"
390    REPEAT
400       K=GET
410    UNTIL K=78 OR K=89
420    IF K=89 THEN T=T+1 : L$(T)=C$(I) : L(T)=C(I)
430 UNTIL T=15 OR I=25
```

Displaying the list

After PROCcompile has produced the shopping list, the items are shown on the screen by PROCdisplay. They are numbered and placed in three columns which occupy the full width of the screen. These positions are used even for shorter lists. If only three items are to be bought, these will be placed at the top of the left hand column leaving the rest of the screen empty. The following diagram shows all 15 possible positions for the items in relation to the screen coordinates:

A Shopping Utility

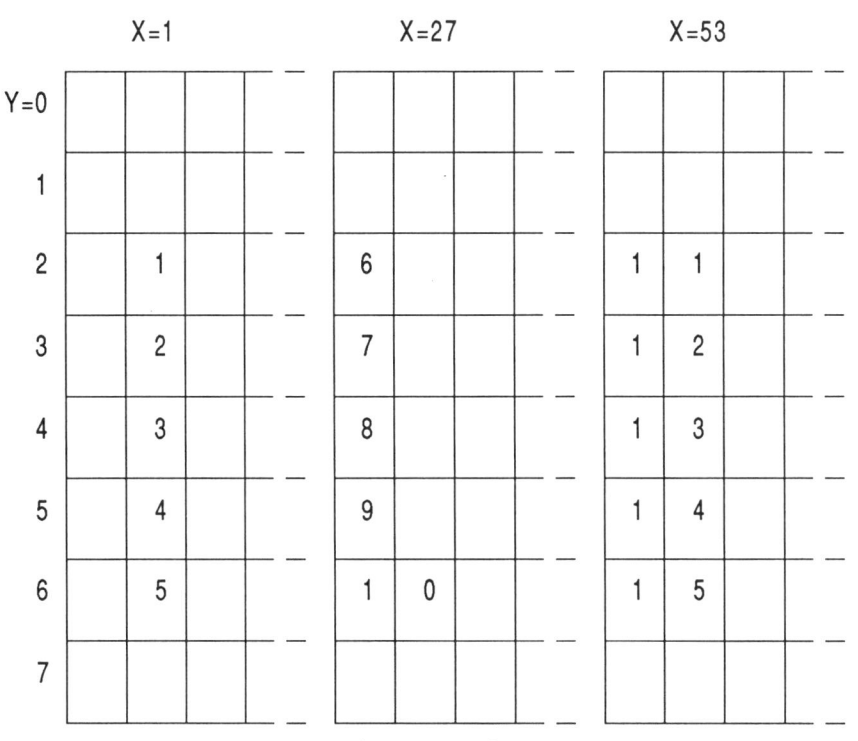

Text coordinates for shopping list

It can be seen that the first character of the each item is placed at X-coordinate 1 for the first column, at 27 for the second column and 53 for the third. The Y-coordinates for the first column are 1 more than the item number. In the second column the Y-coordinates are 4 less than the item number and in the third column they are 9 less. This pattern can be established by first assuming that the coordinates are X=1, Y=I+1 for the Ith item on the list and then adding the two conditional statements:

```
IF I>5 THEN X=27 : Y=I-4
IF I>10 THEN X=53 : Y=I-9
```

PROCinit uses these conditions to calculate the text coordinates needed by all possible 15 screen positions occupied by items of the shopping list. They are placed into two arrays: CX(15) for the X-coordinate and CY(15) for the Y-coordinates:

```
180 REM List coordinates
190 DIM CX(15),CY(15)
200 FOR I=1 TO 15
210    X=1 : Y=I+1
220    IF I>5 THEN X=27 : Y=I-4
230    IF I>10 THEN X=53 : Y=I-9
240    CX(I)=X
250    CY(I)=Y
260 NEXT I
```

These array coordinates are used frequently throughout the operation of the program. They are first required in PROCdisplay to place the shopping list on the Notepad's screen. Note that only the first T of the 15 pairs of CX, CY values are needed:

```
520 FOR I=1 TO T
530   PRINT TAB(CX(I),CY(I); I; CHR$ 32; L$(I)
540 NEXT I
```

The loop variable is included as part of the print statement at line 530 in order to number the items on the list. A space is added between the number and the item itself by CHR$ 32.

Selecting an item from the list

Once the list of items to buy is displayed on the screen, the control routine calls PROCshop. This is the important procedure which allows the user to select items from the list and buy them. At any given time one item is highlighted in inverse text. The item can be bought by pressing <Enter>. It is then erased from the list and its price added to the running total of the bill displayed at the top of the screen. Alternatively the user can scroll up and down the list, highlighting different items in turn until the correct one is identified. This is controlled with the cursor up and cursor down keys. Prompts to explain all of this have already been printed on the top line of the screen by PROCdisplay:

```
480 PRINT "Shopping list:";
490 PRINT " Choose item with cursor.";
500 PRINT " Buy with <Enter>.";
510 PRINT " Bill is"
```

A new variable is required to identify which is the current item highlighted on the list. This 'points' to the item and so is called the pointer, P. Its initial range of values will be between 1 and T, representing all the items on the list. However as items are bought, gaps will appear in this range and the pointer will have to skip over the missing values. The way this is arranged by the program is explained below. Of course, when the shopping list is first presented on the screen it is sensible to highlight the first item. This is done by setting P equal to 1 and over-printing this item in inverse text:

```
600 REM Initialise pointer
610 P=1
620 REM Highlight first item
630 VDU 14
640 PRINT TAB(CX(1),CY(1)); 1; CHR$ 32; L$(1)
650 VDU 15
```

A REPEAT-UNTIL loop now controls the choice of highlighted item. It contains a second, nested REPEAT-UNTIL loop which checks the keypress and limits the user to a choice of four keys, cursor up and down, <Enter> and Q. This is done by looking for the respective ASCII values of 240 for cursor up, 241 for cursor down, 13 for <Enter> or 81 for Q.

A Shopping Utility

Choosing cursor up or down calls the procedure PROChunt, which highlights another item on the list. This keypress also assigns a value to a variable, D, required by PROChunt. Choosing the <Enter> key calls PROCbuy, which deletes the highlighted item from the list and adds its price to the running total displayed at the top of the screen.

Selecting Q, for 'Quit', permits the loop to exit. This returns the program to the control routine and ends the program. The user can do this at any time, but the prompt to remind him or her of this possibility is only printed on the screen when all of the items are bought. The variable 'basket' indicates this, as explained the account of PROCbuy below. The code which orchestrates this perusal of the shopping list is:

```
660 REPEAT
670    REM Scan list
680    REPEAT
690      K=GET
700    UNTIL K=240 OR K=241 OR K=13 OR K=81
710    IF K=240 THEN D=-1 : PROChunt
720    IF K=241 THEN D=1 : PROChunt
730    IF K=13 THEN PROCbuy
740    IF basket=T THEN PRINT "Everything
       bought. Press Q to exit."
750 UNTIL K=81
```

Problems with the list

It is very important to be able to scan up and down the shopping list and highlight any of the items on it. There would be little point in having a shopping list which forced you to buy items in a fixed order. You would need to walk around the supermarket ignoring everything else until you came to the item specified next by your list . . .

The program allows this scanning to take place by using the cursor keys to increase or decrease the value of the pointer, P. This is done by PROChunt. There are two vital details that have to be included:

❏ The pointer must skip past those items in the L$ array which have already been bought.

❏ When the bottom of the list is reached, the pointer must reappear at the top. Similarly when the top of the list is reached, the pointer must reappear at the bottom. So although the shopping list is displayed on the screen as a simple, linear object, in reality it 'wraps around' and rejoins itself.

Skipping purchased items on the list

A further REPEAT-UNTIL loop is used to allow the pointer to avoid coming to rest on an item which has been purchased. The direction in which the pointer should move in the list is determined by the value of the variable D. When the cursor up key has been pressed, D is -1. When cursor down is pressed, D is 1. The new value of P, P+D, will therefore move the pointer in the correct way.

The B(15) array is used to decide when the pointer can stop moving. All the B array locations are zero initially but are reset to 1, in PROCbuy, when an item is bought. The pointer therefore has to keep moving until it finds an item in the list for which the value of B(P) is still zero. This code would achieve what is required:

```
820 REPEAT
830    P=P+D

870 UNTIL B(P)=0
```

'Wrapping around' the list

The shopping list is made into a seamless whole on the screen by adjusting the value of P when it arrives at either end of its range. At the first item of the list, P will have the value 1. If the user continues moving up the list, P will then become 0. This value does not correspond with any item and instead the pointer is switched back to the bottom of the list by setting it to the value T, which represents the last item. The reassignment of P is achieved by this single line of code:

```
850 IF P=0 THEN P=T
```

Similarly when the user is scrolling down the list the last meaningful item is when P has the value T. If the user continues scrolling downwards, P will become T+1. At this point the pointer needs to be placed back at the top of the list and so the code is:

```
860 IF P=T+1 THEN P=1
```

Controlling the highlighted item

PROChunt can now use the two pieces of code described to avoid the problem of the missing items and the list's ends. The procedure also uses VDU 14 and 15 to adjust the highlighting. First it switches off the highlighting of the current item:

```
800 IF B(P)=0 PRINT TAB(CX(P),CY(P)); P; CHR$ 32; L$(P)
```

The condition B(P)=0 is needed to avoid reinstalling old items back on to the displayed list when their empty location is encountered again upon scrolling.

Then, after the correct next item is found, it can be highlighted. VDU 14 toggles on inverse text before printing the item and VDU 15 switches it off again immediately afterwards:

```
890 VDU 14
900 PRINT TAB(CX(P),CY(P)); P; CHR$ 32; L$(P)
910 VDU 15
```

Assembling all these pieces for PROChunt gives:

```
780 DEF PROChunt
790 REM Remove highlighting of current item
800 IF B(P)=0 PRINT TAB(CX(P),CY(P)); P; CHR$ 32; L$(P)
810 REM Search for next item
820 REPEAT
830   P=P+D
840   REM Wrap around
850   IF P=0 THEN P=T
860   IF P=T+1 THEN P=1
870 UNTIL B(P)=0
880 REM Highlight new item
890 VDU 14
900 PRINT TAB(CX(P),CY(P)); P; CHR$ 32; L$(P)
910 VDU 15
920 ENDPROC
```

Adding up the bill

The last procedure in the program is the one which provides the essential display of the running total cost of all the items being purchased. Those who still resist the temptation to buy groceries with a credit card will probably have adopted the policy of leaving luxuries to the last moment and checking their wallet before reaching for the shelf.

The variable used to record the running total is 'bill'. This is initialised in PROCinit:

```
280 bill=0
```

It is updated by the current item's price, L(P), in PROCbuy and printed at the appropriate location on the top line of the screen. As all the item prices are in pence, the value of bill is divided by 100 before it is revealed.

The number of items purchased is recorded by the variable 'basket', which has been initialised in PROCshop:

```
580 REM Initialise items bought
590 basket=T
```

Each time PROCbuy is called, basket is increased by 1. When it reaches the value T, which is the total number of items to buy, it triggers the appropriate prompt already mentioned above.

As well as adding up the bill, and counting the items bought, PROCbuy has to remove the item concerned from the list on the screen. It does this by over-printing the screen position with spaces equal to the length of the item plus the number prefixing it. PROCbuy also alters the B array location to 1 to register that the item has been bought. The total code for the procedure is:

```
 940 DEF PROCbuy
 950 REM Count item
 960 basket=basket+1
 970 REM Remove item from list
 980 PRINT TAB(CX(P),CY(P)); SPC(3+LEN L$(P))
 990 B(P)=1
1000 REM Add price to bill
1010 bill=bill+L(P)
1020 PRINT TAB(66,0); bill/100
1030 ENDPROC
```

Further refinements to the program

The structure of Shopper has been kept deliberately simple so that it may be a useful illustration of programming techniques. If the program were to be adopted as a realistic aid to shopping, further features would need to be added to the program to improve it. The ability to buy more than one of a selected item is important. In its current version the program also makes the assumption that the prices of items remain as stored in the data. This, of course, is unlikely to be the case for long, as supermarkets gradually raise all of their prices. In addition, temporary promotional drives lead to some products being drastically reduced in price.

The program therefore requires the possibility of the user over-riding the price of a particular item and typing in the shelf price. This would need to be an extension of PROCshop, with a further condition allowing the ASCII value of K to call perhaps an additional procedure which alters the value held in the L array. This should not be too difficult to code. A more complicated, but worthwhile, adjustment to the program would permit full file-handling, with new item prices being stored in a separate commodities file. In this way updated information could be carried forward to future shopping expeditions.

A whimsical addition to the program would be an audible warning if the total of the items exceeds a preset figure. Try adding these lines:

```
735 IF bill>2000 THEN PROCwhoops

1041 DEF PROCwhoops
1042 FOR I=1 TO 5
1043    VDU 7
1044    FOR J=1 TO 300
1045    NEXT J
1046 NEXT I
1047 ENDPROC
1048 REM
```

12

Displaying the Time

Information about the date and time forms an integral part of the environment provided by the Amstrad Notepad. In addition, the manual provides a BASIC program (on page 165), for the user to enter, which will place a traditional, analogue clock face on the Notepad's screen. It might therefore seem a little pointless attempting yet another time display.

However the program, Digital, developed in this chapter, is quite useful. It places a very large digital clock face on the Notepad's screen. The numbers occupy the whole height of the display and extend from one end of the screen to the other. This could be quite a useful feature to have available. There could be occasions when you would want to use your Notepad temporarily as a clock and you might need to be able to read the display from a distance.

Working through the program, and the documentation that follows it, gives useful practice in calling procedures with parameters. The program also shows how a two dimensional array can be employed to create a fairly complicated data structure.

Program listing – DIGITAL

```
10 REM DIGITAL
20 REM Control routine
30 PROCinit
40 FOR time=1 TO 10
50     CLS
60     T$=RIGHT$(TIME$,8)
70     VDU 7
80     FOR I=1 TO 6
90         D=(I-1)*80
100        N=VAL(MID$(T$,T(I),1))
110        PROCdigit(N,D)
120    NEXT I
130    FOR P=1 TO 5000
140    NEXT P
150 NEXT time
160 END
```

```
170 REM
180 DEF PROCinit
190 REM Coordinates for segments
200 DIM A(7,4)
210 FOR I=1 TO 7
220   FOR J=1 TO 4
230     READ A(I,J)
240   NEXT J
250 NEXT I
260 REM Segments used in digit
270 DIM B(9,8)
280 FOR I=0 TO 8
290   FOR J=1 TO 8
300     READ B(I,J)
310   NEXT J
320 NEXT I
330 REM Characters required for time
340 DIM T(6)
350 FOR I=1 TO 6
360   READ T(I)
370 NEXT I
380 ENDPROC
390 REM
400 DEF PROCdigit(N,D)
410 LOCAL I
420 FOR I=2 TO B(N,1)
430   PROCsegment(B(N,I),D)
440 NEXT I
450 ENDPROC
460 REM
470 DEF PROCsegment(N,D)
480 MOVE D+A(N,1),A(N,2)
490 PLOT 101,D+A(N,3),A(N,4)
500 ENDPROC
510 REM
520 REM Data for segments
530 DATA 0,53,74,63,0,26,74,36
540 DATA 0,0,74,10,0,31,10,63
550 DATA 64,31,74,63,0,0,10,31
560 DATA 64,0,74,31
570 REM Data for digits
580 DATA 7,1,3,4,5,6,7,0
590 DATA 3,5,7,0,0,0,0,0
600 DATA 6,1,2,3,5,6,0,0
610 DATA 6,1,2,3,5,7,0,0
620 DATA 5,2,4,5,7,0,0,0
630 DATA 6,1,2,3,4,7,0,0
640 DATA 7,1,2,3,4,6,7,0
650 DATA 4,1,5,7,0,0,0,0
660 DATA 8,1,2,3,4,5,6,7
670 DATA 7,1,2,3,4,5,7,0
680 REM Data for time
690 DATA 1,2,4,5,7,8
```

Splitting a digit

The large digital display for the time is produced by printing six large digits on the Notepad's display. Each of these is drawn by the same procedure, PROCdigit(N,D). The procedure employs two variables which are passed to it from the control routine. These are N, the value of the digit to be displayed, and D, which states how many pixels the digit should be displaced across the display to the right.

The diagram shows how each digit is constructed from a possible combination of eight thin rectangles on the screen. Three rectangles are horizontal and four are vertical. Collectively, they are referred to as 'segments' in the program listing. It will be appreciated immediately that the technique is directly copied from the typical LCD type of digital display:

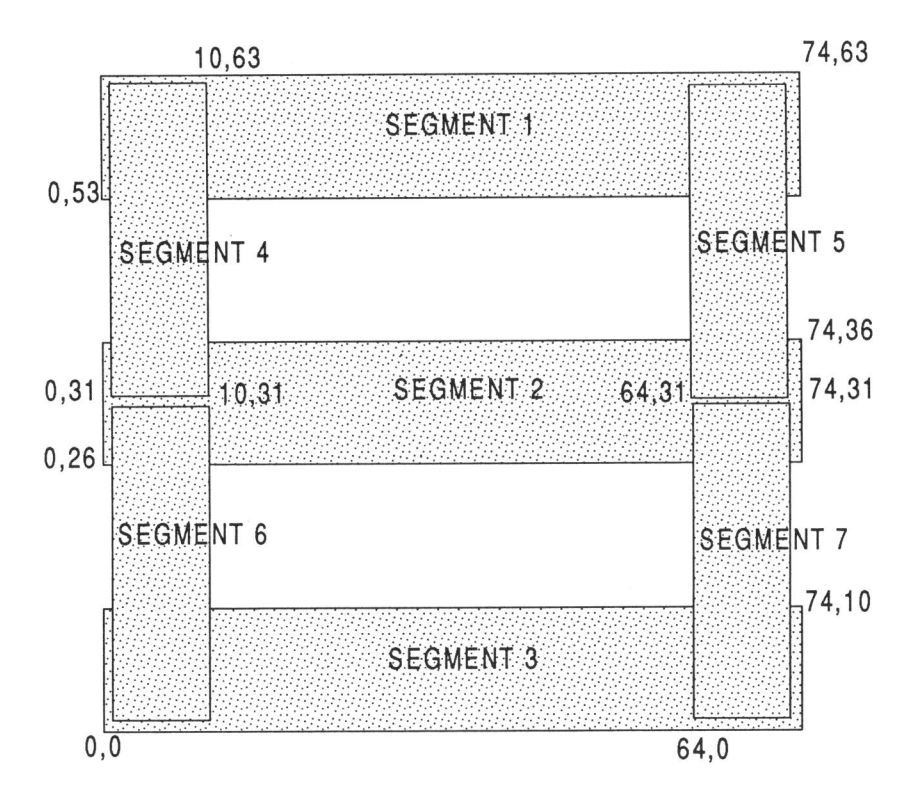

Coordinates for digit segments

The coordinates shown on the diagram are the ones which apply to the extreme left hand digit, the one which will have graphics coordinates (0,0) for its bottom left hand corner. All the other five digits can be constructed from precisely the same set of coordinates, simply by adding an appropriate number of pixels to each X-value.

Each segment can be drawn by a simple use of PLOT 101. First MOVE is used to position the graphics cursor at the bottom left hand corner of the segment. Then PLOT 101, followed by the coordinates of the top right hand corner, fills in a solid rectangle on the display. For example, segment 1 could be drawn by MOVE 0,53 and PLOT 101,74,63. Similarly segment 4 would be drawn as MOVE 0,31 together with PLOT 101,10,63.

A data structure for the segments

A general procedure is required which will draw any segment as required. This means that the coordinates for each segment must be represented in a uniform way. In the diagram each row represents a different digit, starting with segment 1 at the top and ending with segment seven at the bottom. The first column is the X-coordinate of the bottom left hand corner. The second column is the Y-coordinate of this corner. The remaining two columns are the coordinates of the top right hand corner. This is all the graphics data needed to draw any of the segments:

	1	2	3	4
1	0	53	74	63
2	0	26	74	36
3	0	0	74	10
4	0	31	10	63
5	64	31	74	63
6	0	0	10	31
7	64	0	74	31

Array locations for segments

The data recorded in this diagram is held at the end of the program as data statements. The sequence of the numbers is just the same as on the table, starting at the top left and proceeding in the conventional direction. It does not matter that two

Displaying the Time 133

rows of the table have sometimes been placed into the same data statement. Only the sequential order is important:

```
520 REM Data for segments
530 DATA 0,53,74,63,0,26,74,36
540 DATA 0,0,74,10,0,31,10,63
550 DATA 64,31,74,63,0,0,10,31
560 DATA 64,0,74,31
```

This data needs to be readily available as the program is executed. Using RESTORE to a given line number would be hopelessly inefficient and so all the values are read into an array, A(7,4), by two nested loops in PROCinit. The range of the loop variables, I and J, matches exactly the rows and columns of the table. This means, for example, that the number stored at location A(3,4) of the array will be 10:

```
190 REM Coordinates for segments
200 DIM A(7,4)
210 FOR I=1 TO 7
220   FOR J=1 TO 4
230     READ A(I,J)
240   NEXT J
250 NEXT I
```

Drawing a chosen segment

The procedure which will create any selected segment is PROCsegment(N,D). This will draw segment number N and place it at the correct displacement, D, across the screen to correspond to the relevant digit in the six numbers forming the time display.

The coordinates of the bottom left hand corner of the Nth segment are stored at the array locations A(N,1) and A(N,2). The Y-coordinate is not affected by the horizontal displacement across the screen. However the X-coordinate must be increased by D. The statement required to place the graphics cursor at this corner of the segment is therefore:

```
                MOVE D+A(N,1),A(N,2)
```

Similarly, the coordinates of the upper right hand corner of the segment are A(N,3) and A(N,4). After modification by D, this gives the statement needed to fill in the segment as:

```
                PLOT 101,D+A(N,3),A(N,4)
```

The whole procedure to draw the Nth segment is therefore:

```
470 DEF PROCsegment(N,D)
480 MOVE D+A(N,1),A(N,2)
490 PLOT 101,D+A(N,3),A(N,4)
500 ENDPROC
```

A data structure for the digits

Each digit, from 0 to 9, can be constructed as a suitable combination of the segments. For example the digit 4 can be formed from segments 2, 4, 5 and 7. The digit 1 needs just segments 5 and 7. When 8 is drawn, all the segments are required. The program clearly needs a method by which the appropriate segments can be selected for each digit. This method involves a further data structure. Like the coordinate information stored for PROCsegment, this additional data structure uses values held in data statements at the end of the program and placed in a two dimensional array when the program is first executed.

Two distinct types of data need to be recorded for each of the 10 digits that will be drawn. First, the numbers identifying the separate segments composing a given digit must be stored. In addition the total number of segments forming the digit has to be indicated, by some chosen method, in order to inform PROCdigit when it has finished drawing the segments needed to produce the character on the display. This is an 'end of data' signal. How this is achieved in the program will be clear when the table is studied:

	DIGIT	LAST USED LOCATION	1	2	3	4	5	6	7	8 J →
					SEGMENTS REQUIRED					
0	0	7	1	3	4	5	6	7	0	0
1	1	3	5	7	0	0	0	0	0	0
2	2	6	1	2	3	5	6	0	0	0
3	3	6	1	2	3	5	7	0	0	0
4	4	5	2	4	5	7	0	0	0	0
5	5	6	1	2	3	4	7	0	0	0
6	6	7	1	2	3	4	6	7	0	0
7	7	4	1	5	7	0	0	0	0	0
8	8	8	1	2	3	4	5	6	7	0
9	9	7	1	2	3	4	5	7	0	0

I ↓

Array locations for digits

Each row of this table corresponds to one of the digits to be drawn. The top row holds the data required to draw a 0. The bottom row will create a 9. This is made explicit by the first column of the table. (This column is included to make the table clear and does not form part of the data held in the program.)

Displaying the Time

The numbers of the segments required to form a particular digit are held in the third, fourth and succeeding columns to the right. For example the digit 7 needs segments 1, 5 and 7 and these numbers are held in third, fourth and fifth columns of the seventh row. In contrast, the number held in the second column of the seventh row, 4, indicates how many segments are used to make 7. This is done by showing that the fourth item of data in the table is the 'last used location'. (Remember that the first column is not part of the recorded data.)

This method of recording all the segments required is applied rigorously to all 10 digits and all the places in the table are filled in the way described. Zeros must be put into the locations which would otherwise be blank. This is because the numbers will be read from data statements and missing values would disrupt the pattern, leading to incorrect assignment to array locations and an inevitable 'out of data' error message. The content of the table is held in these data statements:

```
570 REM Data for digits
580 DATA 7,1,3,4,5,6,7,0
590 DATA 3,5,7,0,0,0,0,0
600 DATA 6,1,2,3,5,6,0,0
610 DATA 6,1,2,3,5,7,0,0
620 DATA 5,2,4,5,7,0,0,0
630 DATA 6,1,2,3,4,7,0,0
640 DATA 7,1,2,3,4,6,7,0
650 DATA 4,1,5,7,0,0,0,0
660 DATA 8,1,2,3,4,5,6,7
670 DATA 7,1,2,3,4,5,7,0
```

The numbers are placed into an appropriate array. This is initialised as B(9,8). The zeroth set of locations, B(0,1) ... B(0,8) is used in this case because one of the digits that has to be constructed is zero itself. Using the zeroth locations makes the representation of the 10 digits by the array more obvious. The numbers are assigned to the array by two nested FOR-NEXT loops in PROCinit:

```
260 REM Segments used in digit
270 DIM B(9,8)
280 FOR I=0 TO 8
290   FOR J=1 TO 8
300     READ B(I,J)
310   NEXT J
320 NEXT I
```

After these loops have been executed, individual array locations will store different parts of the data structure representing the digits. The first subscript identifies the particular digit. The second shows either each segment required, or the last used location in the array for that digit. For example, B(1,1) has the value 3, which shows that the digit 1 does not use any data after location B(1,3). After this, B(1,2) is 5 and B(1,3) is 7 and so just segments 5 and 7 are needed to draw 1 on the display.

Similarly the fact that the value of location B(5,1) is 6 indicates that locations B(5,2), B(5,3), B(5,4), B(5,5) and B(5,6) are needed to create the digit 5. The values at these locations are 1, 2, 3, 4 and 7 and hence these segments will build up a large 5 on the Notepad's display.

Although working through the ramifications of this data structure is quite complicated for the individual human being, the Notepad can dash through at top speed and draw all digits required for a time display smoothly, without hesitation!

Assembling the digit

Once the data for the digits is stored in the B array, drawing a digit is a simple task for PROCdigit(N,D). First the final array location for the Nth digit is identified from the array as B(N,1). Then a loop determines all the segments required, beginning at B(N,2) and progressing to B(N,B(N,1)). The nomenclature may look a little convoluted, but it is wholly logical! (Programming does tend to be Spockian!)

For each segment identified in the array, a call to PROCsegment draws that part of the digit on the display. The value assigned to D is involved throughout and so each digit is displaced to the appropriate part of the screen. The loop variable, I, is declared local to avoid problem with the loop in the control routine:

```
400 DEF PROCdigit(N,D)
410 LOCAL I
420 FOR I=2 TO B(N,1)
430    PROCsegment(B(N,I),D)
440 NEXT I
450 ENDPROC
```

Obtaining the time

The most complicated part of the program has been achieved once the procedure PROCdigit(N,D) is working, with its calls to PROCsegment(N,D) and the incorporation of all the coordinate and segment data in the arrays A and B. All that is then required is a routine which will access the internal clock to obtain the time and split this up into the individual digits which need to be displayed.

The BASIC function TIME$ gives an output containing more information than is required in this program:

```
>PRINT TIME$
Fri.16 Oct 1992,22:07:47
```

The time itself, hours, minutes and seconds, is contained in the last eight characters of this string. This information is therefore extracted from TIME$ and assigned to the variable T$ by this line of the program:

```
60   T$=RIGHT$(TIME$,8)
```

T$ will consist of eight characters. Only six of these are needed to display the time. The first two give the hours, the fourth and fifth the minutes and the seventh and eighth the seconds. The positions of these relevant characters in the string T$ are held as a final data statement at the end of the program:

```
680 REM Data for time
690 DATA 1,2,4,5,7,8
```

They are placed into an array, T(6), by code contained in PROCinit:

```
330 REM Characters required for time
340 DIM T(6)
350 FOR I=1 TO 6
360   READ T(I)
370 NEXT I
```

The T array then allows each digit required in the time display to be extracted from T$ with the use of MID$. For example, the third digit of the display must be the first digit of the minute figure in T$. This is MID$(T$,4,1). Using the T array allows the digit to be identified as MID$(T$,T(3),1). This is preferable because it can be seen that the Ith digit needed in the display will be MID$(T$,T(I),1). In this form each digit can be found simply inside a FOR-NEXT loop.

MID$ always returns a string. Therefore before the digit can be passed to the procedure PROCdigit(N,D) it must be converted into a numeric variable by operating on it with VAL:

```
100 N=VAL(MID$(T$,T(I),1))
```

Spacing out the digits

The final task is to generate the values for D needed to displace the digits across the screen. As there are six digits and the display is 480 pixels wide, each digit can occupy a section of screen 80 pixels in width.

```
Digit number           I        D
                       1        0
                       2        80
                       3        160
                       4        240
                       5        320
                       6        400
```

The relationship here between D and I is coded in the main control loop of the program:

```
90 D=(I-1)*80
```

Displaying the time

Values for N and D are now available to place the time on the screen. The Ith digit of the date will be placed at the correct screen position by the three lines:

```
 90 D=(I-1)*80
100 N=VAL(MID$(T$,T(I),1))
110 PROCdigit(N,D)
```

The code is embedded inside two nested loops. The I-loop prints out all six digits needed for the time display. The outer loop, controlled by the variable 'time', repeats the time display. It also includes a tone produced by VDU 7 and a further embedded loop to add a pause between each time display:

```
 40 FOR time=1 TO 10
 50    CLS
 60    T$=RIGHT$(TIME$,8)
 70    VDU 7
 80    FOR I=1 TO 6
120    NEXT I
130    FOR P=1 TO 5000
140    NEXT P
150 NEXT time
```

The outer loop repeats only 10 times and is intended simply to demonstrate how the program operates. If Digital were to be used as a serious time display, a REPEAT-UNTIL FALSE loop would be preferable. Other refinements are of course possible.

The shape of the digits displayed is determined entirely by the coordinate data held between lines 530-560 and so alteration here could affect the display considerably. Another modification of the program would be to include an animation sequence triggered at particular times. With a little extra effort a simulation could be developed of the dramatic public clocks which marshal rows of heraldic figures to proclaim the hours.

13

Sorting Numbers and Words

Placing items into numerical or alphabetical order is a common feature of much computer software. Writing a program that will sort a list is quite easy and an interesting exercise. In this chapter a program, Bubble, is developed which uses a standard technique, a 'bubble sort', to order items entered by the user.

Here is a typical output of the program. Not all of this display will be seen at once, but it scrolls up the Notepad's screen slowly enough for everything to be read easily.

```
Type how many numbers to be sorted.
? 8
Type number 1 ? 15
Type number 2 ? 8
Type number 3 ? 11
Type number 4 ? 29
Type number 5 ? 15
Type number 6 ? 11
Type number 7 ? 15
Type number 8 ? 5
Sorting numbers into order:
15, 8, 11, 29, 15, 11, 15, 5
8, 11, 15, 15, 11, 15, 5, 29
8, 11, 15, 11, 15, 5, 15, 29
8, 11, 11, 15, 5, 15, 15, 29
8, 11, 11, 5, 15, 15, 15, 29
8, 11, 5, 11, 15, 15, 15, 29
8, 5, 11, 11, 15, 15, 15, 29
5, 8, 11, 11, 15, 15, 15, 29
Sorting complete. Press key.
```

The program also sorts words entered by the user. These are animated on the display to demonstrate the way in which a bubble sort progressively adjusts the sequence of items in a list until a final numerical or alphabetical order is achieved.

Program listing – BUBBLE

```
 10 REM BUBBLE
 20 REM Control routine
 30 PROCinit
 40 REPEAT
 50   PROCmenu
 60   IF K=78 THEN PROCnumbers : PROCsort
 70   IF K=87 THEN PROCwords : PROCshuffle
 80   IF K<>81 THEN PRINT "Sorting complete. Press key." :
      G=GET : PROCpause(3)
 90 UNTIL K=81
100 PRINT "Program over."
110 END
120 REM
130 DEF PROCinit   140 DIM NUM(20), W$(10), B(10)
150 ENDPROC
160 REM
170 DEF PROCmenu
180 CLS
190 PRINT TAB(37) "BUBBLE"
200 PRINT TAB(27) "Press N.......Sort numbers"
210 PRINT TAB(27) "Press W.......Sort words"
220 PRINT TAB(27) "Press Q.......Quit program"
230 REPEAT
240   K=GET
250 UNTIL K=78 OR K=81 OR K=87
260 IF K<>81 THEN PROCpause(3)
270 CLS
280 ENDPROC
290 REM
300 DEF PROCnumbers
310 PRINT "Type how many numbers to be sorted."
320 REPEAT
330   INPUT N
340 UNTIL N>1 AND AND N<21 AND INT N=N
350 FOR I=1 TO N
360   PRINT "Type number "; I CHR$ 32;
370   INPUT NUM(I)
380 NEXT I
390 CLS
400 ENDPROC
410 REM
420 DEF PROCsort
430 PRINT "Sorting numbers into order:"
440 REPEAT
450   PROCshow
460   SW=0
470   FOR I=1 TO N-1
480     IF NUM(I) > NUM(I+1) THEN PROCswap
490   NEXT I
500 UNTIL SW=0
510 ENDPROC
```

Sorting Numbers and Words

```
520 REM
530 DEF PROCswap
540 REM Rearrange pair
550 A=NUM(I)
560 NUM(I)=NUM(I+1)
570 NUM(I+1)=A
580 REM Reset swap flag
590 SW=1
600 ENDPROC
610 REM
620 DEFPROCshow
630 FOR I=1 TO N
640   PRINT; NUM(I);
650   IF I<N THEN PRINT CHR$ 44; CHR$ 32;
660 NEXT I
670 PROCpause(2)
680 PRINT
690 ENDPROC
700 REM
710 DEF PROCwords
720 PRINT "Type how many words to be sorted."
730 REPEAT
740   INPUT N
750 UNTIL N>1 AND N<11 AND INT N=N
760 B(1)=5
770 FOR I=1 TO N
780   REPEAT
790     PRINT "Type word "; I; CHR$ 32;
800     INPUT W$(I)
810     L=LEN W$(I)
820   UNTIL L<8
830   IF I<N THEN B(I+1)=B(I)+L+1
840 NEXT I
850 ENDPROC
860 REM
870 DEF PROCshuffle
880 REM Show words
890 CLS
900 FOR I=1 TO N
910   PRINT TAB(B(I),6) W$(I)
920 NEXT I
930 PROCpause(3)
940 REPEAT
950   SW=0
960   FOR I=1 TO N-1
970     IF W$(I)>W$(I+1) THEN PROCslide
980   NEXT I
990 UNTIL SW=0
1000 PRINT
1010 ENDPROC
1020 REM
1030 DEF PROCslide
1040 L1=LEN W$(I)
```

```
1050 L2=LEN W$(I+1)
1060 REM Move word up
1070 FOR Y=5 TO 1 STEP -1
1080   PRINT TAB(B(I),Y) W$(I)
1090   PRINT TAB(B(I),Y+1) SPC L1
1100   PROCpause(1)
1110 NEXT Y
1120 REM Move word right
1130 FOR X=B(I)-1 TO B(I)+L2
1140   PRINT TAB(X,1) CHR$ 32; W$(I)
1150   PROCpause(1)
1160 NEXT X
1170 REM Move word left
1180 FOR X=B(I+1) TO B(I) STEP -1
1190   PRINT TAB(X,6) W$(I+1) CHR$ 32
1200   PROCpause(1)
1210 NEXT X
1220 REM Move word down
1230 FOR Y=2 TO 6
1240   PRINT TAB(B(I)+L2+1,Y) W$(I)
1250   PRINT TAB(B(I)+L2+1,Y-1) SPC L1
1260   PROCpause(1)
1270 NEXT Y
1280 A$=W$(I)
1290 W$(I)=W$(I+1)
1300 W$(I+1)=A$
1310 B(I+1)=B(I)+L2+1
1320 REM Reset swap flag
1330 SW=1
1340 ENDPROC
1350 REM
1360 DEF PROCpause(P)
1370 FOR T = 1 TO P*500 : NEXT T
1380 ENDPROC
```

Using a menu

The program is menu-driven. A series of choices appears on the screen and the user can select which of these is required:

```
Press N.......Sort numbers
Press W.......Sort words
Press Q.......Quit program
```

Pressing either the N or W keys calls procedures which permit entry, then sorting, of numbers or words. After this the menu is redisplayed. Pressing Q ends the program.

The control routine calls a separate procedure to display the menu on the screen:

```
170 DEF PROCmenu
180 CLS
190 PRINT TAB(37) "BUBBLE"
```

Sorting Numbers and Words

```
200 PRINT TAB(27) "Press N.......Sort numbers"
210 PRINT TAB(27) "Press W.......Sort words"
220 PRINT TAB(27) "Press Q.......Quit program"
230 REPEAT
240   K=GET
250 UNTIL K=78 OR K=81 OR K=87
260 IF K<>81 THEN PROCpause(3)
270 CLS
280 ENDPROC
```

First the program's title and three prompts are placed centrally on the display using PRINT TAB. A REPEAT-UNTIL loop then waits until one of the N, Q or W keys is detected by its ASCII value. If Q has been selected the procedure ends immediately. In contrast, pressing N or W leads to a brief delay:

```
260 IF K<>81 THEN PROCpause(3)
```

This is intended to make the menu appear a little more deliberate in its action. Rapid screen updating can be disconcerting for the user. The delay is created by an empty FOR-NEXT loop in PROCpause. This procedure is called with a parameter, P, because different length delays are required in various parts of the program:

```
1360 DEF PROCpause(P)
1370 FOR T = 1 TO P*500 : NEXT T
1380 ENDPROC
```

PROCmenu is called from within a REPEAT-UNTIL loop in the control routine:

```
40 REPEAT
50   PROCmenu
60   IF K=78 THEN PROCnumbers : PROCsort
70   IF K=87 THEN PROCwords : PROCshuffle
80   IF K<>81 THEN PRINT "Sorting complete. Press key." :
       G=GET : PROCpause(3)
90 UNTIL K=81
```

Pressing N calls PROCnumbers and PROCsort, which sort a series of numbers. Similarly selecting W calls PROCwords and PROCshuffle. These procedures sort a group of words by animating them on the screen. When either pair of procedures is complete, a further prompt appears on the screen requesting another keypress before the program displays the menu again. This allows the user to inspect the sorted numbers or words in detail. Note that this line of the program is not executed if the Q key has been pressed:

```
80 IF K<>81 THEN PRINT "Sorting complete. Press key." :
     G=GET : PROCpause(3)
```

Entering a series of numbers

When the user presses N, PROCnumbers is called. This first requests that the length of the series of numbers is specified. A REPEAT-UNTIL loop checks that this an integral number between 2 and 20:

```
310 PRINT "Type how many numbers to be sorted."
320 REPEAT
330    INPUT N
340 UNTIL N>1 AND AND N<21 AND INT N=N
```

An array, NUM(20), has already been initialised, together with arrays for PROCwords, by PROCinit:

```
130 DEF PROCinit
140 DIM NUM(20), W$(10), B(10)
150 ENDPROC
```

A FOR-NEXT loop can now place the chosen numbers into the NUM array. Clarity is added by showing the sequential order of the entry and placing the input on the same line of the display. This is achieved with the use of CHR$ 32 and a semi-colon:

```
350 FOR I=1 TO N
360    PRINT "Type number "; I CHR$ 32;
370    INPUT NUM(I)
380 NEXT I
```

A bubble sort

A variety of sorting methods have been developed for computer programs. One of the easiest to understand is the bubble sort and so is used in this program. Before the coding is attempted, it is important to appreciate how such a sorting technique operates. This requires working through a typical bubble sort and performing all the arithmetic steps by hand. Suppose that a short series of six numbers is:

4, 1, 6, 3, 7, 2

Sorting into ascending order can begin by comparing pairs of numbers in turn. If they are in the wrong order, they are reversed and then the next pair is examined. The first pair here is 4 and 1. These must be reversed so that the series becomes:

1, 4, 6, 3, 7, 2

The second pair is now 4 and 6. These are in ascending order already and so no alteration is required. The third pair is checked. The numbers are 6 and 3 and so must be interchanged to give:

1, 4, 3, 6, 7, 2

The fourth pair, 6 and 7, is in the right order but the fifth pair, 7 and 2, needs to be reversed. The series is now:

1, 4, 3, 6, 2, 7

Sorting Numbers and Words

Note that, although there are six numbers, only five pairs have to be checked. However the series is clearly not in order yet. Checking all the pairs just once has achieved a partial ordering, but the task is incomplete. Repeating the whole process a second time gives:

1, 3, 4, 2, 6, 7

A third ordering is:

1, 3, 2, 4, 6, 7

Finally, the fourth attempt finishes the sorting:

1, 2, 3, 4, 6, 7

Looking at all the successive stages of the sorting process displayed together shows a distinct pattern:

4, 1, 6, 3, 7, 2
1, 4, 3, 6, 2, 7
1, 3, 4, 2, 6, 7
1, 3, 2, 4, 6, 7
1, 2, 3, 4, 6, 7

The lower values have progressively 'risen' to the left. The similarity to bubbles rising in a glass leads to the accepted name for this sorting technique.

Performing all the arithmetic is laborious. The method is nevertheless quite easy to adapt for a computer.

Coding the bubble sort

The steps involved above can be coded into the procedure, PROCsort, which is called by the program once the numbers have been entered into the NUM array.

The first step, the process of checking each pair of numbers in turn, is performed by a FOR-NEXT loop. This is executed one time fewer than the length of the series, just as the six numbers in the example above generated five pairs of numbers for comparison, not six:

```
470    FOR I=1 TO N-1
480      IF NUM(I) > NUM(I+1) THEN PROCswap
490    NEXT I
```

Those number pairs which need to be reversed are inverted by code contained in PROCswap:

```
550 A=NUM(I)
560 NUM(I)=NUM(I+1)
570 NUM(I+1)=A
```

An extra variable, A, is introduced to allow the exchange of the two array locations, NUM(I) and NUM(I+1). This variable temporarily holds the value of the NUM(I) location while this is reassigned the value in the NUM(I+1) location. The latter is then given the value of A, which is identical to the initial value of NUM(I). Hence, this routine swaps the two numbers. Anybody who has cooked for several people in a small kitchen will be familiar with this sort of juggling.

The second stage of the routine is necessary because repeating the FOR-NEXT loop just once will probably not be sufficient. This was the case in the example above. Instead, the loop has to keep repeating until all the numbers are in ascending order. The FOR-NEXT loop must be embedded in a REPEAT-UNTIL loop and an exit condition needs to be provided for this outer loop.

Here PROCswap can be used again. When the numbers are in order, PROCswap will no longer be called. Therefore a flag updated by PROCswap can be used to control exit from the REPEAT-UNTIL loop. The variable SW is used as this flag. It is set to zero at the beginning of the REPEAT-UNTIL loop and reset to 1 by PROCswap. If it is still zero at the end of the loop, PROCswap has not been called. If this happens the numbers must be completely sorted. Hence, the exit condition for the loop simply has to check if SW is zero:

```
440 REPEAT
450    PROCshow
460    SW=0
470    FOR I=1 TO N-1
480       IF NUM(I) > NUM(I+1) THEN PROCswap
490    NEXT I
500 UNTIL SW=0
```

The complete coding for PROCswap, including the resetting of the SW flag, is:

```
530 DEF PROCswap
540 REM Rearrange pair
550 A=NUM(I)
560 NUM(I)=NUM(I+1)
570 NUM(I+1)=A
580 REM Reset swap flag
590 SW=1
600 ENDPROC
```

In order to inform the user how the sorting routine is altering the sequence of the numbers, the loop also calls PROCshow to print out their current order on the display:

```
620 DEFPROCshow
630 FOR I=1 TO N
640    PRINT; NUM(I);
650    IF I<N THEN PRINT CHR$ 44; CHR$ 32;
660 NEXT I
670 PROCpause(2)
680 PRINT
690 ENDPROC
```

Sorting words

If W is pressed when the menu is displayed, two procedures are called that will sort words into alphabetical order. The bubble sort employed is identical with the one used for numbers and relies upon BASIC 'overloading' the arithmetical greater-than operator to apply to words as well as numbers.

A different approach is adopted with the display of the words, however. The nature of a bubble sort is emphasised by animating the whole sorting process. Words move about the display and glide into fresh positions in the horizontal list displayed. The sequential interchange of word pairs can be seen quite clearly and this makes the bubble sort very explicit.

Although the algorithm used for the sort itself is unchanged, extra code is incorporated to permit the display of the words. For example, when the user types in the words to be sorted, the total is limited to a maximum of 10 because all the words must fit into the horizontal list:

```
720 PRINT "Type how many words to be sorted."
730 REPEAT
740    INPUT N
750 UNTIL N>1 AND N<11 AND INT N=N
```

When the words are entered into the W$ array their length is limited to eight letters. In addition the X-coordinate of the starting location for each word is calculated from the corresponding coordinate of the previous word, together with its length, and entered into the B array. This array plays a vital role in the animation of the words. The first word in the list is given a B array value of 5 and allowance is made in the calculation of the array values for the gap between each word:

```
760 B(1)=5
770 FOR I=1 TO N
780    REPEAT
790      PRINT "Type word "; I; CHR$ 32;
800      INPUT W$(I)
810      L=LEN W$(I)
820    UNTIL L<8
830    IF I<N THEN B(I+1)=B(I)+L+1
840 NEXT I
```

Animating the words

Before the sort begins, all the words in the W$ array are displayed near the bottom of the Notepad's screen using the coordinates held in the B array:

```
900 FOR I=1 TO N
910    PRINT TAB(B(I),6) W$(I)
920 NEXT I
```

After this the bubble sort takes place. It is just the same as the routine in PROCsort and uses a flag, SW, again to control exit from a REPEAT-UNTIL loop when all the words are in order:

```
940 REPEAT
950   SW=0
960   FOR I=1 TO N-1
970     IF W$(I)>W$(I+1) THEN PROCslide
980   NEXT I
990 UNTIL SW=0
```

PROCslide is analogous to PROCswap in the earlier procedure. It interchanges words and resets the SW flag:

```
1280 A$=W$(I)
1290 W$(I)=W$(I+1)
1300 W$(I+1)=A$

1320 REM Reset swap flag
1330 SW=1
```

In addition, PROCslide contains the animation routines that allow the two words to be interchanged graphically. This diagram, showing W$(I) and W$(I+1) as 'Sarah' and 'Heather', will help in describing the way the animation is achieved:

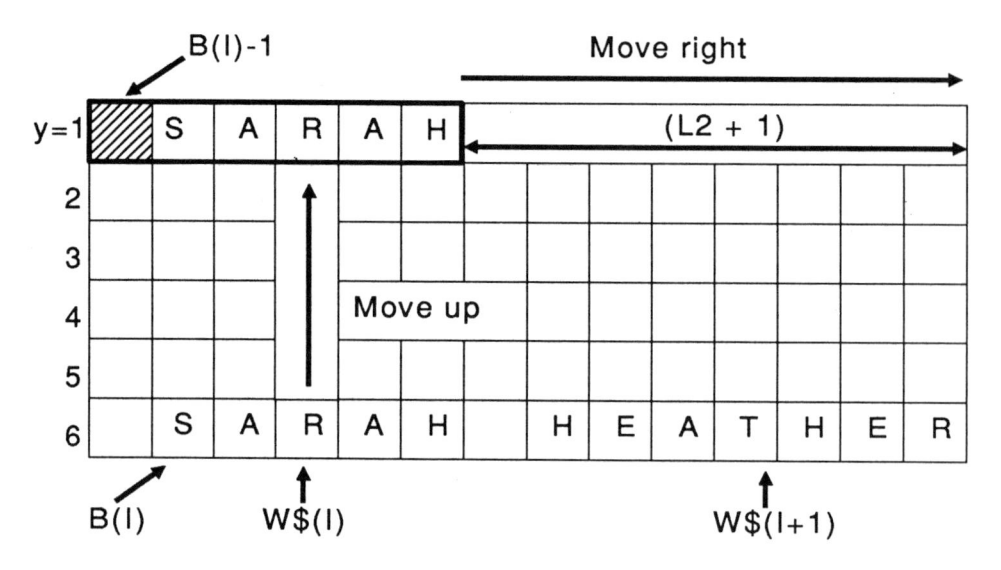

Word animation

First PROCslide assigns the lengths of W$(I) and W$(I+1) to the variables L1 and L2. This simplifies subsequent code:

```
1040 L1=LEN W$(I)
1050 L2=LEN W$(I+1)
```

A FOR-NEXT loop then moves the first word of the pair from the sixth line of the display to the first. Its X-coordinate is retained as B(I) but its Y-coordinate is controlled by the loop. Its previous position is erased by overprinting with the number of spaces determined by its length, L1, and PROCpause is called to create the required animation delay:

```
1060 REM Move word up
1070 FOR Y=5 TO 1 STEP -1
1080   PRINT TAB(B(I),Y) W$(I)
1090   PRINT TAB(B(I),Y+1) SPC L1 1100   PROCpause(1)
1110 NEXT Y
```

Next, W$(I) has to be moved to the right. The distance that it must travel is determined by the length of W$(I+1). From the diagram it can be seen that in order for the last letter of W$(I) to reach a position vertically above the last letter of W$(I+1) the whole word must move a distance of L2 + 1. The word is moved with an extra character, CHR$ 32, prefixed on the left. This is so it will erase itself as it moves, rather than leaving a trail. The extra character means that the animation loop must therefore begin with an X-coordinate of B(I) – 1. As the total distance moved is L2 + 1, the final coordinate reached is (B(I)-1) + (L2+1) or B(I)+L2:

```
1120 REM Move word right
1130 FOR X=B(I)-1 TO B(I)+L2
1140   PRINT TAB(X,1) CHR$ 32; W$(I)
1150   PROCpause(1)
1160 NEXT X
```

At this point W$(I+1) can be animated to occupy the position vacated by W$. It has to move from B(I+1) to B(I), trailing CHR$ 32 to erase its passage:

```
1170 REM Move word left
1180 FOR X=B(I+1) TO B(I) STEP -1
1190   PRINT TAB(X,6) W$(I+1) CHR$ 32
1200   PROCpause(1)
1210 NEXT X
```

Finally W$(I) can be moved down to replace W$(I+1) at the bottom of the display. Its initial letter was originally at an X-coordinate of B(I) and the word has moved L2+1 to the right. Its X-coordinate is therefore now B(I)+L2+1. This value is used in the animation loop. The Y-coordinate must increase from 2 to 6. Again SPC is used to erase the previous position of W$(I):

```
1220 REM Move word down
1230 FOR Y=2 TO 6
1240   PRINT TAB(B(I)+L2+1,Y) W$(I)
1250   PRINT TAB(B(I)+L2+1,Y-1) SPC L1
1260   PROCpause(1)
1270 NEXT Y .
```

At this point W$ and W$(I+1) have become completely interchanged on the screen display. They can now be exchanged in the W$ array as well:

```
1280 A$=W$(I)
1290 W$(I)=W$(I+1)
1300 W$(I+1)=A$
```

The B array values also have to be considered. The 'new' W$(I) is occupying exactly the same position on the screen as the previous W$(I) and so the B(I) value can be left unchanged. However, the 'new' W$(I+1) is not in the same position as the original, unless the two words have the same length. Instead, as explained above, it is at a different X-coordinate, B(I)+L2+1. This final code is required:

```
1310 B(I+1)=B(I)+L2+1
```

14

Useful Number Crunching

Computers operate with such varied software that people now easily forget the machine's original image as the ultimate number cruncher. It seems almost prosaic to ask your Notepad to perform mindless calculations. Yet there are occasions when slipping into BASIC, and adding a little quick programming, can produce a neat routine that saves repetitive pressing on the calculator's keys.

In this chapter a program is introduced which can calculate the average of a series of numbers. This will be not simply the common understanding of average – the 'add all the numbers and divide by how many there were' variety. The formal term for this is the 'arithmetic mean'. Two other averages exist as well, the 'median' and the 'mode'. All three have their own particular use, according to circumstance.

The median is the middle term of a series of numbers when it is arranged in increasing or decreasing order. (For an even numbered series, in which there are two middle numbers, the mean of these is taken to give the median.) The mode is the number which occurs most frequently in the series. The suitability of these different definitions of the average for a particular situation will always need to be considered carefully.

If an engineer needed to decide how springy the suspension of a bus should be, the average with which he or she would be concerned would be the mean of the passengers' weight. However this type of average would be of little use to the owner of a sports' outfitters. A three-place decimal fraction lodged between two regular shoe sizes is unhelpful. Instead the relative numbers of different trainer sizes to stock is needed. It would be necessary to be aware which sizes were most often requested. This would be the mode of the data. The median simply indicates the half way point in any series. It is used in applications like life expectancy, in the calculations of insurance firms, and for quality control in industry.

A program, Average, is shown below which will accept a series of numbers and then analyse it to give these three averages. Calculating the mean of the series is very simple but, in order to calculate the median and the mode, it is necessary to include a sorting procedure. This will place the numbers into ascending order before other procedures decide on the middle term and the most common. For this, Average uses the sorting routine already written for the previous program, Bubble.

Here is a typical output of the program. Not all of this display will be seen at once, but it scrolls up the Notepad's screen slowly enough for everything to be read easily.

```
>RUN
Type how many numbers you want to enter
? 8
Type number 1 ? 15
Type number 2 ? 8
Type number 3 ? 11
Type number 4 ? 29
Type number 5 ? 15
Type number 6 ? 11
Type number 7 ? 15
Type number 8 ? 5
Sorting numbers into order:
15, 8, 11, 29, 15, 11, 15, 5
8, 11, 15, 15, 11, 15, 5, 29
8, 11, 15, 11, 15, 5, 15, 29
8, 11, 11, 15, 5, 15, 15, 29
8, 11, 11, 5, 15, 15, 15, 29
8, 11, 5, 11, 15, 15, 15, 29
8, 5, 11, 11, 15, 15, 15, 29
5, 8, 11, 11, 15, 15, 15, 29
Numbers now sorted.
Finding total of numbers:
5 + 8 = 13
13 + 11 = 24
24 + 11 = 35
35 + 15 = 50
50 + 15 = 65
65 + 15 = 80
80 + 29 = 109
Total = 109
Mean = 109 / 8 = 13.625
Numbers in order are:
5, 8, 11, 11, 15, 15, 15, 29
Median is (11 + 15) / 2 = 13
Mode is 15
Press <Enter> to continue ?
```

It can be seen how the program shows the numbers being sorted. The running total needed for the mean is then displayed and the mean itself. Finally the reordered series is shown again before the median and mode are indicated. In this way the program is not merely stating its answers but attempting to justify them as well. Such

Useful Number Crunching

accountability in software design is an important feature, as it helps the user in keeping track of what is happening in the program.

Program listing – AVERAGE

```
 10 REM AVERAGE
 20 REM Control routine
 30 PROCinit
 40 REPEAT
 50   PROCnumbers
 60   PROCsort
 70   PROCmean
 80   PROCmedian
 90   PROCmode
100 UNTIL FALSE
110 REM
120 DEF PROCinit
130 DIM NUM(20)
140 DIM SET(10,1)
150 ENDPROC
160 REM
170 DEF PROCnumbers
180 REPEAT
190   CLS
200   PRINT "Type how many numbers you
      want to enter."
210   INPUT N
220 UNTIL N>0 AND INT N=N
230 FOR I=1 TO N
240   PRINT "Type number "; I; CHR$ 32;
250   INPUT NUM(I)
260 NEXT I
270 CLS
280 ENDPROC
290 REM
300 DEF PROCsort
310 PRINT "Sorting numbers into order:"
320 REPEAT
330   PROCshow
340   SW=0
350   FOR I=1 TO N-1
360     IF NUM(I)>NUM(I+1) THEN PROCswap
370   NEXT I
380 UNTIL SW=0
390 PRINT "Numbers now sorted."
400 ENDPROC
410 REM
420 DEF PROCswap
430 VDU 7
440 REM Rearrange pair
450 A=NUM(I)
460 NUM(I)=NUM(I+1)
470 NUM(I+1)=A
```

```
480 REM Reset swap flag
490 SW=1
500 ENDPROC
510 REM
520 DEFPROCshow : LOCAL I
530 FOR I=1 TO N
540   PRINT; NUM(I);
550   IF I<N THEN PRINT CHR$ 44; CHR$ 32;
560 NEXT I
570 PROCpause
580 PRINT
590 ENDPROC
600 REM
610 DEF PROCpause
620 VDU 7
630 FOR T=1 TO 2000 : NEXT T
640 ENDPROC
650 REM
660 DEF PROCmean
670 PRINT "Finding total of numbers:"
680 SUM=NUM(I)
690 FOR I=2 TO N
700   PRINT SUM; " + "; NUM(I); " = "; SUM+NUM(I)
710   SUM=SUM+NUM(I)
720   PROCpause <$ob> 730 NEXT I
740 PRINT "Total = "; SUM
750 PROCpause
760 PRINT "Mean = "; SUM; " / "; N; " = "; SUM/N
770 ENDPROC
780 REM
790 DEF PROCmedian
800 REM Set parity flag
810 REM Even: P=1 Odd: P=0
820 IF INT(N/2) = N/2 THEN P=1 ELSE P=0
830 PRINT "Numbers in order are:"
840 PROCshow
850 N1=NUM(N/2)
860 N2=NUM(N/2+1)
870 N3=NUM(INT(N/2)+1)
880 PRINT "Median is ";
890 IF P=1 THEN PRINT; CHR$ 40; N1; " + "; N2;
    CHR$ 41; " / 2 = "; (N1+N2)/2
900 IF P=0 THEN PRINT; N3
910 ENDPROC
920 REM
930 DEF PROCmode
940 REM Fill SET array
950 J=1
960 SET(J,1)=NUM(I)
970 FOR I=1 TO N-1
980   IF NUM(I)=NUM(I+1) THEN SET(J,0)=SET(J,0)+1 :
      ELSE J=J+1 : SET(J,1)=NUM(I+1)
990 NEXT I
```

```
1000 REM Determine whether mode exists
1010 IF J<N THEN PROCmost ELSE PRINT "There is no mode."
1020 REM Wait for further numbers
1030 PRINT "Press <Enter> TO CONTINUE."
1040 INPUT Z
1050 ENDPROC
1060 REM
1070 DEF PROCmost
1080 REM Find most frequent number
1090 MAX=0
1100 FOR I=1 TO J
1110    IF SET(I,0)>MAX THEN MAX=SET(I,0) :   SETVAR=I
1120 NEXT I
1130 PRINT "Mode is "; SET(SETVAR,1)
1140 ENDPROC
```

Computing and self-plagiarism

The composer Serge Prokofiev had an endearing self-confidence which prevented him from ever discarding music he had written. Once a decent tune was notated and jotted down it would reappear somewhere in a published work, perhaps even decades later. He even applied the principle to large scale compositions and, when his opera 'The Fiery Angel' was not an immediate box office smash hit, he rewrote it as his third symphony. The German composer Hans Werner Henze derived his fourth symphony by a similar process.

Programmers, too, can justify such squirrel-like hoarding of their creativity. One of the proclaimed advantages of structured programming is that procedures can be taken from one program and placed in another, if this proves useful. Some computer languages make this particularly easy to do. The programmer builds up a library of useful routines and then links them together to create a new program!

No apology will be made, therefore, when Average borrows some of the procedures from Bubble. PROCnumbers is used again to enter the series of numbers for which the three averages will be calculated. PROCsort and PROCswap will arrange the series into ascending order and PROCshow will display the series on the Notepad's screen. All that will be changed is the line numbers attached to these procedures, because they will appear in a different position relative to the rest of the program.

Controlling the program

Average is controlled by one simple REPEAT-UNTIL loop. After PROCinit has set up two arrays required by the program, this loop calls all the procedures in turn. They request a series of numbers from the user, sort them into order and then calculate the three separate averages with PROCmean, PROCmedian and PROCmode:

```
 20 REM Control routine
 30 PROCinit
 40 REPEAT
 50   PROCnumbers
 60   PROCsort
 70   PROCmean
 80   PROCmedian
 90   PROCmode
100 UNTIL FALSE
```

The procedures PROCnumbers and PROCsort have already been explained in the previous chapter. PROCmean, PROCmedian and PROCmode are explained below.

Finding the common sense average, the mean

The arithmetic mean is calculated in a very obvious way. The FOR-NEXT loop between 690-730 has the added refinement, though, of detailing each stage of the addition as a running total displayed on the screen. The current total of the numbers is represented by the variable SUM. This is initialised as the first of the series, or NUM(1), at line 680. After this, line 700 within the loop actually shows SUM being added on to NUM(I), which is the next number of the series for the current cycle of the loop. The updating of the value of SUM itself is carried out by line 710. Outside the loop, the final total is shown being divided by the number of items in the series to give the arithmetic mean. This is displayed by line 760.

```
670 PRINT "Finding total of numbers:"
680 SUM=NUM(I)
690 FOR I=2 TO N
700   PRINT SUM; " + "; NUM(I); " = "; SUM+NUM(I)
710   SUM=SUM+NUM(I)
720   PROCpause <$ob>730 NEXT I
740 PRINT "Total = "; SUM
750 PROCpause
760 PRINT "Mean = "; SUM; " / "; N; " = "; SUM/N
```

Finding the middle term, the median

As explained earlier, the calculation of the median of a set of numbers differs according to whether the number in the set is odd or even. Line 820 therefore assigns a value of 1 or 0 to the variable P according to whether N is even or odd. This is achieved using the function INT and depends upon the fact that even numbers will divide exactly by 2 without acquiring a trailing decimal fraction.

```
800 REM Set parity flag
810 REM Even: P=1 Odd: P=0
820 IF INT(N/2) = N/2 THEN P=1 ELSE P=0
```

Useful Number Crunching 157

Lines 830, 840 then remind the user of the new order of the series. After this, three important members of the series are identified as the variables N1, N2 and N3. These are needed in the identification of the middle term, for an odd-numbered series and for an even. How values are assigned to the variables can be understood if an example series is considered.

```
Series ......... 10,  13,  14,  15,  34,  45,  56
Number of term ... 1    2    3    4    5    6    7
```

Here there is an odd number of terms, 7, and the median is number 4 in the series. The value 4 is derived from 7 by the expression INT(7/2) + 1. Testing this formula shows that it is correct for all series with an odd number of terms. It is incorporated as N3 by the code:

```
870 N3=NUM(INT(N/2)+1)
```

Here is a series with an even number of terms.

```
Series ......... 10,  13,  14,  15,  34,  45,  56,  77
Number of term ... 1    2    3    4    5    6    7    8
```

The median is now found as the mean of term 4 and term 5. These are obtained from 8 as (N/2) and (N/2+1) respectively. Again this relationship is appropriate for all series of even terms and so is coded into the procedure as N1 and N2 by:

```
850 N1=NUM(N/2)
860 N2=NUM(N/2+1)
```

The relevant combination of N1, N2 and N3 can now be selected according to the value of P and used to display the median. This code could be made far more compact by including the expression for P directly into an IF-THEN-ELSE structure, but it would then be a little more difficult to understand:

```
880 PRINT "Median is ";
890 IF P=1 THEN PRINT; CHR$ 40; N1; " + "; N2;
    CHR$ 41; " / 2 = "; (N1+N2)/2
900 IF P=0 THEN PRINT; N3
```

Finding the most repeated term, the mode

The most common number in the series is found by filling an additional array, SET. This is a two dimensional array. The first subscript records how many of a particular number there are. (To be precise, this total is always one less than the actual number but this is not important.) The second subscript represents the number itself. Initially SET(1,0) will be zero. SET(1,1) is made equal to NUM(1) by the code:

```
950 J=1
960 SET(J,1) = NUM(I)
```

The FOR-NEXT loop which follows then works through the series of numbers. If two adjacent numbers are equal, a conditional statement increments the value in the first array position, SET(J,0). However if the numbers are not equal, the value of J is incremented instead. This means that a new total will be established for the next number in the series to indicate how many times it repeats. The identity of the number is recorded in the second array position by SET(J,1) = NUM(I+1):

```
970 FOR I=1 TO N-1
980    IF NUM(I)=NUM(I+1) THEN SET(J,0)=SET(J,0)+1 :
       ELSE J=J+1 : SET(J,1)=NUM(I+1)
990 NEXT I
```

At the end of the loop the value of J can be used to decide whether or not any of the numbers have repeated. If they have, J will be less than N. If they have not, J will equal N. In the latter case the user is informed that no mode exists for the series. If J is less than N, PROCmost is called to deduce what the mean is.

```
1000 REM Determine whether mode exists
1010 IF J<N THEN PROCmost ELSE
     PRINT "There is no mode."
```

In PROCmost a FOR-NEXT loop uses a variable, MAX, to help determine the largest value in the first position of the SET array. This will correspond to the mode and so all that needs then to be done is to identify the number in the respective second array position in SET. The value of the loop variable associated with the largest value of MAX is recorded as the further variable, SETVAR. The mode will then be simply the number in the second array position of SET which is determined by SETVAR. This is SET(SETVAR,1):

```
1080 REM Find most frequent number
1090 MAX=0
1100 FOR I=1 TO J
1110    IF SET(I,0) > MAX THEN MAX=SET(I,0) :
        SETVAR=I
1120 NEXT I
```

The user is informed which number is the mode by:

```
1130 PRINT "Mode is "; SET(SETVAR,1)
```

Then a simple technique of an irrelevant input, here identified as the variable Z, delays return to the control routine. As soon as the <Enter> key is pressed, Average will request a new series of numbers to analyse.

```
1020 REM Wait for further numbers
1030 PRINT "Press <Enter> TO CONTINUE."
1040 INPUT Z
```

15

Machine Learning

There is a game in which a person has to identify an object imagined by somebody else simply by asking a series of questions. Each question must only invite a 'yes' or 'no' reply. Despite this, a careful choice is able to eliminate successive groups of possibilities until the correct answer is found.

Suppose that the object is a power boat. All the person attempting to guess is told initially is that it is a vehicle. Appropriate questions could proceed as follows. 'Does it fly?' receives a negative answer. This removes the possibility of any type of aircraft. A further inquiry 'Does it float?' is given a positive reply, which then concentrates investigation towards different categories of boat. 'Has it sails?' is answered no. At this point the vehicle could be correctly identified as a power boat.

If the game is played repeatedly, the person will become far more efficient at discovering the objects. The first time the question 'Does it fly?' is answered yes, it might be assumed that the vehicle is a plane. However, it might be a balloon instead. Remembering this, the next time 'Does it fly?' is answered positively the correct action is to ask the further question 'Does it have wings?' An affirmative reply now should suggest the answer 'plane' and a negative one the answer 'balloon'.

Provided that all the questions and replies are noted down, the game will inevitably increase the amount of 'knowledge' that it stores. Every time an incorrect answer is given, the correct reply is added to the list, together with a relevant question to ask in this case. At a given stage the questions and answers could be recorded in a diagram similar to the one on the next page:

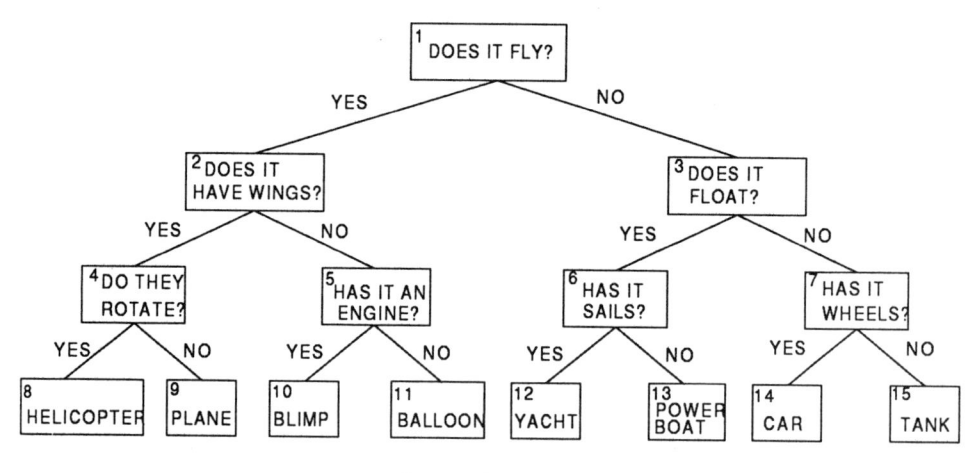

```
                    ┌─────────────┐
                   1│ DOES IT FLY?│
                    └─────────────┘
               YES                    NO
        ┌──────────────┐        ┌──────────────┐
       2│ DOES IT      │       3│ DOES IT      │
        │ HAVE WINGS?  │        │ FLOAT?       │
        └──────────────┘        └──────────────┘
       YES          NO          YES          NO
   ┌────────┐  ┌────────┐   ┌────────┐  ┌────────┐
  4│DO THEY │ 5│HAS IT AN│ 6│HAS IT  │ 7│HAS IT  │
   │ROTATE? │  │ENGINE?  │  │SAILS?  │  │WHEELS? │
   └────────┘  └────────┘   └────────┘  └────────┘
   YES    NO   YES    NO    YES    NO   YES    NO
   ┌──┐ ┌──┐  ┌──┐  ┌──┐   ┌──┐ ┌────┐  ┌──┐ ┌──┐
  8│  │9│  │10│  │11│   │12│  │13│POWER│14│  │15│  │
   │HELICOPTER│PLANE│BLIMP│BALLOON│YACHT│BOAT│CAR│TANK│
```

A guessing game

This is only a temporary situation. Further knowledge can always be added at the bottom of the diagram as an additional question and pair of answers. An important principle involved is that a structured diagram is being established which can be formalised into a computer program that appears to 'learn'. This is an extremely simple illustration of the topic of machine learning but nevertheless fun to program on the Amstrad Notepad. Following the general rule of short file names, the following program is titled Expert.

Program listing – EXPERT

```
 10 REM EXPERT
 20 REM Control routine
 30 PROCinit
 40 REPEAT
 50   REM Set pointer to 1st question
 60   P=1
 70   REM Find answer
 80   REPEAT
 90     CLS
100     REM Calculate further numbers
110     IF P>7 AND F(1)=0 THEN PROCnumbers(P)
120     REM Show diagram
130     PROCdiagram(1)
140     IF P>7 THEN PROCdiagram(2)
150     REM Ask question
160     PRINT TAB(0,0) N$(P,1)
170     PROCkey
180     REM Next level
190     P=2*P+D
200     REM Record route followed
210     G(P)=1
220   UNTIL N$(P,2)="E" OR K=81
230   REM Check answer correct
240   PRINT "Is it a ";
```

Machine Learning

```
250     PRINT N$(P,1)
260     PROCkey
270     REM Program 'learns'
280     IF D=1 THEN PROCextend
290     REM Discard current route
300     PROCerase
310 UNTIL K=81
320 END
330 REM
340 DEF PROCinit
350 REM Initial 'knowledge'
360 DIM N$(63,2)
370 FOR I=1 TO 3
380   FOR J=1 TO 2
390     READ N$(I,J)
400   NEXT J
410 NEXT I
420 REM Coordinates for diagram
430 DIM AX(7),AY(7)
440 FOR I=1 TO 7
450   READ AX(I),AY(I)
460 NEXT I
470 REM Coordinates for box sides
480 DIM BX(4),BY(4)
490 FOR I=1 TO 4
500   READ BX(I),BY(I)
510 NEXT I
520 REM Lines joining boxes
530 DIM C(6,2)
540 FOR I=1 TO 6
550   FOR J=1 TO 2
560     READ C(I,J)
570   NEXT J
580 NEXT I
590 REM Coordinates for box labels
600 DIM DX(7),DY(7)
610 FOR I=1 TO 7
620   READ DX(I),DY(I)
630 NEXT I
640 REM Screen layout
650 DIM E(2,2)
660 FOR I=1 TO 2
670   FOR J=1 TO 2
680     READ E(I,J)
690   NEXT J
700 NEXT I
710 REM Numbers for boxes
720 DIM F(7)
730 REM Route followed
740 DIM G(63)
750 G(1)=1
760 ENDPROC
770 REM
780 DEF PROCerase
790 FOR I=2 TO 63
```

```
800    G(I)=0
810 NEXT I
820 ENDPROC
830 REM
840 DEF PROCnumbers(N)
850 A=0 : B=0.5
860 FOR I=1 TO 3
870    B=B*2
880    FOR J=1 TO B
890       A=A+1
900       F(A)=N*B+J-1
910    NEXT J
920 NEXT I
930 ENDPROC
940 REM
950 DEF PROCkey
960 REPEAT
970    K=GET
980 UNTIL K=78 OR K=81 OR K=89
990 D=-(K=78)
1000 ENDPROC
1010 REM
1020 DEF PROCextend
1030 N$(2*P+1)=N$(P,1)
1040 PRINT "Enter correct answer"
1050 INPUT N$(2*P,1)
1060 PRINT "Type a question for which"
1070 PRINT "this is the answer"
1080 INPUT N$(P,1)
1090 N$(P,2)="F"
1100 N$(2*P,2)="E"
1110 N$(2*P+1,2)="E"
1120 ENDPROC
1130 REM
1140 DEF PROCdiagram(L)
1150 FOR I=1 TO 7
1160    IF L=1 THEN box=I ELSE box=F(I)
1170    X=AX(I)+E(L,1)
1180    Y=AY(I)
1190    IF G(box)=1 THEN PROCfill(X,Y) ELSE PROCbox(X,Y)
1200    PRINT TAB(DX(I)+E(L,2),DY(I));box
1210 NEXT I
1220 REM Add lines
1230 FOR I=1 TO 6
1240    MOVE AX(C(I,1))+E(L,1)+17,AY(C(I,1))
1250    DRAW AX(C(I,2))+E(L,1)+17,AY(C(I,2))+14
1260 NEXT I
1270 ENDPROC
1280 REM
1290 DEF PROCbox(X,Y)
1300 MOVE X,Y
1310 FOR J=1 TO 4
1320    DRAW X+BX(J),Y+BY(J)
1330 NEXT J
1340 ENDPROC
```

Machine Learning

```
1350 REM
1360 DEF PROCfill(X,Y)
1370 MOVE X,Y
1380 PLOT 101,X+35,Y+14
1390 ENDPROC
1400 REM
1410 REM Data for boxes
1420 DATA DOES IT FLY,F
1430 DATA PLANE,E,CAR,E
1440 REM Data for diagram
1450 DATA 63,48,30,24,95,24,0,0
1460 DATA 41,0,82,0,123,0
1470 REM Data for box sides
1480 DATA 35,0,35,14,0,14,0,0
1490 REM Data for lines
1500 DATA 1,2,1,3,2,4,2,5,3,6,3,7
1510 REM Data for box labels
1520 DATA 9,0,7,2,18,2,2,5,11,5
1530 DATA 14,5,23,5
1540 REM Data for layout
1550 DATA 156,26,320,53
```

Storing the information

Examining the information held in the first diagram shows that two categories of text are involved. Most of the boxes hold questions, like 'Does it have wings?' and 'Has it an engine?'. However, the boxes at the bottom of the diagram store a different type of text. Here instead are predictions about what the object is, for example 'helicopter' or 'yacht'.

Despite this difference, though, all the text for the boxes is held in similar array locations. These are in the two dimensional string array, N$(63,2). The first subscript can range up to 63 because this is the total number of boxes possible in a diagram which extends down to the sixth level. A larger set of boxes could not be displayed easily on the Notepad's screen. The reason for employing a two dimensional array, and not simply N$(63), is that the second array location associated with each box can be used to show when an identification of the object is to be attempted rather than another question.

The program begins with the least possible working knowledge. It holds one question, 'Does it fly?', and two potential objects, 'plane' and 'car'. These together with the letter F and E – which indicate whether a box is 'filled' with a question or is an 'end box' with an identification – are stored as data:

```
1410 REM Data for boxes
1420 DATA DOES IT FLY,F
1430 DATA PLANE,E,CAR,E
```

The data is placed into the N$ array in PROCinit:

```
350 REM Initial 'knowledge'
360 DIM N$(63,2)
370 FOR I=1 TO 3
380   FOR J=1 TO 2
390     READ N$(I,J)
400   NEXT J
410 NEXT I
```

Moving to the correct box

The initial question the user is asked is located in the first box of the diagram. This is represented in the program by a 'pointer' variable, P, which is initially assigned a value of 1. The appropriate location in the N$ array can then be printed on the Notepad's screen:

```
50 REM Set pointer to 1st question
60 P=1
```

[Further code]

```
150      REM Ask question
160      PRINT TAB(0,0) N$(P,1)
```

At this stage the user has to press either 'Y' or 'N' and the pointer jumps to the appropriate box. The way that this is achieved is by adopting a systematic way for numbering the boxes. Looking again at the first diagram it can be seen that the number of the box reached after pressing Y is exactly twice the number of the current box.

Similarly finding the box reached after N is pressed requires the current number to be doubled and then 1 added. This relationship applies consistently throughout the whole diagram, irrespective of the level or how far down the diagram the questions and answers extend. This means that the relevant box will be located simply by doubling the number of the current box and adding 1 for negative answers.

Checking for yes or no

A route can therefore be traced down through the diagram if a procedure is added which will monitor the key pressed and return 1 for N and 0 for Y. This value can be added to twice the current pointer position, P, and will then automatically point to the next box. The procedure which achieves this is PROCkey. It assigns the ASCII value of the key pressed to the numeric variable K. A REPEAT-UNTIL loop ensures that N, Y or Q must be pressed. The option of pressing Q is to permit the user to exit the program. (This additional condition is included principally for programming etiquette rather than for necessity. The <Stop> key is an adequate alternative.)

PROCkey returns 1, as the value of a further variable D, when the N key is pressed. D must otherwise be 0. The result is obtained by using the Boolean value of the

Machine Learning

expression (K=78). This will only be true when N, which has an ASCII value of 78, is selected. The expression then evaluates as -1. This means that assigning D the value of -(K=78) will lead to precisely the value of 1 for N and 0 for Y. The complete code for PROCkey is:

```
 950 DEF PROCkey
 960 REPEAT
 970   K=GET
 980 UNTIL K=78 OR K=81 OR K=89
 990 D=-(K=78)
1000 ENDPROC
```

By calling this procedure, the program finds the appropriate box in the next level of the diagram:

```
170 PROCkey
180 REM Next level
190 P=2*P+D
```

Adding further information

Repeated use of the above code permits descent through the diagram. This continues until the lowest level is reached for which information is stored in the N$ array. This fact is registered by the content of the second N$ location changing from F to E:

```
220 UNTIL N$(P,2)="E" OR K=81
```

Again, the second condition present in this line permits exit from the program.

When the program is first run, the lowest level is the second. As the main loop repeats subsequently, lower levels can be reached but inevitably at some point the value of the second N$ array location is E. When this happens, the user is asked to confirm that the answer in the current box is correct. The response is again monitored by a call to PROCkey:

```
230 REM Check answer correct
240 PRINT "Is it a ";
250 PRINT N$(P,1)
260 PROCkey
```

If Y is selected, no modification is made to the N$ array. However, if N is pressed a further procedure, PROCextend, is called:

```
270    REM Program 'learns'
280    IF D=1 THEN PROCextend
```

This procedure will add more information to N$. Consider a typical case where the program offers an incorrect response. Suppose the answer it has provided is 'car', but the user is thinking about a yacht. Then a question to distinguish between the two could be 'Does it float?' Obviously this question must be asked instead of the emphatic 'Is it a car?' Therefore it should be placed into the current box, N$(P,1), and replace 'plane' in that array location. This is done by:

```
1060 PRINT "Type a question for which"
1070 PRINT "this is the answer"
1080 INPUT N$.(P,1)
```

However, before this code overwrites the N$(P,1) location, the incorrect 'car' must be shifted into the 'No' box corresponding to this new question. The box concerned is N$(2*P+1,1) and so the code is:

```
1030 N$(2*P+1)=N$(P,1)
```

In addition, the correct answer, 'yacht' must be assigned to the 'Yes' box, N$(2*P,1):

```
1040 PRINT "Enter correct answer"
1050 INPUT N$(2*P,1)
```

These are not the only alterations required for the N$ array. In addition the second subscript locations need to be adjusted to reflect the extension of the diagram. The N$(P) box is no longer in the end position and must now be represented by F. The N$(2*P) and N$(2*P+1) boxes have become the extremities of the diagram and so require an E. This is coded as:

```
1090 N$(P,2)="F"
1100 N$(2*P,2)="E"
1110 N$(2*P+1,2)="E"
```

The entire procedure which adds the fresh information to the array is:

```
1020 DEF PROCextend
1030 N$(2*P+1)=N$(P,1)
1040 PRINT "Enter correct answer"
1050 INPUT N$(2*P,1)
1060 PRINT "Type a question for which"
1070 PRINT "this is the answer"
1080 INPUT N$(P,1)
1090 N$(P,2)="F"
1100 N$(2*P,2)="E"
1110 N$(2*P+1,2)="E"
1120 ENDPROC
```

Illustrating machine learning

The program will be capable of providing text-only output using the following code to call relevant procedures:

```
40 REPEAT
50    REM Set pointer to 1st question
60    P=1
70    REM Find answer
80    REPEAT
```

```
150     REM Ask question
160     PRINT TAB(0,0) N$(P,1)
170     PROCkey
180     REM Next level
190     P=2*P+D

220     UNTIL N$(P,2)="E" OR K=81
230     REM Check answer correct
240     PRINT "Is it a ";
250     PRINT N$(P,1)
260     PROCkey
270     REM Program 'learns'
280     IF D=1 THEN PROCextend

310 UNTIL K=81
```

The program would run quite effectively, even with these gaps in the line numbers. It becomes far more interesting, though, if a pictorial route through the diagram is added. To achieve this extra sophistication, a number of additional graphics procedures are included.

Unfortunately an immediate problem is encountered when attempting a diagram of this nature on the Notepad's display. The latter is broad, rather than deep, and does not match the inherent shape of a diagram that extends downwards. The situation is resolved by splitting the levels of boxes into two separate groups, each with three levels of boxes, placed alongside one another on the Notepad's screen. A typical display will be like this:

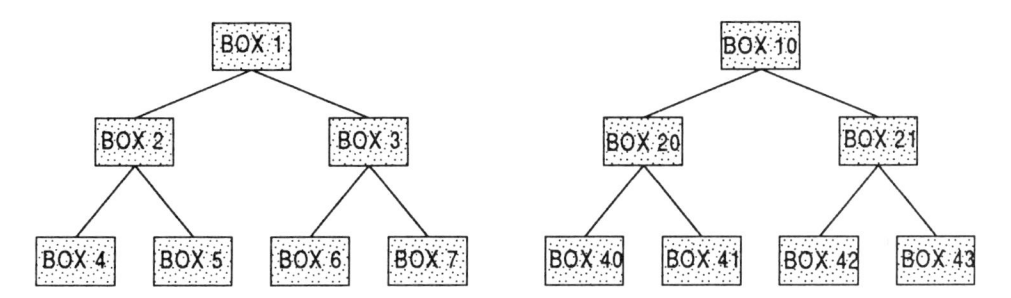

Displaying six levels

The first three levels of the diagram are displayed on the left. These boxes are numbered 1 to 7. The numbering of the left hand boxes will always be the same as this because they show the top of the diagram where possible routes are fewer in number. The three layers of boxes shown on the right, though, represent different sections of the whole diagram because they can have been extensions from any of the four boxes at the bottom level of the first layer.

A 'yes' route from box 4 will begin with box 8 and a 'no' route with box 9. Similarly the other boxes on the left, 5, 6 and 7, can lead on to boxes 10, 11, 12, 13, 14 and 15. This means there are eight possible different numberings for the right hand side of the diagram. Only one of these is illustrated above. This is the 'yes' route from box 5. Inevitably including coding to permit these variations complicates the program in a way unnecessary for a computer with a larger screen.

Drawing a set of boxes

The identical geometry of the two separate sets of boxes means that almost the same coding can be employed to draw both of them. The only modifications that will be required are a shift in the X-coordinates used and separate labelling for the boxes on the right. Each of the two sets is allowed to occupy approximately one third of the display width. The remaining third of the screen is reserved for the text that will also need to be displayed.

The width of each of the boxes is set at 35 pixels. This, together with a spacing of six pixels between the four boxes in the third layer, gives a total width for the set of boxes of (4 x 35) + (3 * 6) or 158 pixels. This is only two pixels less than one third of the screen width. Placing the bottom left hand corner of the lowest box on the left at (0,0) means that the other three boxes on this level are at (41,0), (82,0) and (123,0). The height of each box is chosen to be 14 pixels. Simple arithmetic then permits the coordinates of the bottom left hand corners of the other boxes to be calculated as the values shown in the diagram:

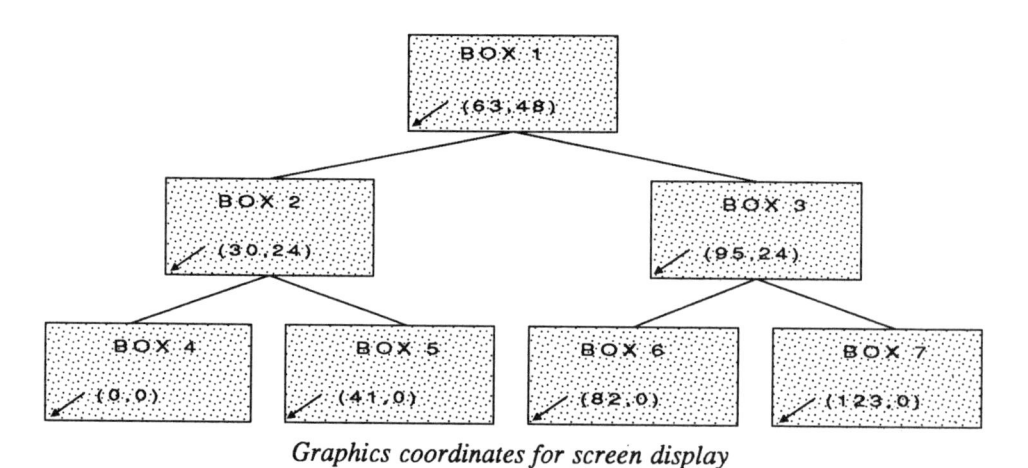

Graphics coordinates for screen display

Of course, the two sets of boxes placed on the screen will have an additional displacement to the right to locate them both in the correct areas of the display.

The coordinates on the diagram are held as data in the program:

```
1440 REM Data for diagram
1450 DATA 63,48,30,24,95,24,0,0
1460 DATA 41,0,82,0,123,0
```

The coordinates are held in the correct order, with the first pair referring to the box in the top level. All seven pairs are read into the AX(7), AY(7) arrays in PROCinit:

```
420 REM Coordinates for diagram
430 DIM AX(7),AY(7) 440 FOR I=1 TO 7
450    READ AX(I),AY(I)
460 NEXT I
```

The Ith box can be drawn by coordinate displacements from the coordinates AX(I), AY(I) of its bottom left-hand corner. In the diagram this is labelled A. The other three corners, moving around the rectangle in an anti-clockwise direction are B, C and D:

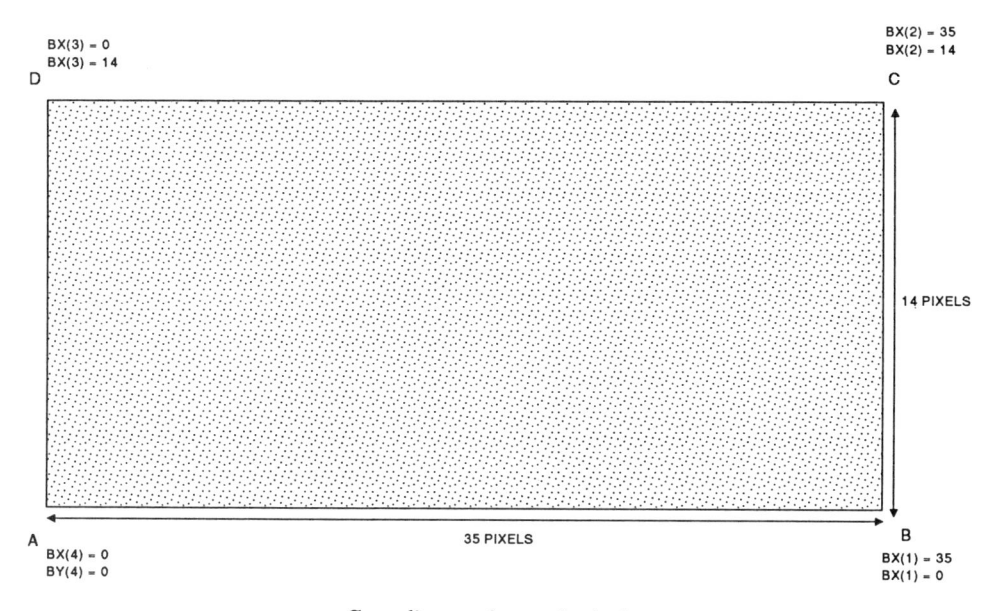

```
BX(3) = 0                                              BX(2) = 35
BX(3) = 14                                             BX(2) = 14
D                                                      C




                                                       ↑
                                                       14 PIXELS
                                                       ↓
A              35 PIXELS                               B
BX(4) = 0                                              BX(1) = 35
BY(4) = 0                                              BX(1) = 0
```

Coordinates for a single box

The coordinates of the graphics cursor relative to A as it moves from corner to corner are needed. The X- and Y- displacements from A to B are (35,0). Similarly the displacements from A to C are (35,14). The remaining two displacements, from A to D and from A back to A again, are (0,14) and (0,0). All these values are stored as a data statement in the program:

```
1470 REM Data for box sides
1480 DATA 35,0,35,14,0,14,0,0
```

PROCinit reads these numbers into the arrays BX(4), BY(4):

```
470 REM Coordinates for box sides
480 DIM BX(4),BY(4)
490 FOR I=1 TO 4
500    READ BX(I),BY(I)
510 NEXT I
```

The B array values can then be used in a separate procedure that will draw a box relative to a general point (X,Y):

```
1290 DEF PROCbox(X,Y)
1300 MOVE X,Y
1310 FOR J=1 TO 4
1320   DRAW X+BX(J),Y+BY(J)
1330 NEXT J
1340 ENDPROC
```

This procedure is called subsequently by PROCdiagram, with values for X and Y derived from the AX and AY arrays, together with the appropriate X-coordinate shift to the right.

Labelling the boxes

The display would lack clarity if the boxes were not identified by the number showing their relative position in the overall diagram. This would be a particular problem with the second group of boxes on the right, because their position in the diagram depends upon the route which has been followed through the group of boxes on the left. It is important to add the box numbers and this in turn requires seven pairs of text coordinates. These are stored as data in the program:

```
1510 REM Data for box labels
1520 DATA 9,0,7,2,18,2,2,5,11,5
1530 DATA 14,5,23,5
```

PROCinit places the coordinates into the DX(7), DY(7) arrays:

```
590 REM Coordinates for box labels
600 DIM DX(7),DY(7)
610 FOR I=1 TO 7
620   READ DX(I),DY(I)
630 NEXT I
```

The values for the actual numbers to be displayed by the boxes are explained in *The second set of numbers* below.

Adjusting the display

The graphics coordinates in the AX, AY arrays and the text coordinates in the DX, DY arrays have been defined with respect to the left hand side of the screen. The X-coordinates now have to be adjusted to permit the display of boxes to appear in two separate screen locations. There may appear to be an element of redundancy in this approach, but the use of the separate arrays does permit further development of the program. For example it would be possible to display a single group of boxes in a third position on the screen. This would be useful for those occasions when an identification of the object was achieved before the fourth level.

These adjustments are held in a two dimensional array, E(2,2). The left hand position for the boxes is identified by a value of 1 for the first subscript and the right hand position by 2. The graphics displacement for X is represented by a value of 1 for the second subscript and the text displacement by 2. This is illustrated by this diagram:

E(1,1) LEFT GROUP GRAPHICS DISPLACEMENT	E(1,2) LEFT GROUP TEXT DISPLACEMENT
E(2,1) RIGHT GROUP GRAPHICS DISPLACEMENT	E(2,2) RIGHT GROUP TEXT DISPLACEMENT

Display adjustments

Again, the values for the E array are held as data:

```
1540 REM Data for layout
1550 DATA 156,26,320,53
```

PROCinit places the values into the array. Two nested loops are required because the array is two dimensional:

```
640 REM Screen layout
650 DIM E(2,2)
660 FOR I=1 TO 2
670    FOR J=1 TO 2
680       READ E(I,J)
690    NEXT J
700 NEXT I
```

Adding the lines

The following code could create the display of both groups of boxes on the screen. The lines are unnumbered because this is not the final version required:

```
FOR I=1 TO 7
  X=AX(I)+E(L,1)
  Y=AY(I)
  PROCbox(X,Y)
  PRINT TAB(DX(I)+E(L,2),DY(I));box
NEXT I
```

The new variable, box, needs to be assigned the correct value the each box in turn. As stated, this is explained below. A value of 1 for the additional variable L creates the left hand group and a value of 2 the right hand group. However, this loop would only show the outline of the boxes and not the lines joining them. Further code is required to achieve this.

Six lines altogether must be added to each group of seven boxes. One line will join the first box to the second. Another line must also attach the first box to the third. A further line is then required between the second box and the fourth. A convenient way to think of all the lines is as a table. The left hand column represents the top box of a linked pair and the right hand column the bottom box:

Top box	Bottom Box
1	2
1	3
2	4
2	5
3	6
3	7

These pairs are held as data:

```
1490 REM Data for lines
1500 DATA 1,2,1,3,2,4,2,5,3,6,3,7
```

The numbers can then be placed in the two dimensional array, C(6,2) by PROCinit:

```
520 REM Lines joining boxes
530 DIM C(6,2)
540 FOR I=1 TO 6
550    FOR J=1 TO 2
560       READ C(I,J)
570    NEXT J
580 NEXT I
```

This array will indicate which boxes have to be linked. How the line should be drawn can be understood by considering the diagram on the next page. Here a line has been drawn for the 'Yes' route. The mathematics is just the same for the 'No' route. The diagram indicates how the Ith line is added to a group of boxes. Using the values in the C array, the upper box of the pair is number C(I,1) and the lower box C(I,2). Remembering that the coordinates of the bottom left hand corner of the Ith box are AX(I), AY(I), and that the X-coordinate will be shifted by E(L,1) pixels to the right, gives the coordinates of the bottom left corner of the upper box as:

```
AX(C(I,1)) + E(L,1), AY(C(I))
```

The coordinates for the same point on the lower box are:

Machine Learning

UPPER BOX GRAPHIC COORDINATES

AX(C(I,1)) + E(L,1), AY(C(I,1))

BOX C(I,1)

17 pixels

LOWER BOX GRAPHIC COORDINATES

BOX C(I,2)

14 pixels

17 pixels

AX(C(I,2)) + E(L,1), AY(C(I,2))

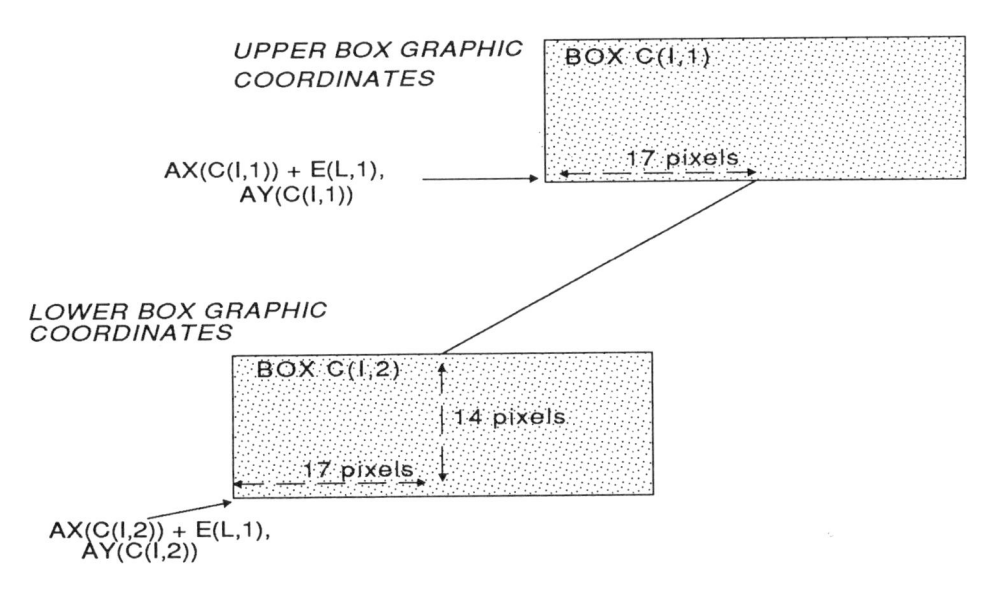

Joining two boxes

```
AX(C(I,2)) + E(L,1), AY(C(2))
```

The two points which have to be joined are displaced from these positions. From the diagram it can be seen that the top of the line has coordinates:

```
AX(C(I,1)) + E(L,1) + 17, AY(C(I))
```

The bottom of the line has coordinates:

```
AX(C(I,2)) + E(L,1) + 17, AY(C(2)) + 14
```

Using MOVE to place the graphics cursor initially at the top, and DRAW to draw to the bottom of the line, leads to this code in PROCdiagram which adds all six lines to the group of boxes:

```
1220 REM Add lines
1230 FOR I=1 TO 6
1240   MOVE AX(C(I,1))+E(L,1)+17,AY(C(I,1))
1250   DRAW AX(C(I,2))+E(L,1)+17,AY(C(I,2))+14
1260 NEXT I
```

The second set of numbers

The DX and DY arrays hold the text coordinates for the numbers of the boxes but they do not store the numbers themselves. As already stated, there is no difficulty in numbering the boxes on the left hand side of the diagram. These are consecutively 1 – 7. Unfortunately, the numbers on the right are more difficult. A typical set of boxes will be numbered 10, 20, 21, 40, 41, 42 and 43. The general rule is that each box determines the numbers of the two boxes below it as being twice its own value and this number plus 1. This means that if the number attached to the first box is N, the numbers for the second and third boxes are N*2 and N*2+1. The numbers identifying the fourth, fifth, sixth and seventh boxes are N*4, N*4+1, N*4+2 and N*4+3. A diagram will now show how these numbers can be generated by a pair of nested FOR-NEXT loops:

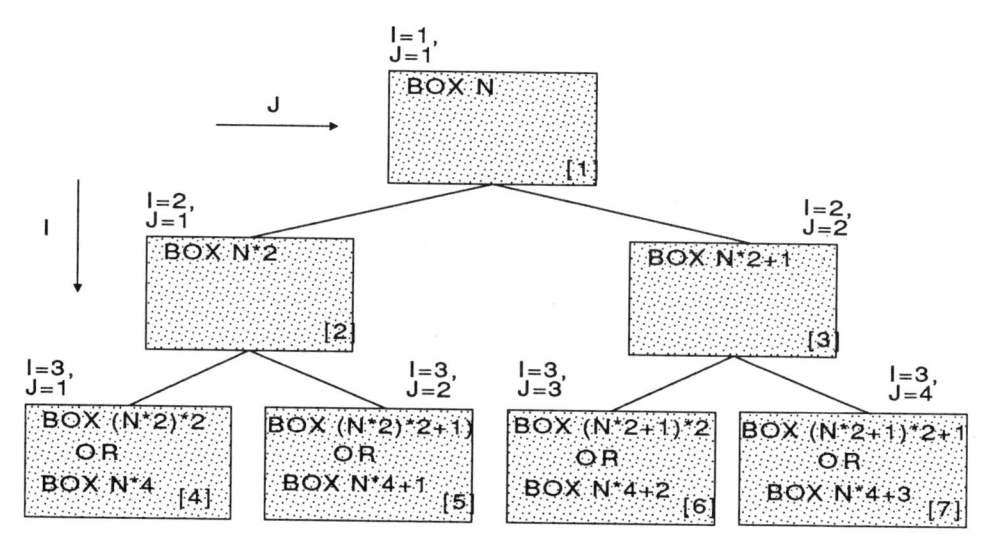

Box numbers for second group

An outer, I, loop determines the level of a particular box and J the position of the box within that level. The value for I and J for each box is shown in the diagram. These values are shown also in the table below. Here the position of the box in the group, the number attached to it, the I and J values for the box and the maximum value for J in the appropriate level are all displayed. A variable, B, is used to represent the maximum value of J:

Position	Number	I value	J value	B
1	N	1	1	1
2	N*2	2	1	2
3	N*2+1	2	2	2
4	N*4	3	1	4
5	N*4+1	3	2	4
6	N*4+2	3	3	4
7	N*4+3	3	4	4

Studying this table shows that the number for any of the seven boxes is calculated by N*B+J-1.

Machine Learning

An expression has to be found for B, the maximum value of J. As I takes the values 1, 2 and 3, the value of B must be 1, 2 and 4. Clearly B is doubling at each cycle of the I loop. If it is initialised as 0.5 before the loop begins, this will give exactly the values required.

Using these ideas, a procedure can be defined to calculate the numbers for the boxes. First an array is required to store them. This is set up in PROCinit:

```
710 REM Numbers for boxes
720 DIM F(7)
```

The procedure, PROCnumbers(N), can then be called when the second group of boxes is about to be placed on the screen and a value is known for N:

```
840 DEF PROCnumbers(N)
850 A=0 : B=0.5
860 FOR I=1 TO 3
870   B=B*2
880   FOR J=1 TO B
890     A=A+1
900     F(A)=N*B+J-1
910   NEXT J
920 NEXT I
930 ENDPROC
```

In the procedure I and J have the range shown on the diagram. The maximum value for J is calculated at line 870. A counter, A, identifies the relevant location in the F array and the appropriate value is assigned by line 900.

Tracing the route followed

The diagram is intended to show the series of boxes encountered as each question is answered. A further array, G(63), is created in PROCinit to represent the route followed. The array locations are set to 1 as a box is selected. The first box must inevitably have a G array value of 1 as the series of questions always begins here:

```
730 REM Route followed
740 DIM G(63)
750 G(1)=1
```

Other boxes included in the route are registered in the main loop of the control routine:

```
200     REM Record route followed
210     G(P)=1
```

When the diagram is drawn, the value of the relevant G array location is used to choose between PROCbox(X,Y), which draws the box in outline, and PROCfill(X,Y). The latter procedure draws a box which is shaded:

```
1190    IF G(box)=1 THEN PROCfill(X,Y)
        ELSE PROCbox(X,Y)
```

PROCfill(X,Y) uses PLOT 101 to fill in an identically sized rectangle to match the outline drawn by PROCbox:

```
1360 DEF PROCfill(X,Y)
1370 MOVE X,Y
1380 PLOT 101,X+35,Y+14
1390 ENDPROC
```

All these additional features can now be incorporated into the final version of PROCdiagram(L). In the previous version this only created the two groups of box outlines, with indeterminate numbering. Now the procedure draws all the boxes, correctly linked by lines to show the structure of the diagram. All boxes are numbered. The second group's numbers accurately reflect where they have originated in the first group. Finally the path through the diagram, as questions are answered affirmatively or otherwise, is shown by boxes being shaded:

```
1140 DEF PROCdiagram(L)
1150 FOR I=1 TO 7
1160    IF L=1 THEN box=I ELSE box=F(I)
1170    X=AX(I)+E(L,1)
1180    Y=AY(I)
1190    IF G(box)=1 THEN PROCfill(X,Y) ELSE PROCbox(X,Y)
1200    PRINT TAB(DX(I)+E(L,2),DY(I));box
1210 NEXT I
1220 REM Add lines
1230 FOR I=1 TO 6
1240    MOVE AX(C(I,1))+E(L,1)+17,AY(C(I,1))
1250    DRAW AX(C(I,2))+E(L,1)+17,AY(C(I,2))+14
1260 NEXT I
1270 ENDPROC
```

Line 1160 assigns the appropriate number to be displayed as the variable 'box'. This will be the same as the value of the loop variable for the left hand group and will be the F array value for the right hand group. Which of these is required is determined by the value of L.

Controlling the program

PROCnumbers(N) and PROCdiagram(L) can now be included in the full control routine, which combines learning with graphical display:

```
40 REPEAT
50    REM Set pointer to 1st question
60    P=1
70    REM Find answer
80    REPEAT
90       CLS
100      REM Calculate further numbers
```

Machine Learning

```
110     IF P>7 AND F(1)=0 THEN PROCnumbers(P)
120     REM Show diagram
130     PROCdiagram(1)
140     IF P>7 THEN PROCdiagram(2)
150     REM Ask question
160     PRINT TAB(0,0) N$(P,1)
170     PROCkey
180     REM Next level
190     P=2*P+D
200     REM Record route followed
210     G(P)=1
220   UNTIL N$(P,2)="E" OR K=81
230     REM Check answer correct
240     PRINT "Is it a ";
250     PRINT N$(P,1)
260     PROCkey
270     REM Program 'learns'
280     IF D=1 THEN PROCextend
290     REM Discard current route
300     PROCerase
310   UNTIL K=81
```

Note that the diagram is redrawn each time a question is set. Only the left hand group of boxes is displayed, by PROCdiagram(1), until the pointer has reached a value of 8. After that PROCdiagram(2) will add the right hand group as well. The numbers for the F array must only be calculated once, when the right hand group is displayed for the first time. After that the F array values must remain the same. The double condition at line 110 ensures this:

```
110 IF P>7 AND F(1)=0 THEN PROCnumbers(P)
```

When a fresh set of questions and answers is to begin, the G array locations greater than G(1) must be reset to 0 to prevent the previous route from being displayed again. This reassignment is performed by PROCerase, called at line 300, and defined as:

```
780 DEF PROCerase
790 FOR I=2 TO 63
800   G(I)=0
810 NEXT I
820 ENDPROC
```

The program assumes that an identification will have been achieved by the sixth level. If this does not happen, an error will occur. One way that this could be prevented is by enlarging the N$ and G arrays and by not attempting further graphical display.

16

Writing a Database

Computers are excellent at storing information and retrieving it quickly. Most people are now familiar with the concept of a database and it is easy to obtain appropriate software for any machine. It would be unrealistic to imagine that the amateur programmer could hope to improve upon what is commercially available. Nevertheless the logic involved in designing and coding a simple database is quite intriguing.

The task stimulates programming techniques. In this chapter a simple database, Store, is developed. A detailed explanation of how the program works follows the listing, but a diagram will illustrate how the information about a particular subject, Lassie the famous trans-Atlantic Collie, can be broken down schematically into a logical structure:

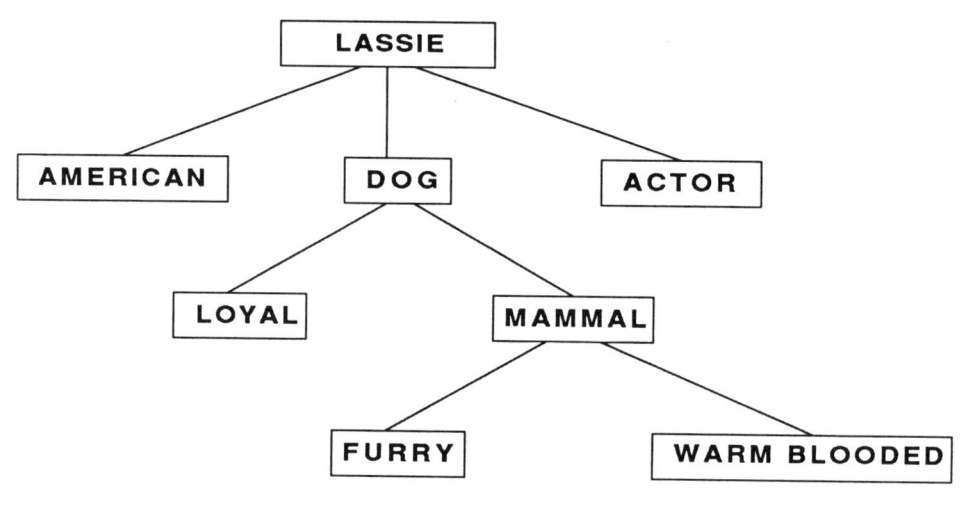

Database for Lassie

Writing a Database

Here the salient features of Lassie's persona have been noted. The diagram has a characteristic shape, very like an uprooted tree which has been turned upside down so that its trunk is at the top and highest twigs at the bottom. For this reason, the structure depicted is called a tree. It proves to be a very important, widely employed concept in computing.

Various, slightly contradictory, terms are used to refer to the component parts of the structure. The information contained in it is located at 'nodes'. The top node is called the 'root' and the lowest the 'leaf' nodes. The links between nodes are referred to as 'arcs' or 'branches'. The relationship between two nodes connected by an arc is described, less consistently, by the non-arboreal terms 'parent' and 'child'.

The way in which Store is written has to reflect the logical structure of the diagram, noting which nodes are linked to which. All the parent node/child node branches must be recorded. This is done as the information is typed in by the user. The mathematically coded tree pattern then has to be available again to allow information to be extracted in a coherent fashion. What Store is expected to achieve is shown in the following typical program run.

The keys I, O and L are adopted as the menu choice for inserting data, obtaining data or leaving the program. Key N returns the program to the menu. Store deliberately uses INPUT rather than GET to read the keyboard. This means that the user's choices are made explicit in the program dialogues:

```
INSERT DATA - TYPE I
OBTAIN DATA - TYPE O
LEAVE  TREE - TYPE L
? I
TYPE NODE
? LASSIE
TYPE CHILD NODE OR N
? AMERICAN
TYPE CHILD NODE OR N
? DOG
TYPE CHILD NODE OR N
? ACTOR
TYPE CHILD NODE OR N
? N
INSERT DATA - TYPE I
OBTAIN DATA - TYPE O
LEAVE  TREE - TYPE L
? O
TYPE NODE FOR WHICH YOU
REQUIRE INFORMATION
? LASSIE
LASSIE IS LASSIE
LASSIE IS AMERICAN
LASSIES IS DOG
LASSIE IS ACTOR
PRESS ENTER TO CONTINUE
?
```

At this stage all the first level information about Lassie has been placed into the program. However, nothing yet has been added to extend the available data on 'dog'. This is shown by the negative response in the following sequence.

```
INSERT DATA - TYPE I
OBTAIN DATA - TYPE O
LEAVE  TREE - TYPE L
? O
TYPE NODE FOR WHICH YOU
REQUIRE INFORMATION
? DOG
NO INFORMATION
PRESS ENTER TO CONTINUE
?
```

More data needs to be entered.

```
INSERT DATA - TYPE I
OBTAIN DATA - TYPE O
LEAVE  TREE - TYPE L
? I
TYPE NODE ? DOG
TYPE CHILD NODE OR N
? LOYAL
TYPE CHILD NODE OR N
? MAMMAL
TYPE CHILD NODE OR N
? N
INSERT DATA - TYPE I
OBTAIN DATA - TYPE O
LEAVE  TREE - TYPE L
? I
TYPE NODE
? MAMMAL
TYPE CHILD NODE OR N
? FURRY
TYPE CHILD NODE OR N
? WARM BLOODED
TYPE CHILD NODE OR N
? N
```

The new information can now be extracted again.

```
INSERT DATA - TYPE I
OBTAIN DATA - TYPE O
LEAVE  TREE - TYPE L
? O
TYPE NODE FOR WHICH YOU
REQUIRE INFORMATION
? DOG
DOG IS DOG
DOG IS LOYAL
```

Writing a Database

```
DOG IS MAMMAL
DOG IS FURRY
DOG IS WARM BLOODED
PRESS ENTER TO CONTINUE
?
```

The information on dog is automatically added to that on Lassie, as illustrated in this exchange.

```
INSERT DATA - TYPE I
OBTAIN DATA - TYPE O
LEAVE  TREE - TYPE L
? O
TYPE NODE FOR WHICH YOU
REQUIRE INFORMATION
? LASSIE
LASSIE IS LASSIE
LASSIE IS AMERICAN
LASSIE IS DOG
LASSIE IS ACTOR
LASSIE IS LOYAL
LASSIE IS MAMMAL
LASSIE IS FURRY
LASSIE IS WARM BLOODED
PRESS ENTER TO CONTINUE ?
```

It can be seen how the available information is extended quite naturally as further data is added to individual nodes. This permits the interactive, dynamic handling of information that is required in a database. The listing for the program is now given.

Program listing – STORE

```
 10 REM STORE
 20 REM Control routine
 30 PROCinit
 40 REPEAT
 50    PROCmenu
 60 UNTIL A$="L"
 70 CLS
 80 END
 90 REM
100 DEF PROCinit
110 REM Initialise node total
120 NT=0
130 REM Initialise node data
140 DIM NODE$(20)
150 REM Initialise child arcs
160 DIM CHILD(20,5)
170 REM Initialise search array
180 DIM SEARCH(20)
190 ENDPROC
200 REM
```

```
210 DEF PROCmenu
220 CLS
230 PRINT "
240 PRINT "INSERT DATA - TYPE I"
250 PRINT "OBTAIN DATA - TYPE O"
260 PRINT "LEAVE TREE   - TYPE L"
270 REPEAT
280    INPUT A$
290 UNTIL A$="I" OR A$="O" OR A$="L"
300 IF A$="I" THEN PROCinsert
310 IF A$="O" THEN PROCobtain
320 ENDPROC
330 REM
340 DEF PROCinsert
350 PRINT "TYPE NODE"
360 INPUT N$
370 REM Identify this node
380 N=-1
390 REPEAT
400    N=N+1
410 UNTIL NODE$(N)=N$ OR N=NT
420 REM Increase node total
430 REM Utilise Boolean value
440 NT=NT-(N=NT)
450 REM Record node content
460 NODE$(N)=N$
470 REM Initialise child subtotal
480 C=0
490 REM Request child nodes
500 REPEAT
510    PRINT "TYPE CHILD NODE OR N"
520    INPUT CH$
530    IF CH$<>"N" PROCchild
540 UNTIL CH$="N"
550 ENDPROC
560 REM
570 DEF PROCchild
580 REM Increment node total
590 NT=NT+1
600 REM Record child as fresh node
610 NODE$(NT)=CH$
620 REM Record arc between parent and child
630 C=C+1
640 CHILD(N,C)=NT
650 ENDPROC
660 REM
670 DEF PROCobtain
680 PRINT "TYPE NODE FOR WHICH YOU"
690 PRINT "REQUIRE INFORMATION"
700 INPUT TARGET$
710 TG=-1
720 REPEAT
730    TG=TG+1
```

Writing a Database

```
740 UNTIL NODE$(TG) = TARGET$ OR TG > NT
750 REM Initialise search counter
760 S=1
770 REM Identify first node in search
780 SEARCH(S)=TG
790 REM Initialise search array total
800 ST=1
810 REM Search whole tree
820 REPEAT
830   FOR I=1 TO 5
840     IF CHILD(SEARCH(S),I)<>0 THEN PROCadd
850   NEXT I
860   S=S+1
870 UNTIL S>ST
880 REM Display all nodes found
890 IF ST=1 THEN PRINT "NO INFORMATION"
    ELSE PROCdisplay
900 PRINT "PRESS ENTER TO CONTINUE"
910 INPUT Z
920 ENDPROC
930 REM
940 DEF PROCadd
950 ST=ST+1
960 SEARCH(ST) = CHILD( SEARCH(S),I)
970 ENDPROC
980 REM
990 DEF PROCdisplay
1000 FOR I=1 TO ST
1010    PRINT TARGET$; " IS ";
     NODE$(SEARCH(I))
1020 NEXT I
1030 ENDPROC
```

The user interface

Control of Store is exercised by means of one REPEAT-UNTIL loop in the control routine of the program:

```
40 REPEAT
50    PROCmenu
60 UNTIL A$="L"
```

The procedure, PROCmenu, repeatedly called by this loop presents a prompt on the Notepad's screen, followed by a further REPEAT-UNTIL loop which requires the user to press key I, O or L, and then <Enter>. Keys I and O call the procedures PROCinsert or PROCobtain. Pressing L permits this loop, and the loop in the control routine, to end:

```
240 PRINT "INSERT DATA - TYPE I"
250 PRINT "OBTAIN DATA - TYPE O"
260 PRINT "LEAVE TREE  - TYPE L"
```

```
270 REPEAT
280   INPUT A$
290 UNTIL A$="I" OR A$="O" OR A$="L"
300 IF A$="I" THEN PROCinsert
310 IF A$="O" THEN PROCobtain
```

How the tree is represented by arrays

The structure of the tree diagram is represented in the program by two arrays, NODE$ and CHILD, and one additional variable, NT. These are initialised in PROCinit:

```
110 REM Initialise node total
120 NT=0
130 REM Initialise node data
140 DIM NODE$(20)
150 REM Initialise child arcs
160 DIM CHILD(20,5)
```

NT records the Node Total, which increases as further information is added to the program. The content of the nodes is stored in the array NODE$. It is assumed that there will not be more than 20 nodes in a typical program run. This number could of course be altered in the listing if necessary.

The array CHILD plays an essential role in the operation of the program because it represents all the arcs between nodes. A two dimensional array is required here. The first array subscript is the parent node, recorded as the number which identifies it in the NODE$ array. The second subscript counts the particular arc going down from this node to the child node. It is assumed that there will not be more than five children for any given node. The locations of the CHILD array hold numbers identifying which are child nodes in the NODE$ array, rather than the actual node content. That is the reason why CHILD is a numeric array and not a string.

Placing information in the nodes

When the user enters I at the prompt, PROCinsert is called. This procedure allows a particular node to be chosen and then data to be entered which will be stored as child nodes descended from that node. The procedure has to be able to deal with two different situations. The user might type an existing node and wish to enter data about it. Alternatively an entirely new node might be added to the tree structure. The procedure uses a REPEAT-UNTIL loop with two separate exit conditions to be able to respond to either situation. These possibilities are explained below.

Finding an existing node

The node typed by the user is assigned to N$. A counter, N, for the REPEAT-UNTIL loop is then initialised as -1. Inside the loop which follows, it is immediately incremented and steadily increased until N$ matches one of the locations in the NODE$ array. This code, omitting the second exit condition, would achieve what is required:

```
350 PRINT "TYPE NODE"
360 INPUT N$
370 REM Identify this node
380 N=-1
390 REPEAT
400   N=N+1
410 UNTIL NODE$(N)=N$
```

Adding a fresh node

The user might type in a node which is not part of the tree structure and so not present in the NODE$ array. In this case the REPEAT-UNTIL loop will exit via the other condition, N=NT. When this occurs, NT itself must be incremented and the new node information entered into the NODE$ array.

NT is incremented when necessary by making use of the Boolean truth value, true = -1, at line 440. If a fresh node is typed by the user, and N keeps increasing until it equals NT, then the value of the expression (N=NT) will be -1. So subtracting this from NT will, in fact, increment it. When the expression is false, NT will not be increased because the logical value is then 0. The code is:

```
420 REM Increase node total
430 REM Utilise Boolean value
440 NT=NT-(N=NT)
450 REM Record node content
460 NODE$(N)=N$
```

Including the child nodes

After this, any child nodes must be included. The REPEAT-UNTIL loop between lines 500-540 accepts these until N is typed. The procedure PROCchild adds them to the tree. Typing N, however, exits back to PROCmenu and thus to the main control loop between lines 40-60.

```
500 REPEAT
510   PRINT "TYPE CHILD NODE OR N"
520   INPUT CH$
530   IF CH$<>"N" PROCchild
540 UNTIL CH$="N"
```

PROCchild does not have to check the new child nodes entered against the existing content of NODE$ because the assumption can be made that any child node is inevitably new to the tree. This follows automatically from the tree structure. Sideways links between children of different nodes would immediately change the tree into a very complicated network which would require more involved algorithms to extract information.

Line 590 increments the node total. Line 610 places the node content into NODE$. Line 640 records the link between the parent and child node in the CHILD array. Here the variable N represents the current parent node. C is simply a temporary variable which locates the appropriate element in CHILD, given the value of N. The content to be placed in the array is the number of the child node, which is, of course, the freshly incremented value of NT.

```
580 REM Increment node total
590 NT=NT+1
600 REM Record child as fresh node
610 NODE$(NT)=CH$
620 REM Record arc between parent and child
630 C=C+1
640 CHILD(N,C)=NT
```

Searching for information

PROCobtain permits the tree to be searched for all the information on a particular node. It is quite a complicated procedure because once a particular node has been identified as a child of the node in question, all the children of this node must be included in the search as well. This process continues to grandchildren, great grandchildren and further descendants. It only stops when the leaf nodes are reached.

The node for which information is required is identified as TARGET$ at line 700:

```
680 PRINT "TYPE NODE FOR WHICH YOU"
690 PRINT "REQUIRE INFORMATION"
700 INPUT TARGET$
```

A REPEAT-UNTIL loop, lines 720-740, then tries to identify the node in the NODE$ array. If it succeeds, it returns the position of the node in NODE$ as the variable TG. If it does not succeed, the loop exits in any case as a result of the extra condition after the UNTIL.

```
710 TG=-1
720 REPEAT
730     TG=TG+1
740 UNTIL NODE$(TG)=TARGET$ OR TG>NT
```

Two variables, S and ST, are then employed in the search, together with the SEARCH array. This array registers the various child nodes discovered as the descendants of the node being examined.

S is the current node being investigated, while ST is the total number of nodes in the SEARCH array. When S eventually 'catches up' with ST, a situation identified by line 870, the search is over. However, it rather resembles the Red Queen's retort: *Here you see it takes all the running you can do to keep in the same place.* This is because as the REPEAT-UNTIL loop between lines 820-870 examines the nodes represented in the SEARCH array, further nodes are added every time a child is found.

The first node to be searched is the one identified by TG. This value is placed in the SEARCH array by line 780. Line 800 registers the fact as well by recording the total number of nodes to be searched as 1. The REPEAT-UNTIL loop can then begin. It contains a nested FOR-NEXT loop which checks each element in the SEARCH array, using the CHILD array, to determine if there are any child nodes. If so, these are added by PROCadd:

```
750 REM Initialise search counter
760 S=1
770 REM Identify first node in search
780 SEARCH(S)=TG
790 REM Initialise search array total
800 ST=1
810 REM Search whole tree
820 REPEAT
830   FOR I=1 TO 5
840     IF CHILD(SEARCH(S),I)<>0 THEN PROCadd
850   NEXT I
860   S=S+1
870 UNTIL S>ST
```

In PROCadd the SEARCH array is increased by any child node located. The value of ST has to be incremented at line 950. Then this new value of ST is employed in placing the identifying number of the new node into the next location of the SEARCH array:

```
940 DEF PROCadd
950 ST=ST+1
960 SEARCH(ST) = CHILD( SEARCH(S),I)
970 ENDPROC
```

The final lines of PROCobtain display either a *No information* message or call PROCdisplay. Here a FOR-NEXT loop prints out all the nodes discovered as descendants of the node under investigation. Note how both the NODE$ and SEARCH arrays are needed to achieve this.

```
 990 DEF PROCdisplay
1000 FOR I=1 TO ST
1010   PRINT TARGET$; " IS "; NODE$(SEARCH(I))
1020 NEXT I
1030 ENDPROC
```

17

A Notepad Arcade

The advent of the first home computers with a colour display, in the early 1980s, led to an infatuation with arcade style games. For a few years the sound of small electronic creatures being pursued mercilessly through the rooms and corridors of an electronic maze echoed in many bedrooms throughout the country. Their dying wail when ambushed by a lurking predator had a special pathos that now seems to represent the innocence of those distant, 8-bit days.

The subsequent arrival of more powerful microcomputers, with huge memory and attendant ultra-sophisticated software, sadly killed off this early genre. However, there is a fascination with the concept of the maze, from Greek mythology to the Elizabethan knot garden and the recent robotic 'micromouse' competitions. The Notepad's long, narrow display is particularly suited to a simple version of an arcade game which will be developed in this programming example.

The game is quite entertaining to play. Typing in the listing itself and working through the explanation of how the various routines are organised will also help the programming enthusiast acquire further skills which could help in the planning and design of other games. The maze is shown in the diagram:

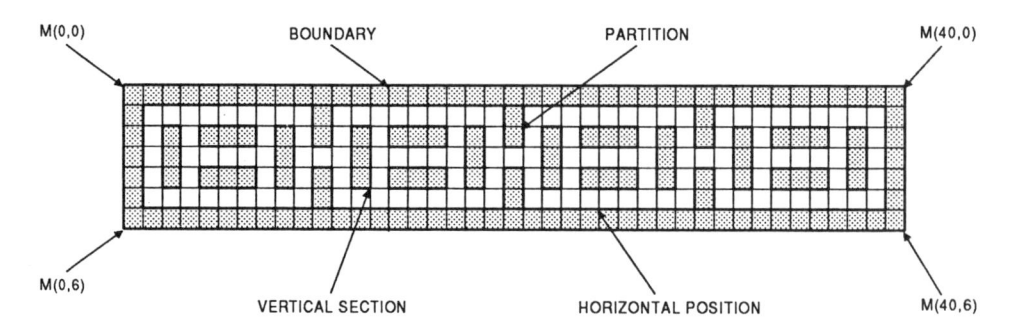

Maze array locations

A Notepad Arcade

It can be seen how a reasonably labyrinthine course is prepared for the chase. The player has to steer a letter O through the maze. The cursor keys are used in the normal fashion to move up, down, left or right, but of course moves can only be made into a free space. The walls of the maze are genuinely impenetrable.

At the beginning of each game the player is located on the far left hand side of the maze and the objective is to progress through the corridors and chambers to the right hand end. If this is achieved, the score is increased by one point. Naturally, as you will be typing in the listing, the appropriate code can be adjusted to award more points for success, if this is regarded as more exciting.

What makes the game a little more difficult is the presence of the 'Minotaur' in the maze, who chases the player with merciless determination. Sadly the Minotaur is shown only as a capital letter M, but it is assumed that the player will employ imagination at this point! The inclusion of the Minotaur is useful in two ways. It does make the maze into more of a game, reminiscent of the early arcades. In addition, the design of the algorithms required to enable the Minotaur to pursue the player is quite a programming challenge and will extend the programmer's skills.

Program listing – MAZE

```
 10 REM MAZE
 20 REM Control routine
 30 PROCinit
 40 PROCdisplay
 50 PROClocation
 60 REPEAT
 70    PROCavoid
 80    IF RND(1)>0.8 THEN PROCfollow
 90    IF ABS(X-BX)<2 AND ABS(Y-BY)<2
       THEN VDU 7 : PROCreset
100    IF X=39 THEN PROCscore
110 UNTIL FALSE
120 END
130 REM
140 DEF PROCinit
150 REM Maze coordinates
160 DIM M(40,6)
170 REM Boundary
180 FOR I=0 TO 40
190    M(I,0)=32
200    M(I,6)=32
210 NEXT I
220 FOR I=1 TO 5
230    M(0,I)=32
240    M(40,I)=32
250 NEXT I
260 REM Partitions
270 FOR I=10 TO 30 STEP 10
280    FOR J=1 TO 2
```

```
290      M(I,J)=32
300      M(I,J+3)=32
310    NEXT J
320 NEXT I
330 REM Vertical sections
340 FOR I=2 TO 32 STEP 10
350    FOR J=2 TO 4
360      M(I,J)=32
370      M(I+6,J)=32
380    NEXT J
390 NEXT I
400 REM Horizontal sections
410 FOR I=4 TO 34 STEP 10
420    FOR J=0 TO 2
430      M(I+J,2)=32
440      M(I+J,4)=32
450    NEXT J
460 NEXT I
470 REM Initialise score
480 S = 0
490 REM Evaluation array
500 DIM E(4)
510 REM Minotaur's move coordinates
520 DIM DX(4) : DIM DY(4)
530 FOR I=1 TO 4
540    READ DX(I), DY(I)
550 NEXT I
560 ENDPROC
570 REM
580 DEF PROClocation
590 REM Initial player coordinates
600 X=1 : Y=3
610 REM Initial Minotaur coordinates
620 REPEAT
630    BX=RND(19)+10 : BY=RND(5)
640 UNTIL M(BX,BY)=0
650 ENDPROC
660 REM
670 DEF PROCdisplay
680 CLS
690 PRINT TAB(2,3) "SCORE 0"
700 VDU 14
710 FOR I=0 TO 40
720    FOR J=0 TO 6
730      PRINT TAB(I+22,J) CHR$ M(I,J)
740    NEXT J
750 NEXT I
760 VDU 15
770 ENDPROC
780 REM
790 DEF PROCavoid
800 PRINT TAB(X+22,Y) CHR$ 79
810 XL=X : YL=Y
```

A Notepad Arcade

```
 820 A=INKEY(100)
 830 IF A=243 AND M(X+1,Y)=0 THEN X=X+1
 840 IF A=242 AND M(X-1,Y)=0 THEN X=X-1
 850 IF A=241 AND M(X,Y+1)=0 THEN Y=Y+1
 860 IF A=240 AND M(X,Y-1)=0 THEN Y=Y-1
 870 PRINT TAB(XL+22,YL) CHR$ 32
 880 ENDPROC
 890 REM
 900 DEF PROCfollow
 910 REM 1st stage of evaluation
 920 REM Find vacant sites
 930 FOR I=1 TO 4
 940   IF M(BX+DX(I), BY+DY(I))=0 THEN E(I)=1
       ELSE E(I)=100
 950 NEXT I
 960 REM 2nd stage of evaluation
 970 REM Calculate distances
 980 FOR I=1 TO 4
 990   E(I)=E(I)*SQR((BX+DX(I)-X)^2 +
       (BY+DY(I)-Y)^2)
1000 NEXT I
1010 REM 3rd stage of evaluation
1020 REM Select closest location
1030 MIN=100
1040 FOR I=1 TO 4
1050   IF E(I)<MIN THEN MIN=E(I) : JUMP=I
1060 NEXT I
1070 REM Move Minotaur
1080 PRINT TAB(BX+22,BY) CHR$ 32
1090 BX=BX+DX(JUMP)
1100 BY=BY+DY(JUMP)
1110 PRINT TAB(BX+22,BY) CHR$ 77
1120 ENDPROC
1130 REM
1140 DEF PROCscore
1150 S = S+1 : PRINT TAB(8,3); S
1160 PROCreset
1170 ENDPROC
1180 REM
1190 DEF PROCreset
1200 PRINT TAB(BX+22,BY) CHR$ 32
1210 PROClocation
1220 ENDPROC
1230 REM
1240 REM Data for Minotaur's moves
1250 DATA 0,-1,1,0,0,1,-1,0
```

Representing the maze walls

When you write any computer program you are forced to think about everything very carefully. You cannot take things at face value or allow yourself to base your actions on woolly, unexamined assumptions. A maze game is a good example of this.

Nothing is more obvious to the person playing a game than the impenetrability of the maze walls. The human player will naturally turn at corners, hide in rooms and loyally follow the direction of corridors. Burrowing through a maze wall from one section to another would not seem to be entering into the spirit.

Theseus was equipped with a ball of twine, not a bazooka. The programmer, however, cannot afford to be this naive. He or she will immediately observe that there is a subtle distinction between seeing a wall in the way and being prevented from moving through it. The programmer realises that each chunk of maze wall has two vital attributes:

❏ It needs a graphic symbol displayed on the screen to indicate that a wall is in that particular location

❏ There has to be an 'internal representation' of the wall. This will be a value held somewhere in the computer's memory. It will play a vital role in the 'move to another place' algorithms employed by the program. The number will state, 'You cannot move here. A wall is blocking you.'

The values which delineate the walls of the maze in this program are held in a two dimensional array initialised at line 160 in PROCinit. The array is M(40,6), which can be seen to correspond to the 41 columns and 7 rows of the maze as shown in the diagram above. Each of the M array locations can have either a value of 0, which represents free space, or 32, which represents part of a maze wall.

This matches the choice of ASCII value chosen for the display example in Chapter 6. Again the values are chosen because by printing the corresponding character on the display the maze will be constructed. CHR$ 32 will place a filled square on the screen, while CHR$ 0 leaves the display unaffected. When the array is initialised by DIM M(40,6) at line 160 all the array locations have values of 0. All that has to be done, therefore, is to place values of 32 in the appropriate locations.

This is achieved in PROCinit by lines 170-460. The maze could have been defined by lines of data read into the M array by two nested loops. This program code would be quite short. The alternative method is chosen, however, because of the high degree of pattern and symmetry possessed by the maze walls. All of the filled array locations can be generated by a series of FOR-NEXT loops using simple arithmetic to calculate the positions of each part of the maze wall. This seems a more elegant solution than holding 41 X 7 items of data. As explained earlier, the method is also less prone to copying mistakes or 'errors of transcription'.

Calculating the array locations

The top and bottom edges of the maze are determined by the FOR-NEXT loop between lines 180 – 210. The loop variable ranges from 0 to 40 and so identifies the top sections of maze wall as M(I,0) and the bottom sections as M(I,6). This can be seen by studying the diagram. A similar loop at lines 220 – 250 completes the two

A Notepad Arcade 193

sides of the maze. The left side is identified by M(0,I) and the right side by M(40,I). The code is:

```
170 REM Boundary
180 FOR I=0 TO 40
190    M(I,0)=32
200    M(I,6)=32
210 NEXT I
220 FOR I=1 TO 5
230    M(0,I)=32
240    M(40,I)=32
250 NEXT I
```

Completing the inner sections of the maze is more complicated and requires three sets of nested FOR-NEXT loops. The first set, between lines 270 – 320, generates the six 'partitions' that project from the top and bottom walls of the maze. The second set, lines 340 – 390, produce eight short vertical sections of wall spaced along the maze. The third pair of nested loops, lines 410 – 460, create similar horizontal maze wall sections.

The three pairs of partitions occur at x-coordinates of 10, 20 and 30. Line 270 uses STEP to give the I loop variable these values. The nested J loop variable takes values of 1 and 2, which means that M(I,J) will identify the top half of the partition and M(I,J+3) the bottom half. Lines 290 and 300 assign values of 32 to these array locations. The program code is as follows:

```
260 REM Partitions
270 FOR I=10 TO 30 STEP 10
280    FOR J=1 TO 2
290       M(I,J)=32
300       M(I,J+3)=32
310    NEXT J
320 NEXT I
```

The eight vertical sections occur in four pairs. In each, the second section is always six character positions to the right of the first section. The outer loop therefore needs to STEP only to the four I-values of 2, 12, 22 and 32. This is done by line 340. The additional section is identified each time within the nested loops as I+6. The inner, J, loop simply represents the y-coordinate of each character position. This is in the range 2-4 for all the eight sections.

Given the values assigned within the loops to the variables I and J, all the character positions forming the vertical sections will therefore be defined by the array locations M(I,J) and M(I+6,J). Lines 360 and 370 place the ASCII value of 32 in these locations. This is the BASIC which creates the vertical sections:

```
330 REM Vertical sections
340 FOR I=2 TO 32 STEP 10
350    FOR J=2 TO 4
```

```
360     M(I,J)=32
370     M(I+6,J)=32
380   NEXT J
390 NEXT I
```

The horizontal sections are also calculated in four pairs by two nested loops. The Y-coordinate of all the character positions in the upper section is 2. This increases to 4 for the lower section. Both loop variables, I and J, are involved in calculating the X-coordinate of the positions. The I loop STEPs through the values 4, 14, 24 and 34 to locate the beginning of each section. The J loop then 'smears' this initial position through three squares to create the horizontal section. All the array locations that require an ASCII value of 32 are identified as M(I+J,2) or M(I+J,4) at lines 430 and 440. Here is the BASIC:

```
400 REM Horizontal sections
410 FOR I=4 TO 34 STEP 10
420   FOR J=0 TO 2
430     M(I+J,2)=32
440     M(I+J,4)=32
450   NEXT J
460 NEXT I
```

Putting the maze on the Notepad's screen

The maze array locations are defined in PROCinit. The control routine then calls PROCdisplay, which generates the maze on the Notepad's screen. All that is required is another pair of nested loops which examine each of the M array locations in turn and print out the corresponding character on the display. The loop variables are I and J again, although of course any variable names could have been selected. The array value is M(I,J) and the character printed is CHR$ M(I,J).

PRINT TAB is employed to determine the actual position on the Notepad's screen. This is not the same as the subscripts in the array because a displacement to the right is required in order to place the maze centrally on the display. Two VDU codes are also required. VDU 14 at the beginning of the loops switches on inverse text so that CHR$ 32 will appear as a dark, filled space rather than just a blank. At the end of the loops VDU 15 toggles off inverse text again. The lines of code are:

```
700 VDU 14
710 FOR I=0 TO 40
720   FOR J=0 TO 6
730     PRINT TAB(I+22,J) CHR$ M(I,J)
740   NEXT J
750 NEXT I
760 VDU 15
```

Adding the player – and the Minotaur!

The two procedures described so far, PROCinit and PROCdisplay, are called just once when Maze is run. There is no need to redefine the maze or to redraw it on the Notepad's screen. Remember that the reason for placing the maze wall coordinates in the M array was to allow the player and Minotaur to move around the corridors without passing through the walls. The array was not intended to allow redrawing of the maze itself.

After these two procedures a REPEAT-UNTIL loop keeps calling the remaining procedures of the program. This is to allow the game to continue after the player has reached the far end of the labyrinth or has been captured by the Minotaur. Such improbable survival is an essential feature for any game which is not going to end too quickly.

The first of these continuously repeated procedures is PROClocation. This keeps placing the player and the Minotaur back into the labyrinth. Putting the player at the left hand end is very simple, because the same starting point is used each time giving values (1,3) to the player's coordinates (X,Y):

```
590 REM Initial player coordinates
600 X=1 : Y=3
```

The Minotaur is located with more subtlety. The game would become very predictable and far too easy to play if the monster always appeared in the same place. To avoid this, a random factor is introduced. The 'beast' coordinates, (BX,BY), are selected with the use of RND within a REPEAT-UNTIL loop. The exit condition for the loop is designed to avoid placing the Minotaur on top of a wall section. The proposed location, M(BX,BY) is checked to see if it is vacant. If it is not, the loop repeats to attempt a new position for (BX,BY):

```
610 REM Initial Minotaur coordinates
620 REPEAT
630    BX=RND(19)+10 : BY=RND(5)
640 UNTIL M(BX,BY)=0
```

(Note that in choosing variable names clarity is always essential and choosing (MX,MY) for 'Minotaur' coordinates could have led to confusion with the M used to identify the maze locations.)

Steering the player

The second procedure called by the loop in the control routine is PROCavoid. This, as suggested by its name, allows the player to manoeuvre around the corridors of the labyrinth and attempt to steer past the Minotaur. The beast, of course, is constantly homing in on the player's position.

The illusion of movement is created by the usual animation technique of printing the player's character, a capital letter O represented as ASCII 79, on the display, erasing it again and then printing once more in a new position. Obviously this requires a loop which repeats constantly. In Maze this loop is already present in the control routine. Two sets of coordinates are also needed, the current position of the player, (X,Y), and the last position, (XL,YL), which will be erased by overprinting with CHR$ 32.

The player's choice of direction, right, left, down or up, is determined by the ASCII value of the cursor key pressed, which is used to adjust the value of X or Y.

The stages involved, written as a formal algorithm, are:

❑ Print an O on the screen at the current position

❑ Record current position as 'last position' coordinates

❑ Note key pressed

❑ Adjust current position, according to key pressed

❑ Erase last position.

This is coded as BASIC by these lines in PROCavoid:

```
800 PRINT TAB(X+22,Y) CHR$ 79
810 XL=X : YL=Y
820 A=INKEY(100)
830 IF A=243 AND M(X+1,Y)=0 THEN X=X+1
840 IF A=242 AND M(X-1,Y)=0 THEN X=X-1
850 IF A=241 AND M(X,Y+1)=0 THEN Y=Y+1
860 IF A=240 AND M(X,Y-1)=0 THEN Y=Y-1
870 PRINT TAB(XL+22,YL) CHR$ 32
```

If the player does not use the cursor keys to adjust the values of X and Y, the letter O will still be erased and reprinted but will blink in a fixed position rather than move.

There is no need to place the player's position in the Maze array. This could, of course, be done with a simple additional statement:

```
M(XL,YL)=79
```

Such a modification of the M array's contents would be required if more than one player were involved and if the separate player's positions had to be kept distinct. However, the only interaction between two moving characters in this version of the game is when the Minotaur captures the player. At that point the game starts again from the beginning. Modifying the M array would therefore be rather pointless.

Giving the player a fair chance...

If the game simply involved drawing a maze on the Notepad's screen and letting the player steer around it, the procedures described above would suffice. Such a game would not be very interesting. What provides entertainment is the way that the Minotaur hunts the player. A letter M closes in on the player's location in the maze and, if evasive action is not taken, will capture the letter O.

The most involved section of the program is devoted to this control of the Minotaur. The letter M representing its position ambushes the letter O as the player attempts to reach the right hand side of the maze. The algorithm which achieves this is coded in PROCfollow. It is quite efficient. To prevent the game from being too difficult to play, the procedure is not called each time the main loop repeats in the control routine. Instead, the value of a random number is used to call PROCfollow for only a fraction of the time. This is done by comparing the value of a random decimal with 0.8. When the fraction is greater, PROCfollow is executed. Hence 80 percent of the time the Minotaur is dozing, or perhaps gnawing the remains of a previous victim. The code is:

```
80 IF RND(1)>0.8 THEN PROCfollow
```

Pursuit by the Minotaur

The method by which the Minotaur is assigned positions which continually reduce its distance from the player is quite simple. Nevertheless when the game is played the mindlessly mechanical algorithm used to control the pursuit seems less obvious and it is tempting to believe that the Minotaur really is thinking about what it is doing! This is a result of the way the creature uncannily follows the corridors. It always makes the correct turn when it encounters a junction, apparently making a choice. The game is an example of how a computer program can mimic intelligent behaviour

The algorithm used to steer the Minotaur involves the use of three arrays, E, DX and DY. Each has four locations (ignoring the zeroth), corresponding to the four possible directions in which the Minotaur can move. Moving up corresponds to the first location in each of the three arrays, moving right to the second, down to the third location and moving left is associated with the fourth.

The E, or 'evaluation', array represents the Minotaur's distance from the player in each of the four possible directions it can move. E is initialised in PROCinit and then values for its four locations calculated in PROCfollow.

The DX and DY, or 'increment', arrays hold the coordinate changes, or increments, that the Minotaur requires if it is to move in a particular direction. For example, if the Minotaur is to move up one square in the maze its X-coordinate will remain the same but its Y-coordinate will decrease by 1. This means that the increment in the

X-direction is 0 and the increment in the Y-direction is -1. The DX and DY arrays hold these values as DX(1)=0 and DY(1)=-1. Similarly a move to the right is represented in the arrays by DX(2)=1 and DY(2)=0. All four pairs of values are illustrated in the diagram.

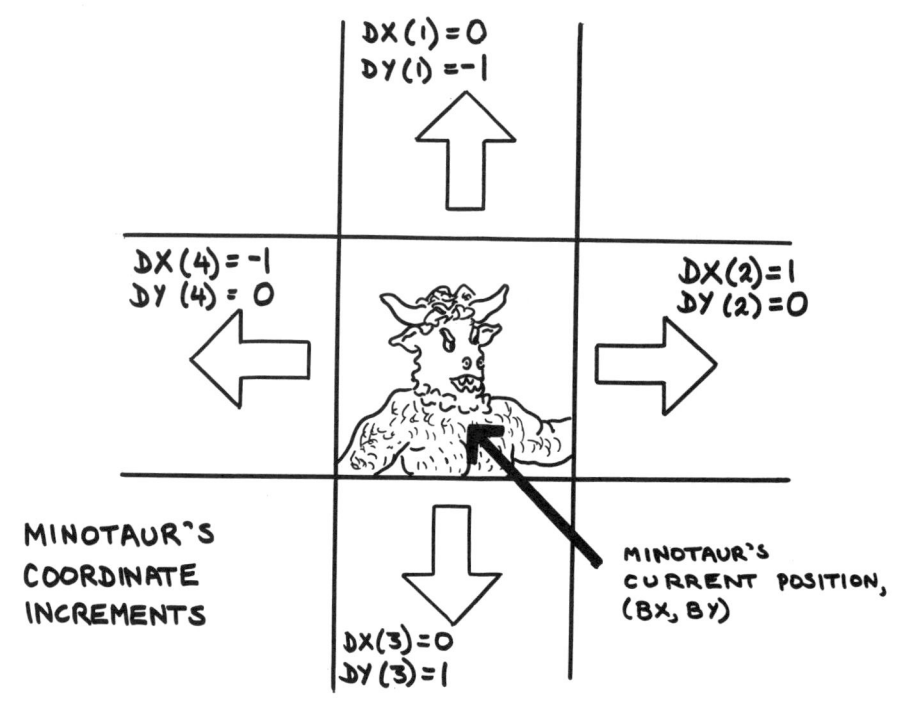

The four pairs of values for the movement array

All eight numbers needed for the DX and DY arrays are held as a data statement at line 1280:

```
1270 REM Data for Minotaur's moves
1280 DATA 0,-1,1,0,0,1,-1,0
```

The evaluation array and increment arrays are established in PROCinit and a FOR-NEXT loop used to read the data into the DX, DY locations:

```
490 REM Evaluation array
500 DIM E(4)
510 REM Minotaur's move coordinates
520 DIM DX(4) : DIM DY(4)
530 FOR I=1 TO 4
540    READ DX(I),DY(I)
550 NEXT I
```

Calculating the evaluation array locations

The evaluation array plays a vital role in controlling the movement of the Minotaur. It not only indicates how far away the player is in any of the four directions but also shows which directions are blocked by maze walls. The Minotaur is then moved in the free direction which is closest to the player. Sometimes this might mean that the Minotaur actually moves further away from the player in order to negotiate its path around a section of maze wall. Nevertheless persistent application of the method will inevitably lead to capture, unless the player has very quick reflexes.

The first stage in filing the evaluation array locations is to discover which directions are blocked by maze walls. This requires inspecting in turn the maze locations above, to the right, below and to the left of the current Minotaur coordinate position, (BX,BY). In order to do this, the values in the DX and DY arrays are required. For example the maze location immediately above the Minotaur has the X-coordinate BX+DX(1). The Y-coordinate is BY+DY(1). Whether this part of the maze is vacant or occupied by a section of wall will depend upon the M array value for this location, M(BX+DX(1),BY+DY(1)). If the array value is 0, the maze is empty space. If it is not 0, there is a section of wall.

A simple representation is used to indicate in the evaluation array whether the maze is free at this point. If it is, a value of 1 is placed in the E array. If it is occupied by a wall section, a value of 100 is used. These values can be used subsequently to show whether the Minotaur can move in that direction. The insertion of the appropriate value into the E array will therefore be performed by the condition:

```
IF M(BX+DX(1), BY+DY(1))=0 THEN E(1)=1 ELSE E(1)=100
```

Similar reasoning shows that the condition which establishes whether there is a free location to the right of the Minotaur, and which represents this accordingly in the E array, is

```
IF M(BX+DX(2), BY+DY(2))=0 THEN E(2)=1 ELSE E(2)=100
```

Clearly an examination of all four directions is best carried out by this FOR-NEXT loop:

```
910 REM 1st stage of evaluation
920 REM Find vacant sites
930 FOR I=1 TO 4
940    IF M(BX+DX(I),BY+DY(I))=0 THEN E(I)=1
       ELSE E(I)=100
950 NEXT I
```

Using Pythagoras

The second stage in selecting values for the evaluation array uses the theorem of

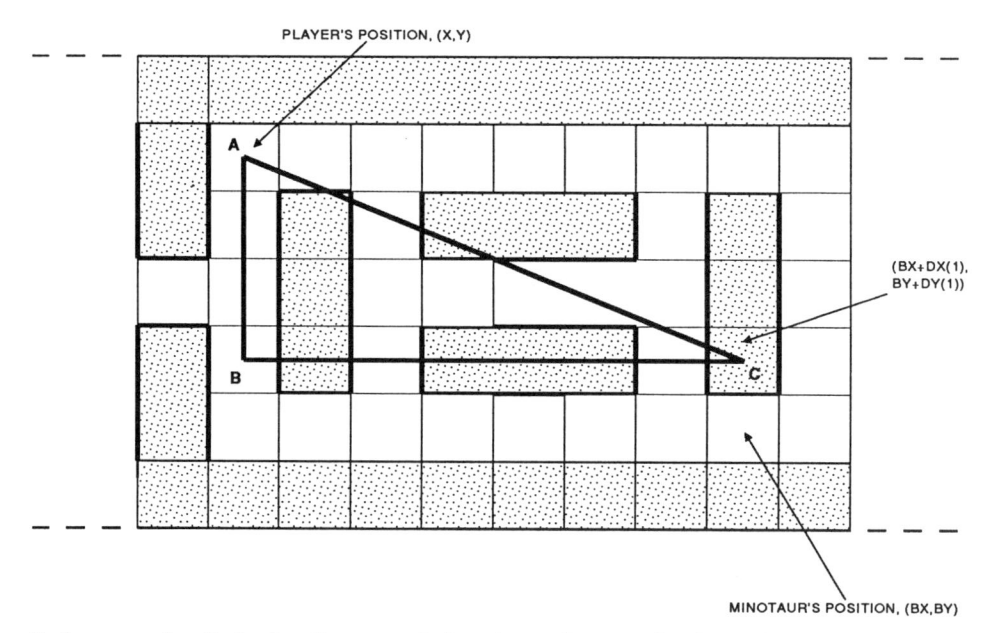

Pythagoras. It finds the distance of the player from each of the four possible maze locations into which the Minotaur could move. This clearly permits a decision to be made about which is the best choice of direction for the pursuit.

The diagram shows how Pythagoras's Theorem calculates the distance between the location above the Minotaur and the player. The right-angled triangle, ABC, has been superimposed on to the maze. Vertex A is at the player's position, coordinates (X,Y). Vertex C is at the maze location immediately above the Minotaur and has coordinates (BX+DX(1), BY+DY(1)). (It will be seen that in this particular case the position above the Minotaur has coincided with one of the vertical sections of maze wall. How these situations are resolved is described below.)

Using Pythagoras to calculate the Minotaur's distance

The lengths of the sides AB and BC can be calculated directly by subtracting the two sets of coordinates. This gives:

```
AB = BY+DY(1) - Y
BC = BX+DX(1) - X
```

The distance between player and Minotaur, the hypotenuse of the triangle, is the square root of the sum of these sides squared:

```
AC = SQR( BC^2 + AB^2 )
AC = SQR( (BX+DX(1)-X)^2 + (BY+DY(1)-Y)^2 )
```

However, it is not this value alone which is placed into location E(1) of the evaluation array. Instead it is multiplied by the value of E(1), either 1 or 100, which is already present in the array. This means that the distance recorded for any location already occupied by a section of maze wall is very large. These E array locations will automatically be ignored in the third stage of evaluation. This multiplicative factor leads to the code:

```
E(1) = E(1)*SQR((BX+DX(1)-X)^2 +(BY+DY(1)-Y)^2)
```

This is then placed into a FOR-NEXT loop to calculate the new evaluation array locations for all four positions around the Minotaur:

```
960  REM 2nd stage of evaluation
970  REM Calculate distances
980  FOR I=1 TO 4
990    E(I)=E(I) * SQR((BX+DX(I)-X)^2 + (BY+DY(I)-Y)^2)
1000 NEXT I
```

Choosing the closest location

By the end of the second stage of evaluation, the E array contains four values giving the Minotaur's distance from the player for each of the four positions into which a move could be made. The impossible positions, those representing a move into a maze wall rather than along a corridor, are identified by a very large distance which has been artificially introduced by the multiplication by 100 in stage two.

All that now needs to be done is to search through the four values and note which is the smallest. This will then represent the best position for the Minotaur to occupy. The searching is done by a simple FOR-NEXT loop. A new variable, MIN, is given an initial large value of 100. The loop then compares each value of E(I) in turn against the current value of MIN. If E(I) is smaller, MIN is reassigned this value for comparison with the next value of E(I). In this way MIN inevitably becomes equal to the lowest E(I) value. Each time MIN's value is reassigned, the value of the loop variable is assigned to another variable, JUMP. In this way JUMP will record the direction, 1, 2, 3 or 4, in which E(I) is smallest. This means that, by the end of the loop, JUMP has determined the direction for the Minotaur to move:

```
1010 REM 3rd stage of evaluation
1020 REM Select closest site
1030 MIN=100
1040 FOR I=1 TO 4
1050   E(I)<MIN THEN MIN=E(I) : JUMP=I
1060 NEXT I
```

Moving the Minotaur

When the three stages of evaluation are complete, the direction in which the Minotaur should move has been established and assigned to the variable JUMP. This will be in the range 1-4 and combined with the values in the DX, DY arrays will permit the Minotaur to be shifted into a more threatening position. First its current location in the maze is erased by overprinting with CHR$ 32. Then the BX, BY coordinates are incremented by the appropriate DX, DY values and the new position marked with a capital letter M:

```
1070 REM Move Minotaur
1080 PRINT TAB(BX+22,BY) CHR$ 32
1090 BX=BX+DX(JUMP)
1100 BY=BY+DY(JUMP)
1110 PRINT TAB(BX+22,BY) CHR$ 77
```

Capturing the player

At this point control of the program returns to the main routine. A proximity condition then compares the Minotaur's coordinates with the player's. Both pairs of X- and Y-coordinates are checked to see how close the Minotaur is. The absolute value of the coordinate difference is calculated to allow for the possibility of the Minotaur closing in from a negative direction with respect to the coordinate frame used on the Notepad's screen. If the Minotaur is close enough a note is sounded and a further procedure called:

```
90 IF ABS(X-BX)<2 AND ABS(Y-BY)<2 THEN VDU 7 : PROCreset
```

PROCreset erases the Minotaur's letter M and calls PROClocation again in order to place the player back at the left hand side of the maze and to select a new random position for the Minotaur:

```
1190 DEF PROCreset
1200 PRINT TAB(BX+22,BY) CHR$ 32
1210 PROClocation
1220 ENDPROC
```

Increasing the score

If the player manages to avoid coming too close to the Minotaur, the condition at line 90 will not be satisfied. In this case line 100 in the control routine checks to see if the right hand side of the maze is reached. If it is, PROCscore is called:

```
100 IF X=39 THEN PROCscore
```

This procedure updates the score shown on the screen. The variable, S, used has been initialised in PROCinit and first shown by PROCdisplay:

```
470 REM Initialise score
480 S=0

690 PRINT TAB(2,3) "SCORE 0"
```

PROCscore now increases the value of S and redisplays it. The procedure also calls PROCreset to allow another game to begin:

18

A Customised Wordsearch

The wordsearch puzzle has become very popular, featuring in many magazines and newspapers. The program, Search, developed in this chapter uses the basic wordsearch theme but allows the user to generate a puzzle based upon words typed into the Notepad.

This has the obvious advantage of tailoring the puzzle to the interests of a particular person. It would be extremely useful for parents of young children because the words could be names of relatives, family pets, local street names and districts or other relevant items. Photocopies of a suitable puzzle would be ideal for a cerebral children's birthday party. It could even be used as a teaching aid, provided that appropriate words were entered. (Possibly the keen programmer could develop the program further to include full file handling linked with the National Curriculum!)

In its current version the program generates a wordsearch on a 30 by 30 grid. The words entered can be up to 15 letters long. Both of these details could be altered quite easily by changing just a few lines in the program. How to do this will be evident after reading through the documentation. No limit is set for the total number of words which can be entered on to the grid, although obviously typing in a very large number will slow down the program and a hopelessly large number of words will lead to an error.

The words are then arranged in the usual way, horizontally, vertically, diagonally and backwards, together with the possible combinations of these, like 'backwards vertically'. The locations are selected entirely at random and so it is a genuine puzzle. It requires the use of a printer, of course. Two pages of print out are generated.

The first shows a blank wordsearch grid, with just the locations of the target words filled in. This is to help those who give up completely on the puzzle itself.

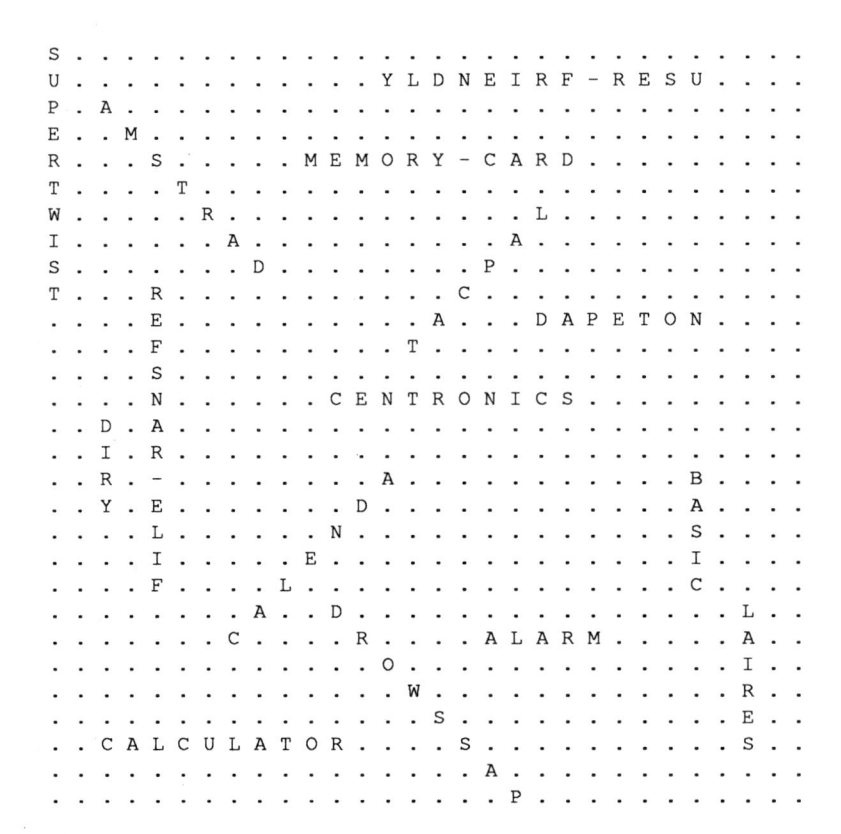

```
S . . . . . . . . . . . . . . . . . . . . . . . . . . . . . . . . . S . . .
U . . . . . . . . . . . . Y L D N E I R F - R E S U . . . .
P . A . . . . . . . . . . . . . . . . . . . . . . . . . . . . . . . . . .
E . . M . . . . . . . . . . . . . . . . . . . . . . . . . . . . . . . . .
R . . . S . . . . . M E M O R Y - C A R D . . . . . . . . . . . .
T . . . . T . . . . . . . . . . . . . . . . . . . . . . . . . . . . . .
W . . . . . R . . . . . . . . . . . . L . . . . . . . . . . . . . .
I . . . . . . A . . . . . . . . . A . . . . . . . . . . . . . . .
S . . . . . . . D . . . . . . . P . . . . . . . . . . . . . . .
T . . . R . . . . . . . . . . C . . . . . . . . . . . . . . .
. . . . E . . . . . . . . . A . . . D A P E T O N . . . .
. . . . F . . . . . . . . T . . . . . . . . . . . . . . .
. . . . S . . . . . . . . . . . . . . . . . . . . . . . .
. . . . N . . . . . C E N T R O N I C S . . . . . . . .
. . D . A . . . . . . . . . . . . . . . . . . . . . . . .
. . I . R . . . . . . . . . . . . . . . . . . . . . . . .
. . R . - . . . . . . A . . . . . . . . . . . . B . . . .
. . Y . E . . . . . . . D . . . . . . . . . . . A . . . .
. . . . L . . . . . N . . . . . . . . . . . . . S . . . .
. . . . I . . . . E . . . . . . . . . . . . . . I . . . .
. . . . F . . . L . . . . . . . . . . . . . . . C . . . .
. . . . . . . A . . D . . . . . . . . . . . . . . L . .
. . . . . . . C . . . . R . . . . A L A R M . . . . . A . .
. . . . . . . . . . . . . O . . . . . . . . . . . . . I . .
. . . . . . . . . . . . . . W . . . . . . . . . . . . R . .
. . . . . . . . . . . . . . . S . . . . . . . . . . . E . .
. . C A L C U L A T O R . . . . S . . . . . . . . . . . S . .
. . . . . . . . . . . . . . . . . . A . . . . . . . . . . .
. . . . . . . . . . . . . . . . . . . P . . . . . . . . . . .
```

The second sheet gives the list of words to find and the completed grid with all the blank spaces filled with randomly selected letters:

```
Find these words:
FILE-TRANSFER
USER-FRIENDLY
MEMORY-CARD
CALCULATOR
CENTRONICS
SUPERTWIST
CALENDAR
PASSWORD
AMSTRAD
NOTEPAD
LAPCAT
SERIAL
ALARM
BASIC
DIARY
```

A Customised Wordsearch

```
S B N U W R Y M K I L S G E O M V Y S U S L H P T J S B R S
U H L E P G C H N Z M I E Y L D N E I R F - R E S U K K M R
P G A J E T U O P P L N Q I Z N K F G S K Y E E I M Z P W P
E G U M Y I L D G Q B M J U P A G D T I E U I F P M I F P T
R S F T S Y I O P M M E M O R Y - C A R D H F T R U W R P Y
T Q Q F Y T T U I B F T T I I L G M A D W R T Y W T Y D G U
W D E T Y L R C B T N D J U L N M W T L O P E G H E T Y S T
I D J U P E N A H F Y W I O M J W U A I B K R Y P Q M C I P
S R U K M X W T D U P V N H W M C P M R Y I E T O K C E T M
T N M Y R E T Y N U K G S T Y U C C B R U J K D T U C B X B
Q S X C E V F D G H V Y E D G A H S W D A P E T O N W S X R
X E R R F R T G D W E D F G T T E X G Y U U X A D R T Y B N
E R T G S G N J T E D N F R E S M C R W A F T S W A G Y H D
A S F G N Y N M T Y U C E N T R O N I C S N V B H U I O V C
Q W D S A B N Y Y V N U I C N M U I T C V R T N X D R G T G
A W I U R G C V N M K I T E W V G O M B E R W X C V Y H V Z
A E A Y T J N M K I O F C V R N J R S X C N M J F R G H N V
X C R F - Y U N N H Y U I A O H S W N H H E S D D B R T H J
A D Y G E H J K L J N M D S D Z C E H K B V F S C A V Y S T
A S D F L H J K L V V N M P W B J V G G U O B J K S P R F L
H J B V I N J K L G E Y Y U L N V E E T D F R X C I T H B D
Z C F G F J K B N L N J R W R I O S D E S F W R H C J J V H
W R T U T H F Z A D F D Y L J U G K H N Y J V X S D G L Y E
X H J N V D E C R R T F R H J C F A L A R M Z D T H V A X S
G D E C V B J O P Y B N W O E T Y U I G C V G Q W F G I G X
V G U U V X D R T Y K I D R W X Z S H J N M C D E R Z R F U
A S H C X E R N M Z E R Y H G S A J E T V B S W P L M E C E
V T C A L C U L A T O R E R T D S B T A H S E N M S T S U I
B N Y O P S W G H K L V G Y L B M A S W R T C D H N J K L M
G H Y K L V M L P R T Y U I C S K B P E K M D T Y D P V W N
```

Program listing – SEARCH

```
 10 REM SEARCH
 20 REM Control routine
 30 PROCinit
 40 PROCwords
 50 PROCorder
 60 PROClocate
 70 VDU 2
 80 PROCtexta
 90 PROCprintout
100 PROCfill
110 PROCtextb
120 PROCprintout
130 VDU 3
140 END
150 REM
160 DEF PROCinit
170 DIM G$(30,30)
180 FOR X=1 TO 30
190   FOR Y=1 TO 30
200     G$(X,Y)=CHR$ 46
```

```
210    NEXT Y
220 NEXT X
230 PRINT "Type number of words for wordsearch"
240 INPUT N
250 ENDPROC
260 REM
270 DEF PROCwords
280 DIM W$(N)
290 FOR I=1 TO N
300    REPEAT
310       PRINT "Type word No";I
320       INPUT W$(I)
330       REM Condition prevents long words
340    UNTIL LEN W$(I)<16
350 NEXT I
360 ENDPROC
370 REM
380 DEF PROCorder
390 REPEAT
400    SW=0
410    FOR I=1 TO N-1
420       IF LEN W$(I)<LEN W$(I+1) THEN PROCswap
430    NEXT I
440 UNTIL SW=0
450 ENDPROC
460 REM
470 DEF PROCswap
480 SW=1
490 A$=W$(I)
500 W$(I)=W$(I+1)
510 W$(I+1)=A$
520 ENDPROC
530 REM
540 DEF PROClocate
550 FOR I=1 TO N
560    W=LEN W$(I)
570    REM
580    REPEAT
590       REM Select starting point for word
600       XS=RND(30) : YS=RND(30)
610       REM
620       REPEAT
630          REM
640          REPEAT
650             REM Select direction for word
660             DX=RND(3)-2 : DY=RND(3)-2
670             REM Condition prevents 'collapsed' word
680          UNTIL NOT(DX=0 AND DY=0)
690          REM
700          REM Locate end of word
710          XE=XS+DX*(W-1)
720          YE=YS+DY*(W-1)
730          REM Condition checks end of word on grid
```

A Customised Wordsearch

```
 740      UNTIL XE>0 AND XE<31 AND YE>0 AND YE<31
 750      REM
 760      REM FOR loop checks spaces vacant
 770      F=1
 780      XL=XS-DX : YL=YS-DY
 790      FOR J=1 TO W
 800         XL=XL+DX : YL=YL+DY
 810         IF G$(XL,YL)<>CHR$ 46 THEN F=0
 820      NEXT J
 830      REM Condition checks no word overlap
 840     UNTIL F=1
 850     REM Place word on grid
 860     REM
 870     XL=XS-DX : YL=YS-DY
 880     FOR J=1 TO W
 890        XL=XL+DX : YL=YL+DY
 900        G$(XL,YL)=MID$(W$(I),J,1)
 910     NEXT J
 920     PRINT "Inserted "; W$(I)
 930 NEXT I
 940 ENDPROC
 950 REM
 960 DEF PROCtexta
 970 PRINT "The wordsearch solution is:"
 980 PRINT
 990 ENDPROC
1000 REM
1010 DEF PROCprintout
1020 FOR Y=1 TO 30
1030    FOR X=1 TO 30
1040       PRINT G$(X,Y); CHR$ 32;
1050    NEXT X
1060    PRINT
1070 NEXT Y
1080 ENDPROC
1090 REM
1100 DEF PROCfill
1110 FOR X=1 TO 30
1120    FOR Y=1 TO 30
1130       IF G$(X,Y)=CHR$ 46 THEN G$(X,Y)=CHR$(RND(26)+64)
1140    NEXT Y
1150 NEXT X
1160 ENDPROC
1170 REM
1180 DEF PROCtextb
1190 CLS
1200 PRINT "Find these words:"
1210 FOR I=1 TO N
1220    PRINT W$(I)
1230 NEXT I
1240 PRINT
1250 ENDPROC
```

Entering the words

In PROCinit the user is prompted to type in the number of words to be involved in the wordsearch. This number is assigned to the numeric variable N. No error trapping has been included here, but it would not be difficult to incorporate a REPEAT-UNTIL loop to prevent unsuitable numbers from being typed:

```
230 PRINT "Type number of words for wordsearch"
240 INPUT N
```

The value of N chosen is then used in PROCwords to dimension an array, W$, to the size required. After this a FOR-NEXT loop requests that the user types in each of the N words in turn. A nested REPEAT-UNTIL loop rejects any entry of words longer than 15 letters:

```
280 DIM W$(N)
290 FOR I=1 TO N
300   REPEAT
310     PRINT "Type word No";I
320     INPUT W$(I)
330     REM Condition prevents long words
340   UNTIL LEN W$(I)<16
350 NEXT I
```

The reason for the length restriction is that very long words are going to block too much space on the wordsearch grid and make it more difficult to fit other words into the remaining spaces.

Sorting the words

The algorithm that places the user's input on to the wordsearch grid will use words which have been sorted into a sequence of descending length. It is easier to place long words on the grid first, and then fit shorter ones around them, than to block vital areas of the grid with short words and subsequently try to find room for the big ones. This rearrangement of the W$ array is performed by PROCorder and PROCswap. The algorithm used here is a standard bubble sort. It should be understood quite easily, especially if the documentation for 'Bubble' in Chapter 13 is read again:

```
380 DEF PROCorder
390 REPEAT
400   SW=0
410   FOR I=1 TO N-1
420     IF LEN W$(I)<LEN W$(I+1) THEN PROCswap
430   NEXT I
440 UNTIL SW=0
450 ENDPROC
460 REM

470 DEF PROCswap
480 SW=1
490 A$=W$(I)
500 W$(I)=W$(I+1)
510 W$(I+1)=A$
520 ENDPROC
```

Preparing the grid

The words will eventually be placed on a 30 by 30 grid printed out on to paper. The grid will also exist as a mathematical object within the program. It is, of course, a two dimensional array, G$(30,30). The first time the grid is printed, it only holds the letters of the words the user selected. The rest of the grid is left empty. This is to provide a solution for the wordsearch. The vacant places in the grid are not left as blank spaces though. It makes the pattern of the grid much easier to understand if these places are filled with full stops. This means that when PROCinit sets up the G$ array, two nested FOR-NEXT loops are used to place full stops into all the locations, as CHR$ 46:

```
170 DIM G$(30,30)
180 FOR X=1 TO 30
190   FOR Y=1 TO 30
200     G$(X,Y)=CHR$ 46
210   NEXT Y
220 NEXT X
```

The letters of the words will overwrite some of these in PROClocate.

A thumbnail sketch of the algorithm

The words in the W$ array can now be placed on the grid. Several distinct stages are involved in the algorithm that does this. First a random location has to be chosen for the first letter of a word. Then a direction has to be chosen for the word to 'unfold' on to the grid.

This is done by giving increments, DX, DY to the word. The values of the increments can be 1, 0 or -1. These are used to alter progressively the location of the letters of the word in the G$ array. Suppose, for example, that the first letter of a particular word has been placed at random at (5,6). If the increments are DX=1, DY=1, then the second letter will be at (6,7) and the third at (7,8). This gradual shift of the letters through the grid locations can be continued until the final letter is reached.

The word will appear diagonally on the grid, sloping down to the right. Now suppose instead that the increments are DX=0, DY=-1. The second letter will now be at (5,5) and the third at (5,4). It can be seen that the word will appear on the grid both backwards and vertical. Different combinations of DX and DY values, always in the range -1, 0, 1, will create all the eight possible directions for the word.

One danger exists in the random choice of DX and DY. If both are zero the word will not advance across the grid at all. Instead all its letters will be placed on top of each other as it 'collapses' on to itself at its initial location. A condition therefore has to be introduced to make sure that DX and DY cannot be doubly zero.

The next stage in the algorithm is to check that this choice of DX and DY does not result in the end of the word falling outside the grid. If this is going to happen, another pair of values for DX and DY must be chosen.

At this point a possible position for the entire word has been found on the grid. However, as several words are going to be entered into the wordsearch, it is quite possible that some of the letters' locations will already have been taken by a letter from a previous word. This means that all the grid locations which will be occupied must be checked to see that they are vacant. Only if this is the case can the word's letters be entered into the G$ array. If there are filled locations, the algorithm has to return to the beginning and choose a new random location for the first letter!

The algorithm is represented by this flowchart:

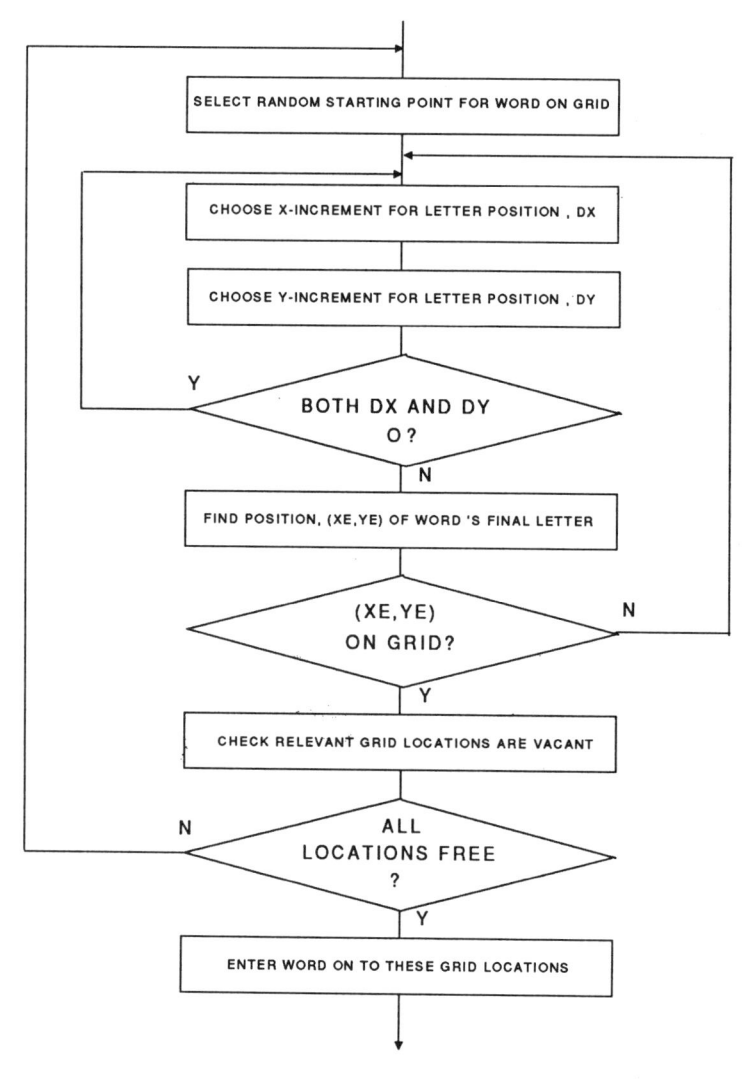

Principal word search algorithm

Coding the algorithm

The initial location for the word is found by the code:

```
590 REM Select starting point for word
600 XS=RND(30) : YS=RND(30)
```

Random values for the increments, DX and DY, then have to be created in the range -1,0,1. The table shows that RND(3)-2 will generate precisely these values:

Value of RND(3)	Value of RND(3)-2
1	-1
2	0
3	1

This expression can be placed inside a REPEAT-UNTIL loop with an exit condition that prevents both DX and DY from being zero at the same time:

```
640 REPEAT
650    REM Select direction for word
660    DX=RND(3)-2 : DY=RND(3)-2
670    REM Condition prevents 'collapsed' word
680 UNTIL NOT(DX=0 AND DY=0)
```

Next, the location of the end of the word has to be found. The number of letters in the word is assigned to the variable W:

```
560 W=LEN W$(I)
```

The location of the final letter, (XE,YE) can now be calculated from this value of W, the increments DX and DY and the initial location, (XS,YS) by:

```
700 REM Locate end of word
710 XE=XS+DX*(W-1)
720 YE=YS+DY*(W-1)
```

The values of XE and YE are then used as the exit condition for the nested REPEAT-UNTIL loop between lines 620-740:

```
730 REM Condition checks end of word on grid
740 UNTIL XE>0 AND XE<31 AND YE>0 AND YE<31
```

All the letter positions along the length of the word are now checked by a FOR-NEXT loop to see if they are vacant. Each position in turn is represented by the array location (XL,YL) and calculated by repeated addition of the increments DX, DY. The content of the grid at this location is G$(XL,YL). If it is not CHR$ 46, then the location is not free and a flag, F, is reset to register this fact:

```
760 REM FOR loop checks spaces vacant
770 F=1
```

```
780 XL=XS-DX : YL=YS-DY
790 FOR J=1 TO W
800    XL=XL+DX : YL=YL+DY
810    IF G$(XL,YL)<>CHR$ 46 THEN F=0
820 NEXT J
```

This routine can be shown as another flowchart:

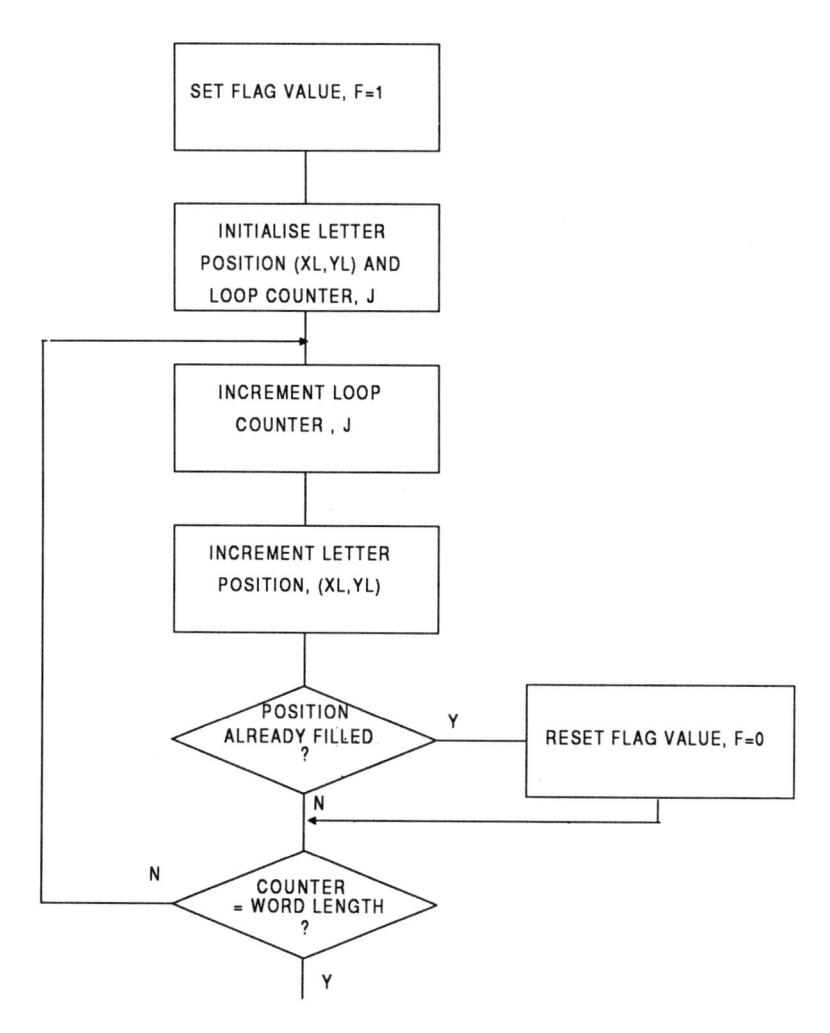

Checking the grid locations are vacant

The value of F is then used to control exit from the outer REPEAT-UNTIL loop:

```
830 REM Condition checks no word overlap
840 UNTIL F=1
```

Putting the word on the grid

The outer, I, loop in PROClocate uses the code detailed above to find a place in turn for each of the words in W$. It then employs a further FOR-NEXT loop to add the letters of the word to the relevant grid locations. MID$ is used to extract the letters in appropriate order. This loop uses J as its variable because it is nested inside the I loop:

```
850 REM Place word on grid
860 REM
870 XL=XS-DX : YL=YS-DY
880 FOR J=1 TO W
890    XL=XL+DX : YL=YL+DY
900    G$(XL,YL)=MID$(W$(I),J,1)
910 NEXT J
```

A prompt is placed on the Notepad's screen to indicate when a word has been added to the grid. This will help the user to follow the operation of the program and will indicate any problem that might arise if too many long words have been included:

```
920 PRINT "Inserted "; W$(I)
```

Printing out the wordsearch

After PROClocate has placed all the words in the G$ array, control returns to the routine at the beginning of the program:

```
 70 VDU 2
 80 PROCtexta
 90 PROCprintout
100 PROCfill
110 PROCtextb
120 PROCprintout
130 VDU 3
```

VDU 2 is used to direct output to the printer, which should be set up correctly and on-line. Two procedures, PROCtexta and PROCtextb place explanatory messages on the screen, including the words which have to be found:

```
1200 PRINT "Find these words:"
1210 FOR I=1 TO N
1220    PRINT W$(I)
1230 NEXT I
```

A procedure, PROCprintout, is called twice to dump the entire G$ array to the printer. The horizontal spacing is increased by the inclusion of an empty space, as CHR$ 32, after each character in the array:

```
1010 DEF PROCprintout
```

```
1020 FOR Y=1 TO 30
1030   FOR X=1 TO 30
1040     PRINT G$(X,Y); CHR$ 32;
1050   NEXT X
1060   PRINT
1070 NEXT Y
1080 ENDPROC
```

Between the two calls to this procedure, the vacant spaces in the G$ array are filled with random letters by a call to PROCfill. The extra letters are generated by line 1130 in the FOR-NEXT loop:

```
1100 DEF PROCfill
1110 FOR X=1 TO 30
1120   FOR Y=1 TO 30
1130     IF G$(X,Y)=CHR$ 46 THEN G$(X,Y)=CHR$(RND(26)+64)
1140   NEXT Y
1150 NEXT X
1160 ENDPROC
```

The condition in the loop identifies those G$ locations which contain a full stop. A random letter is then created by RND(26). The correct ASCII code is derived from this by adding 64, which will bring the random numbers into the correct range for the codes of capital letters.

19

A Game of Logic

The next program to be developed is another game. It involves a degree of logical thought, both in the initial program design and the coding which follows. Creating a game can be a very useful exercise in extending ability in programming techniques. Logic is also involved when the completed piece of software is played with the Notepad as your opponent.

The game should be familiar to most people. It is often played in childhood as an alternative to noughts and crosses. It, too, requires only pencil and paper. However, it possesses an advantage in that its complexity can be increased simply by extending the extent of play.

A rectangular pattern of dots is drawn and then each player takes turns to join adjacent points with short lines. The intention is to enclose as many squares as possible. Like the traditional figure of the gold prospector, each stakes claim to territory. The interesting feature is that an opponent can easily invade and capture an intended square simply by filling in the last side. Soon it is necessary to plan in advance exactly what moves should be made, so that a sufficient number of partially completed squares will cover the game area. Enough of these may conceal the one about to annexed.

The attraction of writing a computer version of this game is that although the basic set of rules involved is relatively simple to code, the actual strategy of play is rather intriguing. In fact it is suggested that after working through the game in the version developed here, the reader experiments with altering those parts of the listing which govern the way the Notepad plans its moves. More and less 'intelligent' implementations of the basic game are certainly possible.

Program listing – BUILD

```
 10 REM BUILD
 20 REM Control routine
 30 PROCinit
 40 PROCdisplay
 50 REPEAT
 60    PROCplayer
 70    PROCmachine
 80 UNTIL SP+SM=24
 90 END
100 REM
110 DEF PROCinit
120 REM Box array
130 DIM BOX(24)
140 REM Side array
150 DIM SIDE(24,4)
160 REM Box coordinates
170 DIM X(24), Y(24)
180 L=0
190 FOR I=1 TO 5 STEP 2
200    FOR J=39 TO 53 STEP 2
210       L=L+1
220       X(L)=J
230       Y(L)=I
240    NEXT J
250 NEXT I
260 REM Side increments
270 DIM DX(4), DIM DY(4)
280 FOR I=1 TO 4
290    READ DX(I), DY(I)
300 NEXT I
310 REM Score variables
320 SP=0 : SM=0
330 ENDPROC
340 REM
350 DEF PROCdisplay
360 CLS
370 REM Show dots
380 FOR I=38 TO 54 STEP 2
390    FOR J=0 TO 6 STEP 2
400       PRINT TAB(I,J) CHR$ 46
410    NEXT J
420 NEXT I
440 FOR I=1 TO 24
450    PRINT TAB(X(I),Y(I)) CHR$(96+I)
460 NEXT I
470 REM Show score positions
480 PRINT TAB(75,1) "PLAYER: "
490 PRINT TAB(75,2) "MACHINE: "
500 REM Show directions of sides
510 PRINT TAB(0,5) "Directions: 1-Up, 2-Right,"
520 PRINT TAB(12,6) "3-Down, 4-Left."
530 ENDPROC
540 REM
550 DEF PROCplayer
```

A Game of Logic

```
 560 REM Outer loop checks side absent
 570 REPEAT
 580   REM Check box in range
 590   REPEAT
 600     INPUT TAB(0,1) "Select box, a - x " B$
 610     B = ASC B$ - 64
 620   UNTIL B>0 AND B<25
 630   REM Check side in range
 640   REPEAT
 650     INPUT TAB(0,3) "Select side, 1 - 4 " S
 660   UNTIL S>0 AND S<5 AND S=INT S
 670 UNTIL SIDE(B,S)=0
 680 REM Display move
 690 M=80
 700 PROCfill
 710 ENDPROC
 720 REM
 730 DEF PROCmachine
 740 REM Avoid losing box
 750 REPEAT
 760   B=RND(24)
 770 UNTIL BOX(B)<>2
 780 REM Seek winning box
 790 FOR I=1 TO 24
 800   IF BOX(I)=3 THEN B=I
 810 NEXT I
 820 REM Select side
 830 FOR I=1 TO 4
 840   IF SIDE(B,I)=0 THEN S=I
 850 NEXT I
 860 PROCpause
 870 REM Indicate machine's move
 880 VDU7
 890 PRINT TAB(0,1) "Computer makes move"
 900 PRINT TAB(0,3) "Box is " CHR$(B+64)
     " - Side is "; S
 910 M=78
 920 PROCfill
 930 PROCpause
 940 REM Clear lower line of text
 950 PRINT TAB(0,3) SPC 20
 960 ENDPROC
 970 REM
 980 DEF PROCpause
 990 FOR T=1 TO 2000 : NEXT T
1000 ENDPROC
1010 REM
1020 DEF PROCfill
1030 REM Update box array
1040 BOX(B)=BOX(B)+1
1050 REM Update side array
1060 SIDE(B,S)=1
1070 REM Update related box and side array
1080 REM Update top box
1090 IF S=1 AND B>8 THEN NB=-8 : NS=3 : PROCnext_box
1100 REM Update right box
```

```
1110 IF S=2 AND B MOD 8 <> 0 THEN NB=1 : NS=4 :
     PROCnext_box
1120 REM Update bottom box
1130 IF S=3 AND B<17 THEN NB=8 : NS=1 : PROCnext_box
1140 REM Update left box
1150 IF S=4 AND B<>1 AND B<>9 AND B<>17 THEN NB=-1
     : NS=2 : PROCnext_box
1160 REM Show new side
1170 REM Select appropriate character
1180 IF S MOD 2 = 1 THEN C=45 ELSE C=124
1190 REM Place side at location
1200 PRINT TAB(X(B)+DX(S),Y(B)+DY(S)) CHR$ C
1210 IF BOX(B)=4 THEN W=B : PROCwin
1220 ENDPROC
1230 REM
1240 DEF PROCnext_box
1250 REM Update box array
1260 BOX(B+NB)=BOX(B+NB)+1
1270 REM Update side array
1280 SIDE(B+NB,NS)=1
1290 IF BOX(B+NB)=4 THEN
W=B+NB : PROCwin
1300 ENDPROC
1310 REM
1320 DEF PROCwin
1330 REM Indicate box is won
1340 PRINT TAB(X(W),Y(W)) CHR$ M
1350 REM Update score
1360 IF M=80 THEN SP=SP+1 ELSE SM=SM+1
1370 PRINT TAB(83,1); SP
1380 PRINT TAB(84,2); SM
1390 REM Award extra move
1400 IF M=80 THEN PROCplayer ELSE PROCmachine
1410 ENDPROC
1420 REM
1430 REM Data for side increments
1440 DATA 0,-1,1,0,0,1,-1,0
```

The initial screen display

This diagram on the next page shows the pattern of dots that appears on the screen when Build is first run. There are four rows of nine dots each. The dots are spaced out to place them at the corners of 24 potential squares, or 'boxes'. Each possible box is identified by a lower case letter, beginning with 'a' at the top left hand corner of the pattern and reaching 'x' at the bottom right. The large rectangle formed by all the dots is not exactly centre of the Notepad's screen, but shifted to the right. This is to allow room for prompts on the screen to the left of the dots as the game is played.

In the diagram, dashed lines have been included to emphasise the outline of the boxes. These are not present at first on the screen. As the game is played, however, the dots are joined together by short lines according to the moves made by the user and the Notepad. Remember, the game is between human and machine!

A Game of Logic 219

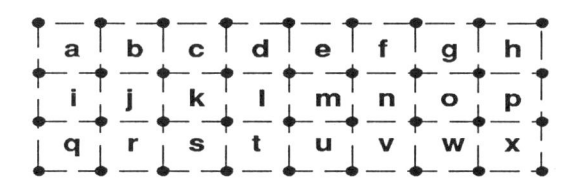

```
┌─•─┬─•─┬─•─┬─•─┬─•─┬─•─┬─•─┬─•─┐
│ a │ b │ c │ d │ e │ f │ g │ h │
├─•─┼─•─┼─•─┼─•─┼─•─┼─•─┼─•─┼─•─┤
│ i │ j │ k │ l │ m │ n │ o │ p │
├─•─┼─•─┼─•─┼─•─┼─•─┼─•─┼─•─┼─•─┤
│ q │ r │ s │ t │ u │ v │ w │ x │
└─•─┴─•─┴─•─┴─•─┴─•─┴─•─┴─•─┴─•─┘
```

The 24 boxes for use in Build

The small letter at the centre of a box remains displayed until it is totally enclosed by four lines. The player completing the fourth side then wins the box and a capital letter is placed in it instead. A capital P shows that the human being has won the square and a capital N marks territory won by the Notepad...

Putting the dots on the screen

A further diagram of the screen display is needed in order to explain how the initial pattern is created by Build. All the character positions involved in the game are shown in this second illustration. The text coordinates are also included along the top of the diagram and on the right. It can be seen that the rectangle of dots begins at an X-coordinate of 38 and finishes at a value of 54. The top row of dots has a Y-coordinate of 0 and the bottom row has a coordinate of 6:

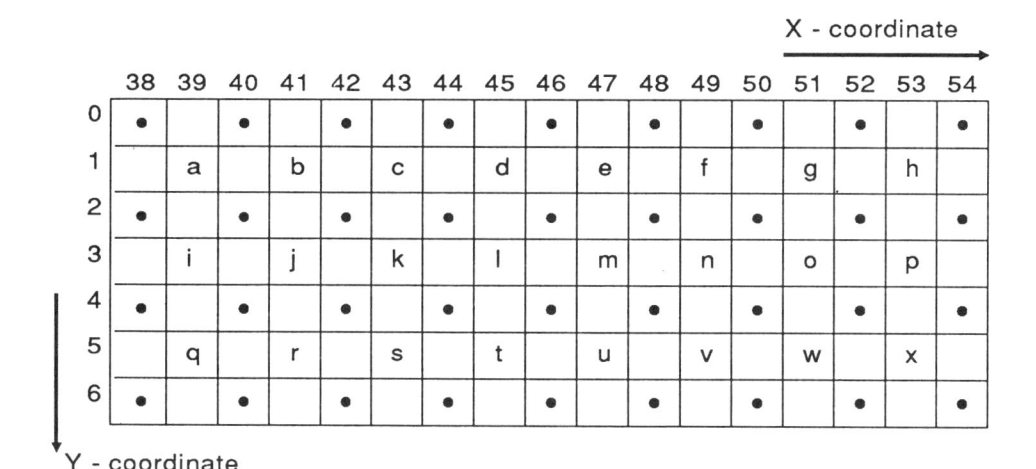

X - coordinate →

	38	39	40	41	42	43	44	45	46	47	48	49	50	51	52	53	54
0	•		•		•		•		•		•		•		•		•
1		a		b		c		d		e		f		g		h	
2	•		•		•		•		•		•		•		•		•
3		i		j		k		l		m		n		o		p	
4	•		•		•		•		•		•		•		•		•
5		q		r		s		t		u		v		w		x	
6	•		•		•		•		•		•		•		•		•

↓ Y - coordinate

Text coordinates for boxes

The X-coordinate range is therefore 38-54 and the Y-coordinate range is 0-6. The pattern of dots alternates with blank spaces throughout the rectangle. Two nested FOR-NEXT loops, each with a step increment of 2, are therefore able to create this pattern on the screen. The dot, or full stop, is printed using its ASCII code of 46. This code is included in PROCdisplay:

```
370 REM Show dots
380 FOR I=38 TO 54 STEP 2
390   FOR J=0 TO 6 STEP 2
400     PRINT TAB(I,J) CHR$ 46
410   NEXT J
420 NEXT I
```

Adding the letters

A similar pair of nested loops could add the letters to the centres of the boxes formed by the dots. The X-coordinates of the letters are in the range 39 to 53 and the Y-coordinates in the range 1 to 5. Step increments of 2 are again needed, In addition, a counter has to be placed inside the loops to identify the ASCII code of the lower case letter required. This gives the BASIC:

```
L=96
FOR I=1 TO 5 STEP 2
  FOR J=39 TO 53 STEP 2
    L=L+1
    PRINT TAB(J,I) CHR$ L
  NEXT J
NEXT I
```

The fact that the code is not used in this direct way emphasises a difference between the dots and the letters. The former simply aid the clarity of the screen display, while the latter perform an important role in the internal representation of the game.

Whenever a line has to be drawn between any pair of dots, it is the text coordinates of an adjacent letter which are used to find the correct position on the screen. This means that the coordinates of all 24 boxes need to be held in two arrays, X(24) and Y(24). The coordinates of any box can then be found when required and used to add lines to a neighbouring square. Modifying the code above gives this routine, which is included in PROCinit:

```
160 REM Box coordinates
170 DIM X(24), Y(24)
180 L=0
190 FOR I=1 TO 5 STEP 2
200   FOR J=39 TO 53 STEP 2
210     L=L+1
220     X(L)=J
230     Y(L)=I
240   NEXT J
250 NEXT I
```

Once these coordinates have been placed in the arrays, a single FOR-NEXT loop is sufficient to add the letters to the dots in PROCdisplay:

```
430 REM Label boxes
440 FOR I=1 TO 24
450   PRINT TAB(X(I),Y(I)) CHR$(96+I)
460 NEXT I
```

Identifying the boxes' sides

Two further arrays are used to represent the status of the game, recording where sides have been added to the pattern of dots. The first of these arrays is BOX(24). This records how many sides of a particular box have been completed. For example BOX(5)=3 would mean that the letter 'e' on the display had three sides added between its surrounding dots. BOX(23)=1 would represent one side added to the dots surrounding the letter 'w'. This array is initialised in PROCinit:

```
120 REM Box array
130 DIM BOX(24)
```

Although this array records how many sides have been completed for any of the boxes, it does not specify which sides these are. The array which does this is SIDE(24,4), also initialised in PROCinit:

```
140 REM Side array
150 DIM SIDE(24,4)
```

This array's role is very important because without a method for determining which pairs of dots have been joined the game would not be feasible. Valid moves could not be checked. SIDE needs to be two dimensional. The first subscript identifies the particular box involved. The second subscript defines which side of the box is represented.

A simple convention is adopted here. The higher, or 'top', side of the box is numbered 1. The right side is 2, the bottom 3 and the remaining, right side is numbered 4. (This notation has to be displayed on the screen to help the user know how to refer to a particular side. As the numbers increase in a clockwise direction, it is not difficult to adjust to the way of identifying the sides.)

Values of 0 and 1 are placed in the SIDE array's locations to indicate whether a particular side is joined up or not. Unjoined dots are represented by 0 and completed sides by 1. The formal way in which the BOX and SIDE arrays record the status of the Nth box of the display is summarised in the diagram on the next page. As a final point to note about the four arrays which define the pattern of dots and boxes, observe the distinct ways in which they are initialised. The X and Y array locations both need to be established with the relevant values to help create the screen display when the program is first run. In contrast to this the two status arrays, BOX and SIDE, must be initialised with zero values.

The different initialisations can be easily justified. The X and Y arrays reflect the 'physical' state of the display on the screen, which will be the same each time the game is played. The values for these two arrays can therefore be calculated in advance. The BOX and SIDE arrays, however, show the 'logical' state of the game.

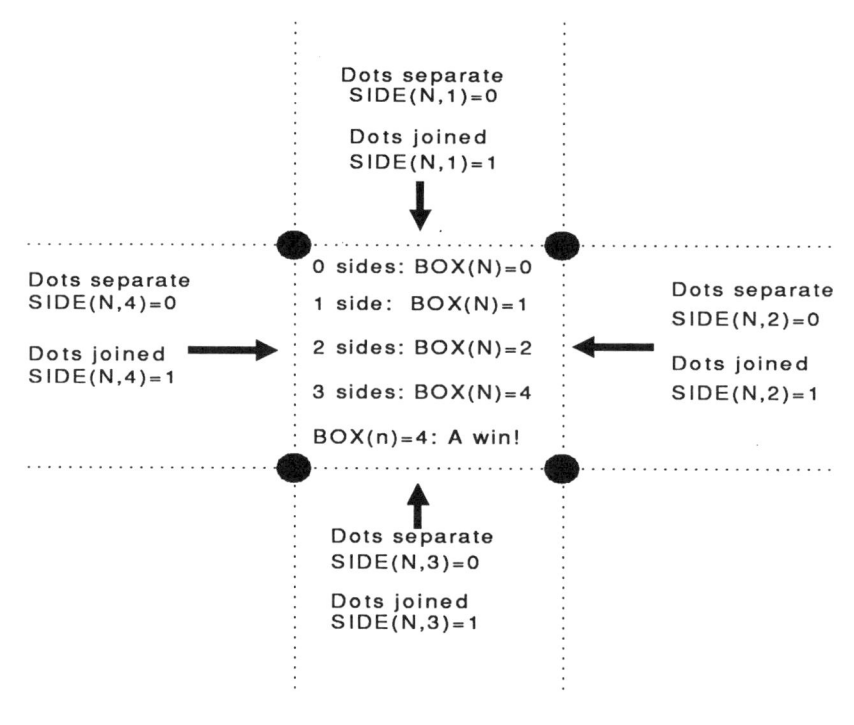

```
                  Dots separate
                  SIDE(N,1)=0

                  Dots joined
                  SIDE(N,1)=1
                        ↓
  .................●.....................●.................
  Dots separate    : 0 sides: BOX(N)=0 :    Dots separate
  SIDE(N,4)=0      :                    :    SIDE(N,2)=0
                   : 1 side:  BOX(N)=1  :
  Dots joined   →  : 2 sides: BOX(N)=2  ←    Dots joined
  SIDE(N,4)=1      :                    :    SIDE(N,2)=1
                   : 3 sides: BOX(N)=4  :
                   :                    :
                   : BOX(n)=4: A win!   :
  .................●.....................●.................
                         ↑
                   Dots separate
                   SIDE(N,3)=0

                   Dots joined
                   SIDE(N,3)=1
```

Status of Nth box

Organising the game

Once the screen display has been established, control of the program alternates between two procedures which permit the player and the machine to make moves. Each in turn will join dots to add sides to the boxes. This continues until the player's score, SP, and the machine's score, SM, add to a total equal to the maximum number of possible boxes. The game is then over:

```
20 REM Control routine
30 PROCinit
40 PROCdisplay
50 REPEAT
60    PROCplayer
70    PROCmachine
80 UNTIL SP+SM=24
90 END
```

Which player has won will be obvious from the screen display, so there is no need for further screen text.

The ramifications of the user's move

A series of four procedures calling each other in turn accompanies the user's completion of a fresh side of a box. PROCplayer accepts the user's move and calls PROCfill. This procedure updates the BOX and SIDE arrays for the chosen box and determines which of the four possible adjacent boxes is also affected by the user's choice. Obviously adding side 3 to box 'b' also involves adding side 1 to box 'j'. PROCfill then calls PROCnext_box and this procedure updates the BOX and SIDE arrays for the neighbouring box. PROCfill and PROCnext_box also call PROCwin if the fourth side has been added to either chosen or adjacent boxes.

Structured programming with discrete procedures makes the domino logic of this processing easier to grasp. It would be very unpleasant if the program had to be written in an earlier dialect of BASIC which attempted to handle all of this with multiple GOTOs!

Accepting the user's moves

In order to make a move, the user has to choose a box and a side for that box. Both choices are made in this program with an input statement rather than using the ASCII value of the keypress. Modifying the procedure to the latter technique would not be difficult.

A REPEAT-UNTIL loop requests a box to be selected. The user's choice is assigned to the string variable B$ and the ASCII value of this checked to see that it corresponds with one of the possible boxes. The box selected by the user will be identified by the value of a numeric variable, B:

```
580     REM Check box in range
590     REPEAT
600       INPUT TAB(0,1) "Select box, a - x " B$
610       B = ASC B$ - 64
620     UNTIL B>0 AND B<25
```

The user is then asked to choose a side. Prompts about the numerical identification of the sides have already been placed upon the screen by PROCdisplay:

```
500 REM Show directions of sides
510 PRINT TAB(0,5) "Directions: 1-Up, 2-Right,"
520 PRINT TAB(12,6) "3-Down, 4-Left."
```

A second REPEAT-UNTIL loop assigns the user's selection to the variable S. The loop repeats until S has an integral value in the range 1-4:

```
630     REM Check side in range
640     REPEAT
650       INPUT TAB(0,3) "Select side, 1 - 4 " S
660     UNTIL S>0 AND S<5 AND S=INT S
```

At this point a box will have been identified by the choice of B and side selected, S. However, it is important that the user does not attempt to add a side which has already been placed on the display. The input routine of PROCplayer is therefore error-trapped to prevent this. The outer REPEAT-UNTIL loop between lines 570 and 670 repeats the entire selection process until the relevant location in the SIDE array is zero. This indicates that unjoined dots have been chosen:

```
560 REM Outer loop checks side absent
570 REPEAT

[Code as above]

670 UNTIL SIDE(B,S)=0
```

The procedure finally assigns a value of 80, the ASCII value for a capital P (for Player), to the variable M and then calls PROCfill.

Adding the new side

One of the functions performed by PROCfill is updating the box chosen by the user. This involves altering the BOX and SIDE array locations for that box. BOX(B) is the relevant value which has to be increased by 1 to show that the box now has an additional side. Similarly SIDE(B,S) is the side chosen and so this location must be changed from 0 to 1:

```
1030 REM Update box array
1040 BOX(B)=BOX(B)+1
1050 REM Update side array
1060 SIDE(B,S)=1
```

Updating the box also involves drawing the line between the two relevant dots on the display. This side will be located with respect to the text coordinates of the letter in the box. These coordinates are X(B), Y(B). The position for the new side will be one character above, to the right, beneath or to the left of this central position. Which of these is the appropriate place depends upon the value of S.

The method adopted for allowing S to control a shift of one position away from the letter is to have two further arrays, DX(4), DY(4) which hold coordinate increments read from data:

```
260 REM Side increments
270 DIM DX(4), DIM DY(4)
280 FOR I=1 TO 4
290   READ DX(I), DY(I)
300 NEXT I

1430 REM Data for side increments
1440 DATA 0,-1,1,0,0,1,-1,0
```

A Game of Logic 225

Adding DX(S) and DY(S) to the letter's coordinates will then identify the side's location as X(B)+DX(S), Y(B)+DY(S). The character to use for the new side will also depend on the value of S. If S is odd the character is added above or below the letter and so must be CHR$ 45 – a horizontal line. Alternatively if S is even the character is added to the left or right of the central letter and so therefore has to be a vertical line, or CHR$ 124. The overall code is:

```
1160 REM Show new side
1170 REM Select appropriate character
1180 IF S MOD 2 = 1 THEN C=45 ELSE C=124
1190 REM Place side at location
1200 PRINT TAB(X(B)+DX(S),Y(B)+DY(S)) CHR$ C
```

Another role for PROCfill is deciding if the new side has led to a box being won. This will happen when BOX(B) is 4. The variable W records which box is won:

```
1210 IF BOX(B)=4 THEN W=B : PROCwin
```

Updating the adjacent box

It is essential that the adjacent box which is affected by the addition of a new side is also updated. This is done by a set of four conditions in PROCfill which identify the number of the neighbouring box, NB, and the number of its common side, NS.

For example if a side is being added to the top of box B, then the neighbouring box is B-8 and its common side is 3. A further complication is the fact that boxes along the top row cannot have neighbouring boxes above them, with similar restrictions on the other boxes along the perimeter of the display. Working out the details of the conditional statements gives:

```
1080 REM Update top box
1090 IF S=1 AND B>8 THEN NB=-8 : NS=3 : PROCnext_box
1100 REM Update right box
1110 IF S=2 AND B MOD 8 <> 0 THEN NB=1 : NS=4 :
         PROCnext_box
1120 REM Update bottom box
1130 IF S=3 AND B<17 THEN NB=8 : NS=1 : PROCnext_box
1140 REM Update left box
1150 IF S=4 AND B<>1 AND B<>9 AND B<>17 THEN NB=-1
        : NS=2 : PROCnext_box
```

Once values are acquired for NB and NS, PROCnext_box can update the BOX and SIDE array values for the adjacent box:

```
1250 REM Update box array
1260 BOX(B+NB)=BOX(B+NB)+1
1270 REM Update side array
1280 SIDE(B+NB,NS)=1
```

The machine's strategy

The Notepad also has to choose a box and a side to complete for this box. PROCmachine does this in two stages. First it selects a value for B to avoid any box with two sides. Such a choice would create a box with three sides. This could be won by the user immediately afterwards. Two sided boxes are avoided by this code:

```
740 REM Avoid losing box
750 REPEAT
760    B=RND(24)
770 UNTIL BOX(B)<>2
```

Immediately after this the Notepad attempts to find a better box. This will be one with three sides filled. If it fails to find one, it will default to its previous choice:

```
780 REM Seek winning box
790 FOR I=1 TO 24
800    IF BOX(I)=3 THEN B=I
810 NEXT I
```

Having found a box, an empty side is located by the code:

```
820 REM Select side
830 FOR I=1 TO 4
840    IF SIDE(B,I)=0 THEN S=I
850 NEXT I
```

The Notepad then declares its choice:

```
870 REM Indicate machine's move
880 VDU7
890 PRINT TAB(0,1) "Computer makes move"
900 PRINT TAB(0,3) "Box is " CHR$(B+64)
    " - Side is "; S.
```

PROCmachine now gives a value of 78, the ASCII value for a capital N (for Notepad), to the variable M and calls PROCfill. The sequence of events is then just as before.

Winning a box

A BOX value of 4 prompts a call to PROCwin. This prints the appropriate letter on to the box, adjusts the score and permits an extra move:

```
1330 REM Indicate box is won
1340 PRINT TAB(X(W),Y(W)) CHR$ M
1350 REM Update score
1360 IF M=80 THEN SP=SP+1 ELSE SM=SM+1
1370 PRINT TAB(83,1); SP
1380 PRINT TAB(84,2); SM
1390 REM Award extra move
1400 IF M=80 THEN PROCplayer ELSE PROCmachine
```

The Tangram Puzzle

The last program developed in this book is based upon a traditional puzzle. The Tangram game comes from China and is very ancient. Books describing it date from the early 19th century and the puzzle itself probably goes back much further into an unrecorded history. It became popular in the West last century and periodically resurfaces as a craze. Martin Gardner's column in the *Scientific American* did much to encourage new enthusiasts in the 1950s, as did his book *More Mathematical Puzzles and Diversions* (Penguin: 1961, reprinted 1990). Joost Elffers' *Tangram: The Ancient Chinese Shapes Game* is a very thorough compendium of Tangram puzzles.

Tangram is the western name, probably invented by a toy manufacturer in the mid 19th century. The Chinese name, ch'i ch'ae pan, means 'Seven-Board of Cunning' and reflects the seven pieces of the game, cut from a square as shown in this diagram:

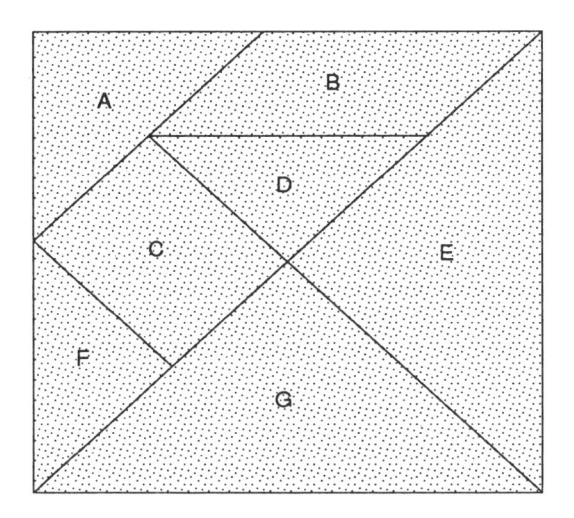

The seven pieces of the Tangram puzzle

The pieces here have been labelled A to G for convenience. Tangram books do not identify the separate pieces, because this would remove the challenge of puzzling out the different Tangram pictures.

The pieces can be rearranged to form stylised shapes. These can resemble people, animals, buildings or anything the player can devise. They can also generate regular geometric forms. The challenge is to recreate a pattern using just the outline of the shape as a guide. For this you need to be set a problem by a fellow practitioner, or work from a book of Tangram puzzles. Some examples are given below. These could be used as practice exercises on the Amstrad Notepad once the program, Tangrams, has been entered.

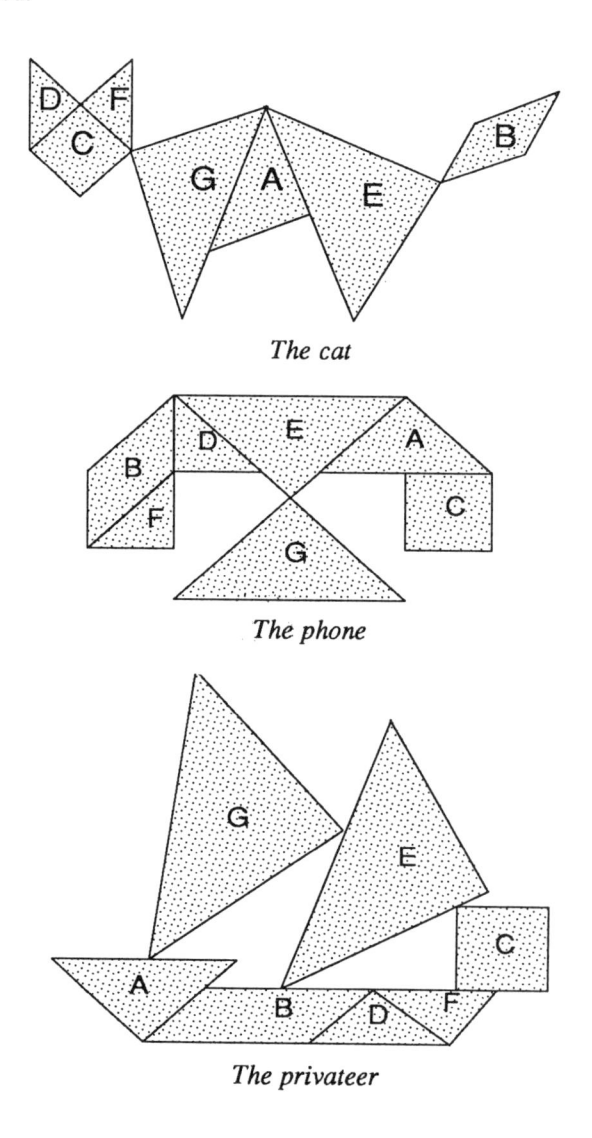

The cat

The phone

The privateer

The Tangram Puzzle

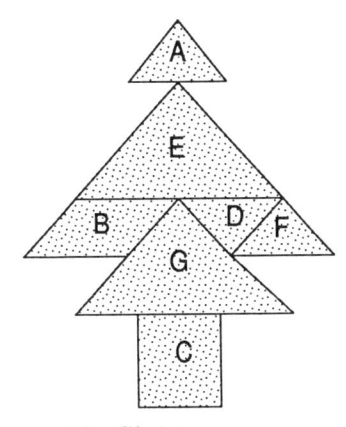

The Christmas tree

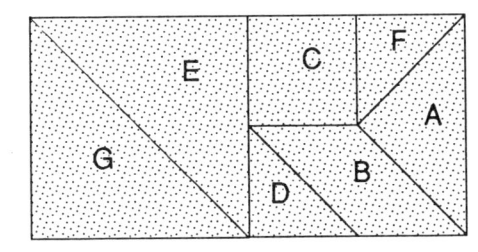

The rectangle

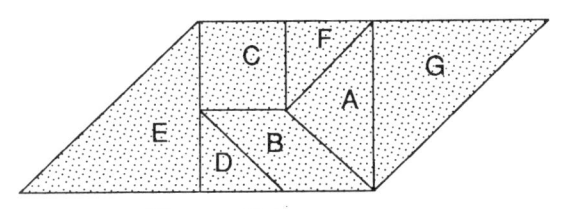

The parallelogram

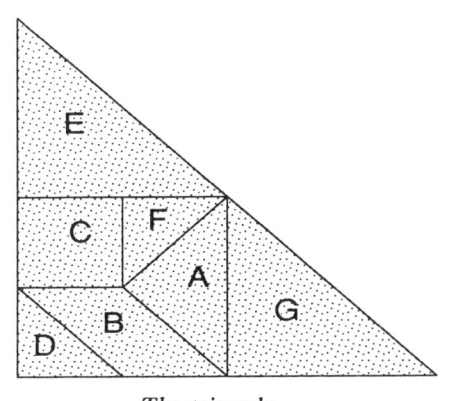

The triangle

Undoubtedly the shapes generated by the Tangram pieces can have the same simplicity and elegance as observed in Origami and oriental architecture. Although in the West Tangram patterns can have only this aesthetic appeal, in traditional Chinese games linguistic meanings may also be conveyed by the shapes produced. The nearest Europeans can come to this is reproducing a company logo!

In the program a complete set of Tangram pieces is displayed on the Notepad's screen. These, although small, can be moved about the display or rotated to fit against one another. Any pattern which you could make with a set of pieces can also be arranged on the screen. (Tangrams can become an obsessive interest, so possibly this program could be the 1990s' equivalent of Space Invaders . . .)

Program listing – TANGRAMS

```
10 REM TANGRAMS
20 REM Control routine
30 PROCinit
40 PROCdisplay
50 REPEAT
60    PROCkeypress
70    IF N<>0 THEN D=7 : PROCshape(N,D)
80    PROCtransform(N)
90    IF N<>0 THEN D=5 : PROCshape(N,D)
100 UNTIL CH=8
110 CLS
120 PRINT "Program over"
130 END
140 REM   150 DEF PROCinit
160 REM Initialise standard configuration
170 DIM A(7,9), B(7,9), C(7,9)
180 FOR I=1 TO 7
190    FOR J=1 TO 9
200       READ A(I,J)
210       C(I,J)=A(I,J)
220       IF J<>1 THEN C(I,J)=C(I,J)*4
230    NEXT J
240 NEXT I
250 REM Initialise transformation array
260 DIM T(7,3)
270 FOR I=1 TO 7
280    T(I,1)=250
290    T(I,2)=20
300 NEXT I
310 REM Initialise hot keys
320 DIM K(14)
330 FOR I=1 TO 14
340    READ K(I)
350 NEXT I
360 REM Initialise chosen shape
370 N=0
380 ENDPROC
390 REM
400 DEF PROCdisplay
410 CLS
420 REM Draw standard configuration
430 FOR S=1 TO 7
440    PROCshape(S,5)
450    PROCtransform(S)
460 NEXT S
470 REM Add labels
```

The Tangram Puzzle

```
 480 FOR I=1 TO 7
 490   READ X,Y
 500   PRINT TAB(X,Y) CHR$ (I+64)
 510 NEXT I
 520 PRINT TAB(11,0) "TANGRAMS"
 530 ENDPROC
 540 REM
 550 DEF PROCkeypress
 560 REM Detect keypress
 570 REPEAT
 580   F=0
 590   CH=0
 600   K=GET
 610   FOR I=1 TO 14
 620     IF K=K(I) THEN F=1 : CH=I
 630   NEXT I
 640 UNTIL F=1
 650 REM Select tangram piece
 660 IF CH<8 THEN N=CH
 670 REM Adjust piece's coordinates
 680 IF N<>0 AND CH>10 THEN T(N,2+(CH>12))
     =T(N,2+(CH>12))+10*(CH MOD 2 -.5)
 690 REM Adjust piece's orientation
 700 IF N<>0 AND (CH=9 OR CH=10) THEN
     T(N,3)=T(N,3)+((CH=9)+.5)*PI/9
 710 ENDPROC
 720 REM
 730 DEF PROCshape(N,D)
 740 LOCAL I
 750 MOVE C(N,2),C(N,3)
 760 FOR I=1 TO C(N,1)
 770   PLOT D,C(N,2*I+2),C(N,2*I+3)
 780 NEXT I
 790 PLOT D,C(N,2),C(N,3)
 800 ENDPROC
 810 REM
 820 DEF PROCtransform(N)
 830 REM Rotate shape
 840 FOR I=2 TO 9
 850   IF I MOD 2=0 THEN B(N,I)=A(N,I)*COS(T(N,3))
       -A(N,I+1)*SIN(T(N,3))
 860   IF I MOD 2<>0 THEN B(N,I)=A(N,I-1)*SIN(T(N,3))
       +A(N,I)*COS(T(N,3))
 870 NEXT I
 880 REM Translate shape
 890 FOR I=2 TO 9
 900   IF I MOD 2=0 THEN C(N,I)=B(N,I)+T(N,I) ELSE
       C(N,I)=B(N,I)+T(N,2)
 910 NEXT I
 920 ENDPROC
 930 REM
 940 REM Data for standard configuration of tangrams
 950 DATA 2,0,7,0,15,7,15,0,0
 960 DATA 3,3,11,7,15,15,15,11,11
 970 DATA 3,0,7,3,11,7,7,3,3
 980 DATA 2,3,11,11,11,7,7,0,0
 990 DATA 2,7,7,15,15,15,0,0,0
1000 DATA 2,0,0,0,7,3,3,0,0
1010 DATA 2,0,0,7,7,15,0,0,0
1020 REM
1030 REM Data for hot keys
1040 DATA 65,66,67,68,69,70,71,81
1050 DATA 88,90,240,241,243,242
1060 REM
1070 REM Data for labels
1080 DATA 1,1,5,1,2,4,5,3,8,4,1,6,5,6
```

A data structure for the tangram pieces

The basic Tangram pattern is defined for the program using a square with sides 16 pixels long. The square is divided to create the pattern of the seven pieces. Then all the vertices for the pieces are calculated to the nearest whole number of pixels. This is illustrated on the diagram:

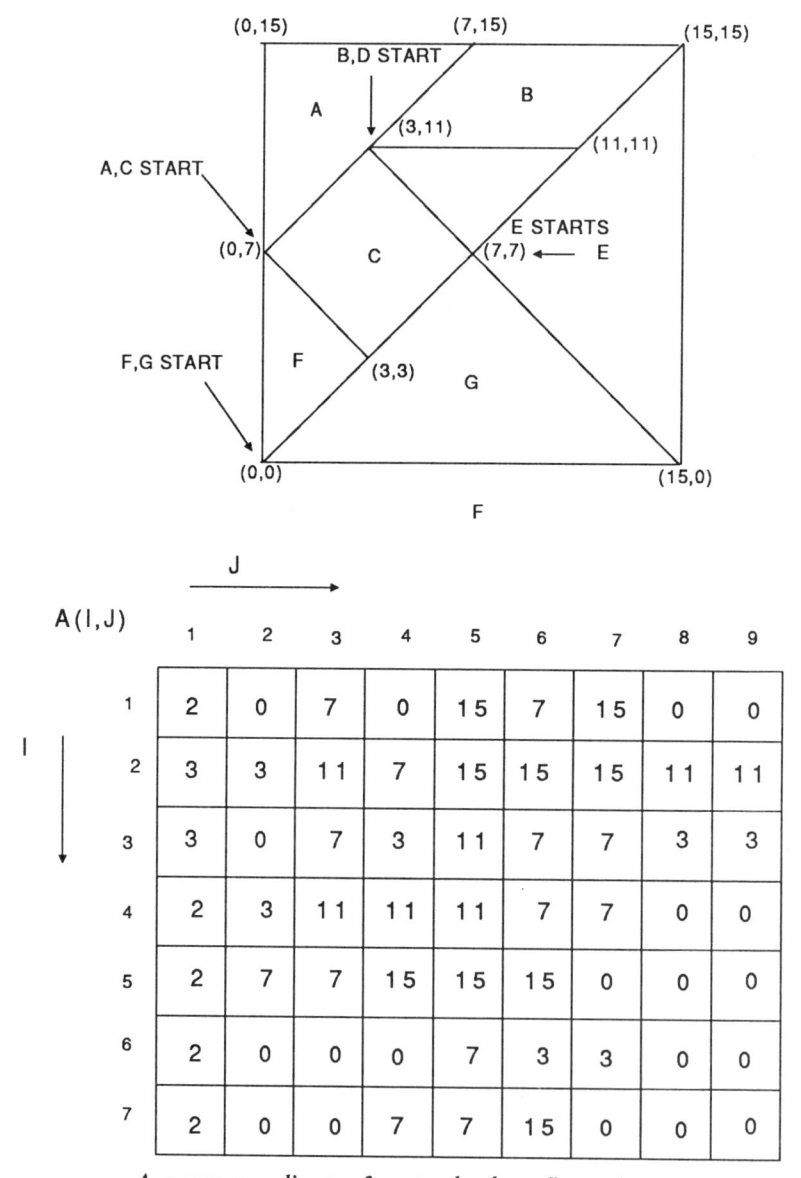

A(I,J)	1	2	3	4	5	6	7	8	9
1	2	0	7	0	15	7	15	0	0
2	3	3	11	7	15	15	15	11	11
3	3	0	7	3	11	7	7	3	3
4	2	3	11	11	11	7	7	0	0
5	2	7	7	15	15	15	0	0	0
6	2	0	0	0	7	3	3	0	0
7	2	0	0	7	7	15	0	0	0

A-array coordinates for standard configuration

For example, piece A has vertices at (0,7), (0,15) and (7,15). A convenient data structure has to be devised which will store the coordinates for all the pieces in a regular way and allow them to be drawn by the same procedure. A data structure cannot really be decided, of course, until an algorithm for drawing any of the Tangram pieces has been established.

One algorithm that might be considered would involve using a FOR-NEXT loop that repeated for the number of sides possessed by the shape. A line would be drawn to each a set of points stored in an array in an appropriate order. This algorithm requires an initial move to one of the points. However, on reflection a slightly more elegant drawing sequence, involving a loop which repeats one time fewer, is the following:
    1. Move to the initial vertex of the piece
    2. Draw a line to the next vertex
    3. Repeat 2 until no new vertices are left
    4. Draw a line to the initial vertex.

The coordinates for each Tangram piece are therefore stored in a sequence which reflects this method. The table of values beneath the diagram shows all the data required. The top row is the coordinate information for piece A, the second row the data for piece B, with the table extending down to piece G at row 7.

The process of drawing can be illustrated with piece C. The first number in the third row is 3, which indicates that the loop drawing sides repeats three times. The pair of numbers that follow in the second and third columns of the table show that the initial move is to point (0,7), as can be seen on the diagram. The loop will then draw to the next three pairs of coordinates, adding lines to points (3,11), (7,7) and (3,3). Finally a line will be drawn to the initial point again, (0,7). On the diagram it will be clear that this has produced the small distinctive diamond shape of piece C.

On the table some locations will be left blank. This happens with the last two columns for all of the triangular pieces. Zeros are inserted into the data at these places to avoid an *Out of data* error when the program loads the data into its array.

The content of the table is stored as data statements at the end of the program. The term 'standard configuration' for the coordinates is used to emphasise the fact that during the progress of the program pieces will move about the screen, and rotate, and that therefore other sets of coordinates will also be involved:

```
 940 REM Data for standard configuration of tangrams
 950 DATA 2,0,7,0,15,7,15,0,0
 960 DATA 3,3,11,7,15,15,15,11,11
 970 DATA 3,0,7,3,11,7,7,3,3
 980 DATA 2,3,11,11,11,7,7,0,0
 990 DATA 2,7,7,15,15,15,0,0,0
1000 DATA 2,0,0,0,7,3,3,0,0
1010 DATA 2,0,0,7,7,15,0,0,0
```

Using three arrays

This data will be placed into an array, A(7,9) by PROCinit. However, one array is not sufficient for the entire operation of the program. As the pieces are moved about the screen their coordinates change and so a second array is needed to store the current coordinates, in contrast with the values in the A array. This array is C(7,9) and is the one used when the pieces are drawn. A third array is also required. This is used for intermediate storage locations when the C array values are being calculated from those in the A array. All three arrays are dimensioned in the same statement:

```
DIM A(7,9), B(7,9), C(7,9)
```

The array locations in B(7,9) are left as zero by PROCinit. Two nested loops are used to read the data into the A(7,9) array. Throughout the execution of the program this array is used as a 'reference point' for the calculation of the current C(7,9) array values. The first time that anything is drawn using the C array is when the initial screen display is produced. This shows the Tangram pieces four times the size they are on the 16 X 16 pixels square on which they are defined. The C locations are therefore initially assigned four times the value of the A locations, with the exception of those locations corresponding to the first column of the data table. The numbers here must be left the same because they are related to the number of sides of each piece and this obviously is the same whatever size the piece is drawn. The code in PROCinit which establishes the three arrays is:

```
160 REM Initialise coordinate arrays
170 DIM A(7,9), B(7,9), C(7,9)
180 FOR I=1 TO 7
190   FOR J=1 TO 9
200     READ A(I,J)
210     C(I,J)=A(I,J)
220     IF J<>1 THEN C(I,J)=C(I,J)*4
230   NEXT J
240 NEXT I
```

Drawing a Tangram piece

The procedure which draws each piece is PROCshape(N,D). The first of the two parameters, N, identifies which of the seven is to be drawn. The second parameter, D, is assigned either of two possible values. When D is 5 the piece is drawn on the screen in 'black'. When D is 7 it is drawn in white. A value of 7 can be used to erase a previously drawn piece by overwriting in white. This is an essential role for PROCshape and permits animation to take place.

The Nth piece is constructed according to the algorithm described above. First the graphics cursor is moved to the initial vertex of the shape. The coordinates of this point are in the second and third columns of the table. Using the locations of the C array, this is the point C(N,2), C(N,3) and so the statement required is:

```
MOVE C(N,2),C(N,3)
```

A loop then draws lines to successive vertices, using PLOT with a value of D which will either draw a line or erase an earlier one. The range of the loop is determined by the first array location for the Nth piece, or C(N,1). The coordinates of the vertices to which lines are drawn have to be determined with care. The X-coordinate of the first vertex can be seen to be in the fourth column of the table. The Y-coordinate is in the fifth column. The sequence of values for all possible vertices is:

	Loop variable, I	X-coord's location	Y-coord's location
1st vertex	1	4	5
2nd vertex	2	6	7
3rd vertex	3	8	9

The general expression giving the location of the X-coordinate of the Ith vertex can be seen to be 2*I+2. For the Y-coordinate the expression is 2*I+3. The Ith vertex therefore has the coordinates C(N,2*I+2), C(N,2*I+3). These are the values that need to be given to PLOT D in the loop.

After the loop, the final line has to be drawn back to the starting point, C(N,2), C(N,3). This is again done by PLOT D. The entire code for PROCshape(N,D) is:

```
730 DEF PROCshape(N,D)
740 LOCAL I
750 MOVE C(N,2),C(N,3)
760 FOR I=1 TO C(N,1)
770    PLOT D,C(N,2*I+2),C(N,2*I+3)
780 NEXT I
790 PLOT D,C(N,2),C(N,3)
800 ENDPROC
```

The initial display

When the program is first run, PROCdisplay calls PROCshape(N,D) seven times to place all the Tangram pieces on the left hand side of the screen. They are viewed here large enough to fill the entire height of the Notepad's display. The enlarged values have previously been placed in the C array by PROCinit. Note that PROCtransform is called to readjust the C array values immediately after each piece is drawn. This is because the next time any piece is displayed it will be the smaller size and in the middle of the display:

```
420 REM Draw standard configuration
430 FOR S=1 TO 7
440    PROCshape(S,5)
450    PROCtransform(S)
460 NEXT S
```

The large set of Tangram pieces remains on the screen throughout the execution of the program. They are used as a key to help identify the individual pieces. This is necessary because, as an inevitable result of the small size of the Notepad's screen, the actual shapes which are moved about the display are far too small to label. Instead, the letters A-G are placed on the large set of pieces. This could be done by seven separate PRINT TAB statements (using text coordinates discovered by experiment) like this:

```
PRINT TAB(1,1) "A"
PRINT TAB(5,1) "B"
PRINT TAB(2,4) "C"
PRINT TAB(5,3) "D"
PRINT TAB(1,6) "F"
PRINT TAB(5,6) "G"
```

This method is feasible, but whenever repeated statements are used in a program it is more interesting to find a loop that will do the work! First, the seven pairs of text coordinates are placed into a data statement:

```
1070 REM Data for labels
1080 DATA 1,1,5,1,2,4,5,3,8,4,1,6,5,6
```

Then a FOR-NEXT loop repeats seven times, reading a pair of coordinates and placing them in a PRINT TAB statement. If the letter to be placed on the screen had been stored as data, together with the coordinates, a loop like this could have been used to add the letters to the display.

```
FOR I=1 TO 7   READ A$,X,Y
  PRINT TAB(X,Y) A$
NEXT I
```

This loop would need the data:

```
DATA A,1,1,B,5,1,C,2,4,D,5,3,E,8,4,F,1,6,G,5,6
```

There is no need to adopt this approach. It is simpler to remember that letters can be identified by their ASCII codes. Those of the sequence A-G begin at 65. As the loop variable, I, starts at 1 all that has to be done is to add 64 to the I value to give the ASCII code of each letter. The letters can then be printed as CHR$ (I+64). The final code used in the program is:

```
470 REM Add labels
480 FOR I=1 TO 7
490    READ X,Y
500    PRINT TAB(X,Y) CHR$ (I+64)
510 NEXT I
```

PROCdisplay ends with a single print statement placing the name TANGRAMS beside the set of large pieces:

```
520 PRINT TAB(11,0) "TANGRAMS"
```

A further refinement here would be to add further text explaining which keys control the program. This would, indeed, match the 'User friendly' logo stamped across the Amstrad Notepad. It is, though, left as an additional exercise for the programmer!

Obeying the keyboard

After PROCdisplay has placed the large set of Tangram pieces on the display and added labels to them, the control routine enters a REPEAT-UNTIL loop between lines 50-100. This permits the user to select a particular piece and move it about the screen. A large number of keys are employed in order to permit the level of control required. Letters A to G are needed initially so that the user can select a piece to move. They are required again whenever he or she changes to any other of the seven pieces. The four cursor keys are also employed to allow the piece to be moved up and down or left and right. Two further keys, X and Z , allow the selected piece to be rotated clockwise or anti-clockwise. Finally, pressing Q allows the program to end.

The need to monitor constantly 14 separate hot-keys means that the method described in Chapter 5 is adopted. The ASCII values of the keys are stored in an array and the content of this array scanned in a FOR-NEXT loop against the current key pressed. First, the ASCII values are placed into data statements at the end of the program:

```
1030 REM Data for hot keys
1040 DATA 65,66,67,68,69,70,71,81
1050 DATA 88,90,240,241,243,242
```

These are then read into an array, K(14), in PROCinit:

```
310 REM Initialise hot keys
320 DIM K(14)
330 FOR I=1 TO 14
340    READ K(I)
350 NEXT I
```

The K(14) array locations are then used in a procedure, PROCkeypress, repeatedly called by the program's control routine to determine whether the current key selected is an appropriate choice. The ASCII value of the keypress is assigned by GET to the variable K. A FOR-NEXT loop then compares K with the array. If a match is found, the value of the loop variable is assigned to CH. A non-zero value for CH permits the key monitoring routine to end and program execution to continue:

```
560 REM Detect keypress
570 REPEAT
580    CH=0
590    REM Scan keys
600    K=GET
610    FOR I=1 TO 14
620       IF K=K(I) THEN CH=I
630    NEXT I
640 UNTIL CH<>0
```

CH is used to select the appropriate action that has to be taken next. This is determined by the values originally placed in the data statements. For example if CH is 1, the key pressed must have been A, because 65 is the first item of data at line 1040. A value of 1 for CH therefore means that Tangram piece A must be selected.

Similarly the action to be taken for each of the 14 possible values for CH is directly related to the data items. A list of the 14 actions is:

Value of CH	Action
1	Select piece A
2	Select piece B
3	Select piece C
4	Select piece D
5	Select piece E
6	Select piece F
7	Select piece G
8	Exit program
9	Rotate clockwise
10	Rotate anti-clockwise
11	Move up
12	Move down
13	Move right
14	Move left

Selecting a tangram piece

As already stated above in *Drawing a Tangram piece*, the variable N is used to identify the current piece to be moved. The initial value of this will be 0 and it changes to the range 1-7 after the user has selected a piece by pressing one of the keys A-G.

In BBC BASIC, as implemented on other machines like the Acorn Archimedes family of computers, the BBC Micro or the Cambridge Z88, any variable is assumed to have the value zero until the programmer assigns some other value to it. BBC BASIC does not produce an 'undefined variable' error if reference is suddenly made to a new variable which has not previously been initialised. However, this does seem to be rather poor programming practice and would not be tolerated in other computer languages. Most of these insist that variables are formally introduced before they start work in a program. In accordance with this, the initial value of N is established in PROCinit:

```
360 REM Initialise chosen shape
370 N=0
```

As soon as the program is run and the user has selected a key in the range A-G, the CH value then acquired is assigned to N. At that point a Tangram piece has been formally chosen and recognised by the program:

```
650 REM Select tangram piece
660 IF CH<8 THEN N=CH
```

The Tangram Puzzle

Preserving the information

In deciding the algorithms to employ in this program, an important decision is needed about the way in which coordinate information for each piece is preserved as the shapes are moved about the display. One approach would be to have a set of coordinates for each piece stored in a single two dimensional array. Each time the user moved a piece on the screen, mathematical calculations would be carried out, according to the keys pressed, and the relevant array values updated. The piece would then be redrawn according to these array values.

The problem according to this method is that successive copies of the coordinate data are constantly being made. Every time a piece 'translates' (moves) on the display, or rotates, its coordinates have been recalculated from their previous values. These values in turn are the result of recalculating from the values preceding them. The process of calculation itself inevitably introduces error. Computers do not have total accuracy but only an ability to deal the best they can with numbers within a certain range. Rounding and approximation becomes unavoidable. After successive manipulation of the same data it will become hopelessly distorted. This is like the children's party game where a message is whispered from person to person and becomes randomly translated. Similarly faxing copies of faxes from one laboratory to another around the world has been shown to be less than reliable.

To avoid the problem of pieces losing their shape and geometrical interest, they are recalculated after each move according to a different algorithm. A fresh calculation is made for the new position beginning each time with the original coordinate data. This initial data, the standard configuration, is stored in the A(7,9) array. The newly calculated coordinates are placed in the C(7,9) array, ready to be used in PROCshape(N,D). The transition from the A array values to the C array values is made, in PROC transform(N), with the help of a 'transform' array, T(7,3), which stores the change in X-coordinate, Y-coordinate and angle of orientation for each piece.

Representing the transformation

This further array, T(7,3) is depicted in the table on the next page. Each row of the table represents one of the Tangram pieces, A-G. The first column holds the current X-displacement of a piece from the standard configuration held in the A array. The second holds the Y-displacement. The third column stores the angle of rotation of the piece away from the orientation shown on the large set of pieces constantly displayed on the left of the screen. The angle of rotation is not stored in degrees, but in radians.

The array is initialised in PROCinit and given location values that will move any of the Tangram pieces, when first selected, to the centre of the screen and away from the diagram on the left. The centre is where they can be reassembled into the different possible patterns. All the pieces are assigned the same X-displacement of 250 pixels and Y-displacement of 20 pixels. These values are placed into the T array locations identified by a 1 or a 2 for the second subscript. The third array location for each piece is left as zero because none of the pieces is rotated until the user makes this choice:

```
250 REM Initialise transformation array
260 DIM T(7,3)
270 FOR I=1 TO 7
280    T(I,1)=250
290    T(I,2)=20
300 NEXT I
```

	x - displacement	y - displacement	Rotation
A	T(1,1)	T(1,2)	T(1,3)
B	T(2,1)	T(2,2)	T(2,3)
C	T(3,1)	T(3,2)	T(3,3)
D	T(4,1)	T(4,2)	T(4,3)
E	T(5,1)	T(5,2)	T(5,3)
F	T(6,1)	T(6,2)	T(6,3)
G	T(7,1)	T(7,2)	T(7,3)

Transformation array

Altering the tangram coordinates

New coordinates and angles of rotation have to be placed into the T array according to the value obtained for CH. First it will be shown how the cursor keys, returning CH values of 11, 12, 13 or 14, can adjust the X and Y coordinates of a selected piece.

The number of pixels for each increment to the coordinates is chosen to be 5. This could, of course, be adjusted by the user if the pieces were to be moved by a greater or lesser amount. Using five pixels for the moves, and remembering that a subscript of 1 in the T array refers to the X-coordinate and 2 to the Y-coordinate, leads to this interpretation of the CH value:

The Tangram Puzzle 241

Value of CH	Action
11	Move up......Increase T(N,2) by 5
12	Move down....Decrease T(N,2) by 5
13	Move right...Increase T(N,1) by 5
14	Move left....Decrease T(N,1) by 5

One way in which this could be coded into BBC BASIC for the Notepad would be:

```
IF CH=11 THEN T(N,2)=T(N,2)+5
IF CH=12 THEN T(N,2)=T(N,2)-5
IF CH=13 THEN T(N,1)=T(N,2)+5
IF CH=14 THEN T(N,1)=T(N,2)-5
```

However, these four conditions can be reduced to just one, if Boolean values are used as explained in Chapter 2.

Simplifying with a Boolean expression

First a Boolean expression is devised which will generate the correct T array subscript from the value of CH. This means that when CH is 11 or 12 the expression must give 2 for the subscript. When CH is 13 or 14 the expression must lead to a subscript of 1. A little thought shows that the expression (CH>12) will be evaluated as 0 when CH is 11 or 12 and as -1 for CH values of 13 or 14. Adding 2 to this expression will give the right value for the subscript. This can be shown as a table:

Value of CH	Truth value of (CH>12)	Evaluated in BASIC	Value of 2+(CH>12)
11	False	0	2
12	False	0	2
13	True	-1	1
14	True	-1	1

The expression will therefore correctly identify the required T array location as T(N,2+(CH>12)).

Using MOD in the condition

Next the increment of plus or minus 5 must also be related to the value of CH. When CH is 11 or 13 the increment must be positive. When CH is 12 or 14 it must be negative. The sign of the increment clearly depends on whether CH is odd or even. This is an obvious indication that the expression must involve CH MOD 2. As this is the remainder when CH is divided by 2, it will be 1 for odd numbers and 0 for even. Subtracting 0.5 will lead to 0.5 for odd and -0.5 for even. All that is then required in order to generate the increment of 5 or -5 is to multiply by 10. The arithmetic is summarised on this table:

CH	CH MOD 2	CH MOD 2 – 0.5	10 * (CH MOD 2 – 0.5)
11	1	0.5	5
12	0	-0.5	-5
13	1	0.5	5
14	0	-0.5	-5

Assembling a complex condition

The two expressions just derived have to be placed into a final condition which will adjust the Tangram piece's coordinates. Two further conditions have to be incorporated. The reasoning above has assumed that CH is in the range 11-14. However, it might be anywhere in the range 1-14. Therefore the final condition must only be invoked if CH>10. In addition there is the possibility that a cursor key is pressed at the beginning of the program before a piece has been chosen. In this situation N will be zero and increments will be placed in invalid (though existing) zeroth array locations. The problem is avoided by adding a further condition, N<>0, to the final BASIC code. This becomes:

```
670 REM Adjust piece's coordinates
680 IF N<>0 AND CH>10 THEN T(N,2+(CH>12))=
    T(N,2+(CH>12)) +10*(CH MOD 2 -0.5)
```

This single condition replaces the four separate conditions shown earlier. It is often possible to design more elegant code, like this, if a regularity appears in the numerical values held in individual expressions. It is rather like the challenge of reducing a display problem to a series of FOR-NEXT loops. Practice makes it easier to simplify arithmetic into a more condensed code.

Using a Boolean expression to adjust the orientation

PROCkeypress also adjusts the angle of the displayed Tangram piece. A CH value of 9 rotates the piece clockwise and a value of 10 rotates it anti-clockwise. PROCkeypress has to update the third location in the T array, or T(N,3) for the Nth piece. When X is pressed, making CH equal to 9, the value of T(N,3) must decrease. When Z is pressed, and CH is 10, the value of T(N,3) must increase. The angle chosen for the change in orientation is 10 degrees. As 360 degrees is 2 * PI radians, the increment for T(N,3) must be plus or minus PI/18 radians. A condition which would adjust the T array is therefore:

```
IF CH=9 THEN T(N,3) = T(N,3) - PI/18
    ELSE T(N,3) = T(N,3) + PI/18
```

As before a lengthy piece of code like this can be compacted into a shorter condition by using a Boolean expression. If CH is 9, the expression must evaluate as -1. If CH is 10, the expression yields 1. From the table below it can be seen that the required expression is 2*((CH=9)+0.5):

CH	(CH=9)	Value	(CH=9) + 0.5	2*((CH=9) + 0.5)
9	True	-1	-0.5	-1
10	False	0	0.5	1

This expression can therefore be used to increment the value of T(N,3) and will automatically add or subtract, according to the value of CH. It has to be multiplied by the size of the angle, PI/18 radians. The fraction 2/18 becomes 1/9 to give:

```
T(N,3)=T(N,3)+((CH=9)+0.5)*PI/9
```

As before, further conditions have to be added to prevent the T array being adjusted when no tangram piece has been selected and to limit the Boolean expression to the situation where CH is only either 9 or 10:

```
690 REM Adjust piece's orientation
700 IF N<>0 AND (CH=9 OR CH=10) THEN
    T(N,3)=T(N,3)+((CH=9)+0.5)*PI/9
```

The role of the transformation procedure

PROCkeypress records the user's choice of translation and rotation of a chosen piece and places new values in the T array to represent how the display should now appear. It does not affect the screen display itself, or adjust the values in the C array which will be needed to draw the piece in its new position.

The updating of the C array is tackled by PROCtransform(N). This procedure takes the T array modifications of X- and Y-coordinates for the shape and its angle of orientation, and applies them to the standard configuration stored in the A array. First PROCtransform(N) rotates the Tangram piece and stores its new coordinates in the temporary array, B(7,9). Then it displaces these coordinates in X- and Y-directions and places the further set of coordinates in the C array. Only then can the piece be redrawn on the display.

Before explaining how the B array values are generated by the rotation, some mathematics is developed.

The mathematics of a rotation

The most complicated part of the Tangrams program is probably the calculations involved in working out the way the coordinate values are altered when a rotation is selected. For those who loathe sines and cosines, this section can be skipped and the two vital equations at the end taken on trust. Those who do follow the argument are implored to accept the laboured approach and not wonder why a brief matrix solution is not presented instead.

This diagram, combined with some basic trigonometry, should help:

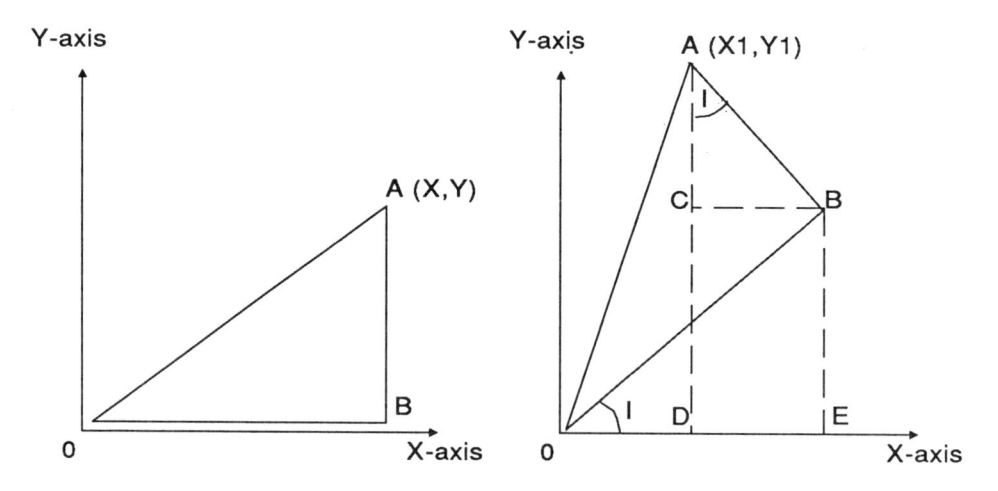

Coordinates transformed by rotation

On the left a pair of coordinate axes are shown. Where they cross, the origin of the coordinate frame, is point O. The triangle AOB has been drawn to show explicitly the coordinates, (X,Y), of a point at A. The side OA of the triangle is equal to X. The side AB is equal to Y.

On the right is the same triangle, AOB. Now it has been rotated anti-clockwise through an angle, I. (Radian measure is used in the program, but for the purpose of this argument the units for the rotation are unimportant.) The coordinates of point A after this rotation have become (X1,Y1). The task is to find equations that will give the value of X1 and Y1 in terms of the original coordinates, X and Y, and the angle of rotation, I. Once this has been achieved, the same equations can be applied to the relevant locations in the A and T arrays to derive the current values needed in the C array.

To achieve these equations, some extra lines have to be added to the diagram. Perpendicular lines are drawn from points A and B to the X-axis, meeting it at the new points D and E. A third line is drawn from point B, perpendicular to the extra line AD. It meets it at point C. This has created a new triangle, BAC, which is 'similar' to the triangle, BOE. Although the two triangles are different sizes, they have identical angles. Importantly, the angle at A is the same as the angle at O and is equal to I.

First, an equation will be found for X1. In the diagram this is the line OD. This can be shown as a subtraction:

X1 = OD = (OE − DE)

In triangle BOE:

COS (I) = OE / OB

The Tangram Puzzle 245

This means that:

$$OE = OB * COS\ I$$

In triangle BAC:

$$SIN\ (I) = BC / AB$$

This gives the equation:

$$BC = AB * SIN\ (I)$$

However, BC is equal to DE. Therefore values for DE, and for OE, can be substituted into the original expression for X. This gives:

$$X1 = OE - DE = (OB * COS\ (I)) - (AB * SIN\ (I))$$

From the first diagram, OB = X and AB = Y. The equation for X1 becomes:

$$X1 = X * COS\ (I) - Y * SIN\ (I)$$

This is one of the two equations required for the program. Next, an equation needs to be found for Y1. In the right hand diagram:

$$Y1 = AD = (AC + CD)$$

In triangle BAC:

$$COS\ (I) = AC / AB$$

This means that:

$$AC = AB * COS\ (I)$$

In triangle BOE:

$$SIN\ (I) = BE / OB$$

Rearranging the equation gives:

$$BE = OB * SIN\ (I)$$

Since BE is equal to CD, values can be substituted into the equation for Y1:

$$Y1 = AC + CD = (AB * COS\ (I)) + (OB * SIN\ (I))$$

Again, AB = Y and OB = X, and so:

$$Y1 = Y * COS\ (I) + X * SIN\ (I)$$

This is rearranged so that X and Y are in the same order as the equation for X1:

$$Y1 = X * SIN\ (I) + Y * COS\ (I)$$

The two expressions needed in PROCtransform(N) are therefore:

$$X1 = X * COS (I) - Y * SIN (I)$$
$$Y1 = X * SIN (I) + Y * COS (I)$$

Rotating the Tangram

These two equations now have to be applied to the particular situation involved in the program. The mathematics remains the same, but the variable names become far more complicated in a way which can easily obscure the principles involved. Remember that the A array values are being rotated to give B array values. This means that all the X and Y in the equations become A locations. All the X1 and Y1 become B locations. In addition, of course, two subscripts have to be associated with every location. The angle, I, is replaced by the third location of the T array.

The first point in the A array for the Nth tangram piece is A(N,2), A(N,3). This is rotated into the point B(N,2), B(N,3). Careful substitution into the two rotation equations gives:

$$B(N,2) = A(N,2) * COS (T(N,3)) - A(N,3) * SIN (T(N,3))$$
$$B(N,3) = A(N,2) * SIN (T(N,3)) + A(N,3) * COS (T(N,3))$$

Despite the complexity of the notation, these two equations are exactly as derived above. Similarly the transformation of the second point in the A array into its rotated image in the B array is:

$$B(N,4) = A(N,4) * COS (T(N,3)) - A(N,5) * SIN (T(N,3))$$
$$B(N,5) = A(N,4) * SIN (T(N,3)) + A(N,5) * COS (T(N,3))$$

For the third point the transformation is

$$B(N,6) = A(N,6) * COS (T(N,3)) - A(N,7) * SIN (T(N,3))$$
$$B(N,7) = A(N,6) * SIN (T(N,3)) + A(N,7) * COS (T(N,3))$$

Studying these equations will show a repeated pattern. If I is used to represent the second subscripted array variable, two different equations are apparent. For even values of I the equation is:

$$B(N,I) = A(N,I) * COS (T(N,3)) - A(N,I+1) * SIN (T(N,3))$$

For odd values of I the equation is:

$$B(N,I) = A(N,I-1) * SIN (T(N,3)) + A(N,I) * COS (T(N,3))$$

At this point a generalisation has been achieved which can be coded into a FOR-NEXT loop to transform the whole of the A array. Using MOD to determine the parity (even or oddness) of I, the BASIC becomes:

```
830 REM Rotate shape
840 FOR I=2 TO 9
850   IF I MOD 2=0 THEN B(N,I)=A(N,I)*COS(T(N,3))
      -A(N,I+1)*SIN(T(N,3))
860   IF I MOD 2<>0 THEN B(N,I)=A(N,I-1)*SIN(T(N,3))
      +A(N,I)*COS(T(N,3))
870 NEXT I
```

Moving the Tangram piece

The code needed to move the piece after it has been rotated is far simpler. All the B array values are translated by the displacements in the T array to give the final C array values which can be used by PROCshape(N,D) to draw the tangram piece. The first point in the B array is B(N,2), B(N,3). This is translated into the point in the C array C(N,2), C(N,3). As X-coordinates have to be increased by T(N,1) and Y-coordinates increased by T(N,2), this gives the two equations:

C(N,2) = B(N,2) + T(N,1)

C(N,3) = B(N,3) + T(N,2)

Similarly the second point is translated by the equations:

C(N,4) = B(N,4) + T(N,1)

C(N,5) = B(N,5) + T(N,2)

Replacing the second subscripted variable again by I, this gives the general equation for even I:

C(N,I) = B(N,I) + T(N,1)

This becomes for odd I:

C(N,I) = B(N,I) + T(N,2)

A simple condition inside a FOR-NEXT loop can therefore translate all of the points:

```
880 REM Translate shape
890 FOR I=2 TO 9  900    IF I MOD 2=0 THEN
    C(N,I)=B(N,I)+T(N,I) ELSE C(N,I)=B(N,I)+T(N,2)
910 NEXT I
```

Designing Tangram patterns

The procedures that have been developed can be used now in the final program to move different pieces around the screen and investigate various patterns. A simple REPEAT-UNTIL loop in the control routine first calls PROCkeypress to allow the user to select, translate or rotate a shape. PROCshape(N,D) is employed with a D value of 7 to redraw the previous shape's position in white and thereby erase it. Then PROCtransform(N) calculates the fresh C array values. After this PROCshape(N,D) is called again with a D value of 5. This will draw the shape in its new position. The constant double calls to PROCshape(N,D), together with the alternating D values of 7 and 5, create the animation effect. Pressing Q causes a CH value of 8 which permits the program to end:

```
 50 REPEAT
 60   PROCkeypress
 70   IF N<>0 THEN D=7 : PROCshape(N,D)
 80   PROCtransform(N)
 90   IF N<>0 THEN D=5 : PROCshape(N,D)
100 UNTIL CH=8
110 CLS
120 PRINT "Program over"
130 END
```

Further development of the program

The program could be extended to include more features. One very useful facility would be the option of increasing the size of the pieces as they are assembled. It would not be too difficult to introduce two additional hot-keys which provided a 'zoom in' and 'zoom out' feature. A new variable would be required which was controlled by these keys and which itself adjusted a scale factor applied to the C array values. It might be possible, then, to magnify the display and check how well two Tangram pieces fitted together. It would also be convenient to be able to enlarge a completed puzzle to fill as much of the display as possible.

One feature which has deliberately not been included in the current version is any limiting of screen coordinates for the pieces. It was felt to be unnecessary, since the user will be concentrating carefully on the positions of all the pieces in any case. Limiting the coordinate range might appeal to some users, however.

Another possibility for extending the program would be to have a set of challenges held as data statements, or perhaps in a data file. The outline of different possible Tangram arrangements could be displayed on the Notepad's screen, without the individual pieces being shown, and the user would have to try and assemble them. Introducing a random selection of patterns could lead to the program becoming more of a game of skill, perhaps even with a checking routine and a time factor. Similarly a library of standard patterns could be stored for demonstration. The location and orientation of each of the seven pieces would be required for every arrangement stored, but this would not be excessively difficult.

In its present form the program does not prevent shapes from overlapping. This could be prevented by including a side checking routine which used the BASIC instruction POINT to examine the screen background before displaying a piece in a new location.

INDEX

*CAT, 11
*DELETE, 12
*EXEC, 112
*KEY, 13
*SPOOL, 111

A
abbreviations, command, 12
ABS, 42
absolute values, 42
AND, 25
animation, 82, 92
    filled shape, 92
arithmetic, 15
arrays, 47
    two-dimensional, 49
ASC, 22
ASCII, 22, 55
ASCII file, 112
assignment operator, 15

B
bar charts, 66
BBC BASIC, 1, 9
    reserved words in, 48
bold text, 6
Boolean values, 25
brackets, use of, 15

C
channel, sound, 94
chords, 95
CHR$, 22

circles, drawing, 68, 77
clock, internal, 136
CLOSE #, 100
CLS, 4
comments, 7
concatenation, 39
conditions, 16
control variable, 19
COS, 68
cursor keys, 24
cursor, graphics, 67

D
DATA, 51, 59
    and sound, 96
data file, 110
data pointer, 52, 87
database, 102, 178
decisions, 15
DEF PROC, 36
DEG, 68
DELETE, 9
DIM, 47
DIV, 25
DRAW, 67

E
EDIT, 10
ELSE, 17
END, 10
ENDPROC, 36
EOF (end of file), 101
error messages, 12

error trapping, 43
errors
    syntax, 114
    tracing, 115
Euclid's algorithm, 29

F
FALSE, 25
fields, 102
file handling, 98, 128
flags, 43
flowcharts, 31
FOR-NEXT, 19
FORTRAN, 1

G
gender changer, 108
GET, 22, 55
GOSUB, 17
GOTO, 18
graphics, 58
    coordinates, 67, 170
    cursor, 169

H
hot-keys, 56, 237

I
IBM PC, 108
IF ... THEN, 15
INKEY, 23, 42, 55
INPUT, 2
INT, 42
interactive programs, 54
inverse text, 6, 117

K
keyboard, scanning, 55
keys, defining, 13

L
Lapcat, 107
LEFT$, 39, 74
LEN, 39
line numbers, 4, 8
LIST, 3
LOAD, 11
LOCAL, 35
loops, 19
    conditional, 21
    nested, 21, 24, 61

M
machine learning, 159
matrix, 50
mean, 151, 156
median, 151, 156, 156
menu-driven programs, 104
MID$, 40
MOD, 25
mode, 151
MOVE, 67
multistatement lines, 24, 25

N
NEW, 11
NOT, 25
OLD, 11
ON ERROR, 53
ON GOSUB, 18, 41, 46
OPENOUT, 100
OR, 25
output, 2

P
parameters, 37, 87
pixels, 67
PLOT, 76, 85, 92
pointer, 124
PRINT #, 100
PRINT TAB, 5, 58
PRINT, 1, 3
printers, 107, 213
PROC, 36
procedures, 35
pseudocode, 31
Pythagoras, 199

R
RAD, 68, 74
random numbers, 43
ray optics, 88
READ, 51
records, 102
rectangle, drawing, 77
REM, 7
RENUMBER, 7, 9
REPEAT-UNTIL, 21
RESTORE, 51
RETURN, 17
RIGHT$, 40
RND, 43
rotation, 243
RUN, 2

Index

S
SAVE, 11
screen dumps, 113
semicolon, use of, 16
simulation, 88
SIN, 68
sine curve, 75
sort, bubble, 139, 144
sound, 94
sound, duration, 94
sound, pitch, 94
SPC, 42
SQR, 43
STEP, 20
STOP, 10
STR$, 40
string variable, 2
structured programming, 34
subroutine, 17
system settings, 11

T
TAB, 5
tangram puzzle, 227
text coordinates, 6, 123
text, inverse, 118
TIME$, 42, 136
TRACE OFF, 116
TRACE ON, 116
tree structure, 179
trigonometry, 68
TRUE, 25

U
user interaction, 54

V
VAL, 40
variables, 14
   global, 35
   integer, 14
   local, 35
   numeric, 14
   string, 14
   subscripted, 48
VDU statement, 6
VDU 2, 107, 213
VDU 3, 107
VDU 7, 94
VDU 14, 6, 126
VDU 15, 6, 126
VDU 17, 6
VDU 19, 6
VDU 20, 6

W
Wittgenstein, 109
word processor, use of, 106

X
Xmodem, 108

Z
Z80, 1

SIGMA PRESS

NOT IN YOUR LOCAL BOOKSHOP?

ORDER DIRECT!

Your preferred choice for book-buying will always be your local bookshop, but sometimes you can't find just waht you want.
To solve this problem, you can now order all your favourite Sigma books direct from Sigma Press. It's fast and convenient and we charge only £1 towards p&p for one book (and nothing at all for two or more to the same address).

Usually, we despatch books on the day we receive your order, and you can pay by cheque or credit card. For the fastest service, phone or fax your order quoting the cardholder name and address, the credit card number and expiry date; please also leave us a daytime telephone number so that we can contact you in case of any queries. Our phone and fax lines operate a 24 hour service. We accept most cards, but not Diners, Amex or debit cards such as Switch.

P.S. There's a **special bonus** for direct postal purchasers: a FREE disk of over 100 Clip Art images in PCX format to liven up your word processing or DTP. When you place your order, just ask for your free SMARTART disk and tell us the size of PC disk you prefer – 3.5" or 5.25".

All part of the service!

For orders and further information on all Sigma books – contact:

Sigma Press,
1 South Oak Lane
Wilmslow
Cheshire
SK9 6AR

Phone: 0625-531035; Fax: 0625-536800